SELFING THE CITY

SELFING THE CITY

SINGLE WOMEN MIGRANTS AND THEIR LIVES IN KOLKATA

IPSHITA CHANDA

Los Angeles | London | New Delhi
Singapore | Washington DC | Melbourne

First published in 2017 by

SAGE Publications India Pvt Ltd
B1/I-1 Mohan Cooperative Industrial Area
Mathura Road, New Delhi 110 044, India
www.sagepub.in

STREE
16 Southern Avenue
Kolkata 700026
www.stree-samyabooks.com

SAGE Publications Inc
2455 Teller Road
Thousand Oaks, California 91320, USA

SAGE Publications Ltd
1 Oliver's Yard, 55 City Road
London EC1Y 1SP, United Kingdom

SAGE Publications Asia-Pacific Pte Ltd
3 Church Street
#10-04 Samsung Hub
Singapore 049483

Published by Vivek Mehra for SAGE Publications India Pvt Ltd, typeset in 11/13 pt Garamond by Zaza Eunice, Hosur, Tamil Nadu, India and printed at Sai Print-o-Pack, New Delhi.

Library of Congress Cataloging-in-Publication Data Available

ISBN: 978-81-906760-4-5 (HB)

SAGE Stree Team: Madhuparna Banerjee, Supriya Das and Alekha Chandra Jena

To the memory of Professor Jasodhara Bagchi
and
to Professor Nabaneeta Dev Sen

Thank you for choosing a SAGE product!
If you have any comment, observation or feedback,
I would like to personally hear from you.
Please write to me at **contactceo@sagepub.in**

Vivek Mehra, Managing Director and CEO, SAGE India.

Bulk Sales

SAGE India offers special discounts
for purchase of books in bulk.
We also make available special imprints
and excerpts from our books on demand.

For orders and enquiries, write to us at

Marketing Department
SAGE Publications India Pvt Ltd
B1/I-1, Mohan Cooperative Industrial Area
Mathura Road, Post Bag 7
New Delhi 110044, India

E-mail us at **marketing@sagepub.in**

Get to know more about SAGE

Be invited to SAGE events, get on our mailing list.
Write today to **marketing@sagepub.in**

This book is also available as an e-book.

Contents

Acknowledgements

This book records and analyses the ways in which single women who come to Kolkata from smaller towns, cities and villages across eastern India experience the metropolis. Since this is something I have myself lived through, I was curious about the variety and sameness of the experiences of other women like me, their negotiations with the urban and urbanization, and their relation with the women's movement and feminism. Much of the discussion and analysis is based on the results of a survey, carried out between 2004 and 2007. The city of Kolkata, the spatial and cultural location of these negotiations, is itself a character in this survey, almost as much a respondent as the women who participated in group discussions or filled in questionnaires, or allowed us access to their thoughts and feelings. These respondents and the resource persons are the actual authors of this book: the formulations, theorizations and tentative conclusions for future ways of engagement and negotiation may be mine, but in the very literal sense, there would have been no book without their participation and generosity. The process of data collection was kept as anonymous as possible; and given the wide cross-section of women accessed and the nature of the questions and responses, the resource persons themselves felt that this anonymity was helpful as well as proper. Some of the respondents and all resource persons are amongst my friends, my debt to all of them is equal, and I would hope that the reader of this book will feel the same. I am not naming any of them separately, but would like to record my gratitude for their time, trust, patience and willingness, which have made this research possible.

How do discourses and activities related to feminism and the women's movement, impact upon the actual life practices of women, as they conceptualize relationships and conduct their lives in and across spaces designated as 'private' and 'public'? This question forms the core of the book, and provides a theoretical frame for this study. But in many places, the reader may find practices and theory confronting each other with questions. This has prompted speculations on theory, ideological positioning and future strategy. In my view, since it includes gender within its problematique, feminist research has by definition a responsibility to move the issues it considers out of institutionalized and 'normalized' forms and structures of feeling, both in the academic and in the larger sense. Thus for me, this study has thrown up questions regarding notions of the 'self' and the process of constructing and inhabiting the 'self' in specific conjunctures. It has also occasioned some reflection on pre-conceived notions of empowerment, intimacy and security. These are just rudimentary thoughts, which the material has made visible: if they cause further engagement, then too, the credit for bringing them onto the agenda through allowing access to the experiences on which these speculations are based goes to the respondents and resource persons. I would like to reiterate my gratitude to them. This is in every sense their book, though the actual writing is mine: hence any disagreements and discrepancies that the reader finds are entirely my responsibility.

The book is dedicated, in alphabetical order, to Jasodhara Bagchi and Nabaneeta Dev Sen, who, through their encouragement, support and when necessary, summary correction, have enabled me to find a space to speak and be spoken to in the city. The grant from the Studies in Cultural Processes Programme funded by the University with Potential for Excellence Programme at Jadavpur University made the survey possible. Nilanjana Gupta's various offices in the Faculty of Arts and at the School of Media Communication and Culture at Jadavpur University provided mobile homes for the project, and Nila herself has been and remains a catalyst for many things. Anindita Bhaduri, Chaitali Basu and Judhajit Sarkar have helped with minute and important details. The anonymous reviewers have been generous and sympathetic, and I thank them inasmuch as one can thank the unknown. All at Stree have done what they always do to make a finally presentable product, leaving me blissfully unconcerned.

Sayantan couldn't care less, for which I am properly grateful. My mother and aunt provided long distance support and handy household tips endlessly, and after twenty years in the city, I seem to be learning to use their wisdom. The one person who will not give an inch but has been unfailingly willing to listen to complaints, has expressed a desire to be acknowledged as a prime number, and deferring to his wishes, I acknowledge him thus.

Introduction

'At sixteen, I was determined to fall in love—
not with a person but with a place. Not any place.
A city.'
'Any city?'
'Well, yes.'

I had decided by then that no power on earth could keep me within the confines of the series of small towns in which I had grown up and acquired an education and a view of life that I later realized was as adequate and expanding as it was constraining and romanticized. But I was not to know that then. At that time I wanted to be the frog that left the well and become—what else—the princess of my own dreams. Today, thirty-odd years later, another sixteen-year-old woman-in-the-making turns to her parents and says that she will not continue her education if they don't send her out of the town in which she was born and brought up—if she is not sent to the city. Her parents ask me what they should do. They ask me because I have been teaching in the city for twenty years now, and by virtue of several little things, seem to be in a position to 'advise' people of different persuasions. I returned to the town of my birth after having spent more than two years in hostel and staying with relatives in a city, which seemed a transformative experience for a sixteen-year-old girl in the late 1970s. There were things I did thirty years ago that my students who are now in their early twenties will not dream of doing because they are infinitely more sensible and balanced; they take more for granted because we were willing to live alone in the city and they have much less reason to follow our example because their parents have now provided them with more money than we had. My readers will not exactly identify with my entire experience, but they will recognize strands and facets of it. That is inevitable, and that is one reason why such an exercise as this one can be undertaken on a larger than personal scale: to discern what remains similar despite our struggles, to understand what has changed and how to contextualize the changes and then to ask, what can be done and how.

As I meander through the last thirty years of wrong turns, missed opportunities, end-of-month empty pockets, of walking the streets alone, learning of and from people, I hesitate for a moment. Another young woman stands on the threshold of identifying herself as a person in the community of persons she will choose to live with. Not those whom fate has chosen for her as family, but those whom she will choose herself, the life that she will make for herself, not the life that birth or marriage have ordained for her: should such a girl be 'allowed' to venture alone into the city? One is reminded of Butler's idea of 'social scripts' (Butler 1988) which prescribe ideals that are unrealizable but which provide frameworks for our activities. The 'sedimented acts' (ibid.) that define 'gender' as a way of being and sex as a way of embodying this being, provide the context for these frameworks. How are women who grow out of the sediment and seek styles of their own, like those in the study, by embarking upon the adventure called the city, changing these social scripts? What role has three decades of feminist engagement played in engineering this change?

This book is, to reiterate, on the lives of women who came to the city of Kolkata from 'outside': the suburbs, other smaller towns and villages of West Bengal and other states in the eastern region of India.[1] Kolkata is the capital of West Bengal (now Paschim Banga), a state in the Indian union. It has a long tradition of metropolitanism because of its historical position as a port on the river Ganges. Its political importance was consolidated when the British East India Company defeated the nawab of Bengal, Siraj-ud-daula, and wrested for itself the diwani of Bengal, Bihar and Orissa. (See Appendix 2 for city history.) In other words, the East India Company took for itself the right to collect taxes in the area once ruled by Siraj-ud-daula. Thereafter, it used the city, an amalgamation of three villages, as the centre of its operations in India. Calcutta thus became the first outpost of colonial capital and the jewel in the British colonial enterprise in South and Southeast Asia and subsequently, for a while, the first city of the British empire.[2]

Calcutta has, historically, been the nursery of an urbanity built up by colonial capital. That it was one of the first such cities that came into existence across what was until recently known as the 'third world' is a fact that seems to have lodged itself in the city's life history. Only recently has a globalized 'postmodernity' begun to appear on the cityscape and within the city's mental and material make-up. This has led to a change in the number of women coming to the city, and in the nature of their 'habitation' (see Chapter 3) of the city, from the time they come to the length and quality of time they spend here. The number of women who came to the city from smaller towns and from the rural areas of the state, aspiring to be doctors and teachers, has now been increased by women from different states, from larger and fast-paced cities. Their professions are no longer traditional in the sense that they are not limited to medicine or teaching. However, women who have come here, for professional reasons from larger cities across India do not occur in the study except sometimes for purposes of contrast.

The survey was conducted among women who come from smaller towns and semi-rural areas not only from this state, but also from the whole of eastern India. As the first urban centre representing the nineteenth-century notion of a colonial city, Calcutta has since the British period itself been the urban focus in eastern India. This continues into the present: in independent India, the state government's attempts to construct other urban centres in the state have yielded limited results. Calcutta for a long while used to serve as the gateway to the rest of India for the seven Northeastern states inhabited by people of different communities, generally perceived (if no longer directly referred to) as 'primitive tribes'; whether this nomenclature is acceptable or not, the attitude of the Indian union to these seven states which are difficult to access because of their mountainous location, is reflected in the fact that the establishment and development of urban centres in these states along with attempts to 'preserve' their cultures, has only recently begun to be a matter of general, widespread concern. One reason for this could be that middle-class Bengalis provided with easy access to English education at the earliest opportunity, staffed the British administrative services and entered professions like law and medicine, spreading out to all parts of India. At least those who went to the other eastern Indian states like Bihar and Odisha seemed to find Calcutta a safe option as far as the education of daughters was concerned. Later we shall meet some of these women who have told us that their parents were willing to let them leave home to study further only if they came to Calcutta: no other city was considered 'safe'. The other part of this story is that these small towns in Bihar and Odisha were (and still are to some extent) considered either 'unsafe' or backward and conventional. Therefore the attraction of Calcutta as an urban destination, for all its decaying glory and glamour worn thin through the passage of centuries, still remains strong and this was spread unevenly over the entire eastern region of the country.

Perhaps it will be appropriate to begin with the idea of 'outsider', a word that I wish to emphasize over available words like 'diasporic' and 'migrant' (despite the latter being part of the title of this book see note 1 and also Appendix 1). Between the time this book was first drafted and the time of going to press, a wealth of literature on female migrants has appeared, focusing mainly on the economic impetus for their movement to different cities (Raju and Banerjee 2009, Banerjee 2011). Indian geographers have engaged with the relation between gender and space (Raju 2011, Raju and Lahiri-Dutt 2011), exploring these relations in specific urban settings (Sil 2011) and even in Kolkata (Paul 2011). The survey on which this study is based was completed many years before the publication of the insights offered by these writers, some of which are corroborated here, albeit from an entirely different perspective. Feminist interventions in the discipline of geography emphasize that interactions between gender and place produce a 'lived experience' of space (Nelson and Seager 2004: 4), a premise from which this study begins. According to Lefebvre (2003: 209) space as a concept links the mental and the cultural, the social and the historical by the processes of discovery of new spaces, producing a spatial organization unique to each society and creating spaces like landscape or city. We have explored women's discoveries and creations of space through their quest for dwelling in the modern city, in the literal and the existential sense. This book depends on the narratives of the lives of single, middle-class women who have moved to a specific city from small towns, suburbs and villages. Though work, which is central to the literature about migrancy, emerges as an important aspect of their lives (see Chapter 5), it is the process of self-construction in relation to the city that forms the main focus of the book. Hence, unless we are dealing with material about employment and movement, where the descriptive word used in the statistical data is 'migrant', I have avoided this word. Where I discuss the nature of women's mobility from the perspectives of class and ethnicity, the existing literature refers to the women as migrants, but where it refers to their experience of city space and city life, I stick to my somewhat inelegant adjectival clause: 'women who come from outside'.

Bachelard (1994: 4), writing on the poetics of space, differentiates a geographical or an ethnographical study of 'home' from a phenomenological one which would 'seize upon the germ of the sure, immediate well-being it encloses'. But feminist philosophers cited throughout this book have pointed to the silence on gender in such studies, and thus questioned the very construction of an affective economy (Ahmed 2004) of 'well-being', as well as its expression in language. This book uses what Benhabib (1999) would describe as a 'narrative conception of self' to read the accounts provided by the participants in the survey. In doing so, it aims to consider the implications of gender as a social category and as lived experience in achieving or refiguring the 'sure, immediate well-being' that phenomenological studies of 'home' claim to 'seize upon'. Many of the women who have spoken to us have wondered where their home really is: a primary dislocation from home apparently leads to lifelong perception of a self constructed as being 'outside' established circuits and circles, first experienced and reflected upon in the aftermath of the struggle to relocate in another place. In this study, the individual participant is a member of a community of female subjects who are characterized by their own sense of being 'outsiders', with all the attendant existentialist connotations. The horizon formed by the city is the background for the individual participant's fashioning of self in response to the affective and material economies of the place she has chosen to inhabit. The narratives of self-fashioning form the raw material on which the study is based.

A word on how the book has been constructed: important because it is also related to the formation, practical and theoretical, within which the material might be placed. I have given introductory markers to individual speakers where and when I have thought these might illuminate the reader's understanding of the speaker's position. Some women will emerge, by the end of the book, as familiar figures who are articulate and intensely fashion their 'selves' in dialectical relation with the city, every day. It is because of this that the theorists of everyday life offer important resources for this study; they provide subtle insights into the level of lived experience we have sought to explore, insights sometimes corroborated, sometimes contradicted when located in specific gendered space different from the original location of the theories themselves. Both corroboration and contradiction have facilitated reinvestigation of experience and its role in theory formation, and helped to locate the experience of negotiating the city as a female 'outsider' in the context of global consumerist capitalist patriarchy, where feminist agendas have been differentially articulated into the social fabric.

The project was born out of both participation in and curiosity about the culture forged by our experiences as women from outside, staying alone in the city and our desire, testified to by the responses to the survey, to acknowledge and understand it. We began with memories of sharing: hostel rooms, confidences, double dates, boyfriend problems, local guardian woes and many such realities that had not existed in the sheltered lives we had left behind in order to chase a dream; the dream of the city. In later years, this was the experience of many students and friends that I could identify with, only now the scene shifted to PG accommodation, shared flats, rented accommodation, and the problems could all be classified under the large, loose category of 'staying or sticking on'. Somewhere along the way, Kolkata had caught us, and we were fighting tooth and nail not to have to go back to the homes we had left behind. Many of us have succeeded; many of us are on the verge of breakthroughs; some of us have married city men; some have decided to club together our lives with other 'outsider' women: but in all cases, we are women who have come from outside, and are now in various stages of intimacy with, various degrees of 'selfing' the city in which we have chosen to chart our future.

While on the subject of charts, let me quickly make a few functional clarifications. This book is about women living in Kolkata: while the city is known by name and even history to some, the intimate details of topography, culture and lifestyle that flesh out the experiences narrated here may not be known to many. I will refer to the history of the city and the details of its topography and lay-out in the relevant places. I have included some very cryptic descriptive material in the body of the text, but this may well be taken as impressionistic; some data about specific areas has also been included in the body of the text as well as in the form of tables and charts. But if the reader wants, literally to 'walk' through the streets of the city, in Appendix 2 there are maps of the areas that have been most frequently mentioned. We shall refer to their exact utility in the chapter about finding accommodation in the city. Here it will be sufficient to say that the maps are to lay out the topography of the city visually. This is the topography out of which the practices of space produce a 'habitation'.

Chapter 1 introduces the conceptual framework which guided both the survey providing material for this study, and the mode of transforming that material into the book before you. The existing theories of urban affect are put in the perspective of insights from feminist geography that argue that place does not reflect geography but produces it (Nelson and Seager 2004: 4). The attempt is to understand spatialization (Lefebvre 2003) through participants' narratives relating place and self, thus creating a poetics of spatialization that foregrounds the gendered context. This chapter outlines the seemingly gender-neutral theoretical frames forged earlier and elsewhere and uses the experience of gender reported by the women in this survey to locate and then interrogate these existing theoretical frames. Cognitive science, which studies how we come to 'know' what the world outside offers us, offers theories to understand how such narratives may be constructed. We begin from these theories, since our aim is to record the participants' understanding of the process of 'selfing' rather than propose a general theory of self or self-fashioning;

hence philosophical insights into the phenomenon of 'self' have not been considered in this chapter, but appear as and when they speak to the experiences narrated by the respondents to the survey. The complementary section of Chapter 1 outlines the method underlying data collection and documentation, that is, the process of making this book itself. What disciplinary category do the results fit into? In Chapter 1, I consider the relation of this project with feminist interventions in sociology and ethnography. Historicizing ethnology, Foucault (1970: 376–77) located it at a 'point in the western ratio', asserting that it is only possible on the basis of a certain situation and an absolutely singular event, which properly belongs to a singular culture. This singular and singularly situated event establishes its fundamental relation to the whole of history. Linking itself to other cultures in a mode of pure theory it 'provides a foundation for the relation it can have with all other sciences, even with the society in which it historically appeared'. Chapter 1 records my discomfort with calling this study an ethnography based upon the foundational ideas of ethnology. As Foucault sees it, the necessary conditions of possibility for ethnology is the unquestioned acceptance 'always restrained but always present' of the 'historical sovereignty ... of European thought and the relation that can bring it face to face with all other cultures as well as with itself' (ibid.: 377). This leaves no doubt about the traces of colonial domination in the very structure of the science itself: without the colonizing episode of Europe, there may have been no ethnology. Though later generalizations have occurred, and Foucault too sees their presence within the discourse of the science, he is under no illusion that the circumstances in which ethnology is practised can change the organization and method of its practice, which bear traces of the history of its origin during the period of European colonization. These practices are not completely discontinuous with the social science theorizing that occurs in European languages within non-European postcolonial academia, either. The attempt in this study has been to engage with theorization from apparently gender-neutral 'European' sites using lived responses from specific Indian sites in order to sharpen the focus on the lack of fit between the two. Throughout this study, the lack of fit is reflected in the narratives of the participants' experiences of the city. Hence, it becomes necessary to inflect critiques of ethnography with an acknowledgement of the surreptitious discursive trope of neutrality which de-genders the subject by claiming for it an abstract humanity. It is in this context that we may locate, understand and present the construction of the codes of femininity and masculinity, in public and private urban space in a 'modern' globalizing postcolonial city marked by the interaction between imposed and local practices of patriarchy.

Chapters 2 and 3 attempt to place the respondents in within this specific urban space, elucidating the process of 'selfing' through an exploration of their initiation into the affective economy of the city. Chapters 4 to 7 directly introduce the reader to the women themselves, who speak as they have spoken/written in the survey questionnaire or in discussions with resource persons. No attempt has been made to change their language or style of expression, and explanatory notes have been provided where necessary. Chapters 8 and 9 are envisaged as parts of a very broad conclusion, addressing the change in the cityscape as a result of the experience of the female citizen, for whom no common noun exists in the language spoken in the city in which this survey is located. Here, we shall step back from the concrete details, gleaned from the fabric of everyday life and ruminate upon the gains and losses for women in general, individual women whose experiences we have been privileged to share, and ponder upon the way forward. Many of the women whose daily experiences and thoughts that we have shared are students; some of them are in the early stages of their careers, some look forward to scaling greater heights; what have they achieved, in their own opinion, what remains to be done? How have they 'appropriated' the city, and how has the city changed to accommodate them? These are the concerns of Chapters 8 and 9. In these two chapters, we shall look at the women's own prescriptions for the city: what should be done to make inhabiting the city easier for these women; how should women institutionalize the micro-level gains that they themselves have engineered and use them as inputs for lasting change, both in social fabric and organization, towards economic empowerment and progress? Finally, related to these questions, what is the role played by feminism as an ideology and by the women's movement in India? Having anointed a woman as President in the sixtieth year after independence, India made a cosmetic statement about political empowerment. As women we know the power of the cosmetic; to ignore it is only to fall into the trap of patriarchal trivialization of all that women feel is important, including beauty. But as women we also know that cosmetic, skin-deep beauty is viable only as limited and short-term goal achievement strategy. For long lasting, fundamental transformation, for enabling the cosmetic to take roots in the soil of the everyday, to make it part of the way people perceive the shared environment and understand the world, and lodge there as change, a longer and more tenacious effort is required.

This is the story of that process, not one that has ended, by any means, but one that has begun in such earnest that it can no longer be ignored. The women who have lived their dreams and dreads 'unprotected' in the city have proved the possibilities and shown us the problems. It remains now to act on that knowledge.

NOTES

[1]   This study was funded by the University Grants Commission's University with Potential for Excellence Plan and carried out under the larger project, Studies in Cultural Processes. The name of this project was 'Selfing the City: Gender and Urban Space', carried out between 2004 and 2007 with a sample size of 350, which included respondents who answered questionnaires in either English or Bangla and participated in interviews. Besides the women who actually came to the city from outside and were living there alone; interviews were also taken, as suggested by the women themselves, of landlords, paying guest accommodation owners, employers, parents and friends of women who lived in the city on their own. A preliminary paper entitled 'Selfing the City: The Myth of Calcutta and the Culture of Everyday Life' was published in Nilanjana Gupta, ed. *Cultural Studies* vol. 1 (Delhi: Worldview 2003); and another aspect of the study was printed in 'Selfing the City: Single Women Outsiders in Calcutta and the Processes of Everyday Urban Life' in *Calcutta Mosaic: Essays and Interviews on Minority Communities in*

Calcutta, edited by. N. Gupta, H. Banerji, and S. Mukherjee (London: Anthem 2009).

2   The anglicized name Calcutta has been recently replaced by Kolkata. But when this study was conducted, the old name still persisted, and since the name of the destination is crucial to weave an image of it, as will be made clear in the following pages, we use both names in this study. This study is based upon interviews of women who originally came to the city not for 'domestic' (read marriage) but for 'public' (education or work) purposes. The older name, Calcutta, was more easily used even when the interviews were conducted in Bangla, though in Bangla, the local language, the city has always been called Kolkata. In official documents, and hence in crucial names like Calcutta University, for instance (once known as the University in Asia with the most number of colleges under its jurisdiction) or the Calcutta Corporation, which used to look after civic amenities when the city was small and manageable, the English name remained. Hence I use both Calcutta and Kolkata variably, quoting from the interviews and surveys used in this study.

WORKS CITED

Ahmed, Sara. 2004. 'Affective Economies', *Social Text* 79 22, 2 (Summer) Duke University Press: 119–35.

Bachelard, Gaston. 1994. *The Poetics of Space*, trans. Maria Jolas, Boston: Beacon Press.

Banerjee, Arpita. 2011. 'Mobilities and Spaces: Gendered Dimensions of Migration in Urban India', in S. Raju and K Lahiri-Dutt, eds., *Doing Gender Doing Geography: Emerging Research in India*, New Delhi: Routledge: 89–109.

Benhabib, Seyla. 1999. 'Sexual Difference and Collective Identities: The New Global Constellation', *Signs* 24: 335–61.

Butler, Judith. 1988. 'Performative Acts and Gender Constitution: An Essay in Phenomenology and Feminist Theory', *Theatre Journal* 40, 4 (December): 519–31.

Foucault, Michel. 1970. *The Order of Things: An Archaeology of the Human Sciences*, New York: Pantheon.

Lefebvre, Henri. [1986] 2003. 'Preface to the New Edition', in S. Elden, E. Lebas and E. Kofman, eds., *The Production of Space. Key Writings*, Athlone Contemporary European Thinkers Series, London: Continuum: 206–13.

Nelson, L., and J. Seagar. 2004. *A Companion to Feminist Geography*, London: Wiley Blackwell.

Paul, Tanusree. 2011. 'Public Spaces and Everyday Lives: Gendered Encounters in the Metro City of Kolkata', in S. Raju and K. Lahiri-Dutt, eds., *Doing Gender Doing Geography: Emerging Research in India*, New Delhi: Routledge: 250–69.

Raju, S. 2011. *Gendered Geography: Space and Place in South Asia*, New Delhi: Oxford University Press.

Raju, S., and Arpita Banerjee. 2009. 'Gendered Mobility: Women Migrants and Work in Urban India', *Economic and Political Weekly* 44, 8 (11 July): 115–23.

Raju, S., and K. Lahiri-Dutt, eds. 2011. *Doing Gender Doing Geography: Emerging Research in India*, New Delhi: Routledge.

Sil, Pallabi. 2011. 'Creating New Places: Women in the Globalising Town of Burdwan, West Bengal', in S. Raju and K. Lahiri-Dutt, eds., *Doing Gender Doing Geography: Emerging Research in India*, New Delhi: Routledge: 10–129.

ONE

Entering the Space: Diversity through a Gender Lens

Mapping the way gender is experienced over time, against the backdrop of burgeoning urbanity fuelled by industrial-capitalist 'modernity' and, gradually, by 'post' modernity resulting from globalization, in India, we find that we are living through the period when in some metropolitan urban spaces, the gains of the first wave of feminism have become so naturalized that middle-class women have forgotten that these rights were struggled for. Given the age range of the respondents, varying between 18–21 and 65–67 in the period in which the survey was conducted (2004–07), we seem to have a history of this phenomenon through narratives of the changing relations among women, employment, education and the city. The narratives of these relations are expressed through a set of symbols common to the discourses of women's emancipation and empowerment, to the organized women's movement and feminism as ideology. How we understand and use the terms 'emancipation', 'empowerment', 'movement' and 'ideology' depends upon the different forms of stratification. Bondi (1990) points out that once the 'homogenizing screen of universal discourse' has been revealed as fraudulent by critical positions such as the feminist, 'we are faced with the concrete world of people and events situated in particular times and places'. This is the world that we attempt to enter through the narratives of events and places by people who experience them. As a group, the respondents share their 'outsider' status, as women, as unattached to a family and as women who have come to the city from elsewhere. In each case, the universalizing discourse of equality, progress and emancipation is brought to question by the experiences these women undergo in their attempt to seize the fruits of equality, emancipation and progress. Simultaneously, these narratives also attempt to understand the negotiations between feminism as ideology and practice and the world where women's lives are lived.

This could be termed a sociological study in the sense that, in an attempt to address concerns raised by reviewers' comments on an earlier draft of this manuscript, I drew upon a textbook by Newman and Grauerholz (2002). Considering myself in nowise any more than a student in the field, I have attempted to follow their advice about 'inductive' writing and learning: make the personal connection first, is their advice (ibid.: xix). As the reader of these pages has already discerned, I have attempted to use the personal connections to the city of Calcutta, made by individuals (including myself) and communities of women who come to the city from outside. The city has been seen as a dynamic urban space in its own right, but through the eyes and experiences of these women, which makes it symbolic of the part of their lives, of which they allowed us to get a glimpse. In that sense, sociologists may name the perspective from which the study is undertaken symbolic interactionism (Blumer 1969): human interaction occurs within a community formed through consensus on symbols, which are used for communication between members of the community among whom the consensus exists. The repertoire of symbols is influenced by the location of the maker and receiver of symbols, by their relative positions in and vis-à-vis the larger world. These symbols become our key to interpreting the behaviour of others within and even outside the community—leading to criticisms of the theory being overtly impressionistic. We have chosen the city as the focus of interaction, source and ground for the symbolic economy connecting commonly held notions of equality, emancipation, progress. For the women who participated in the survey, these notions were often goals to be realized if they were to become city women. They were represented also by the affective states resulting from the success, failure, acceptance or rejection of these activities as ways of becoming city women. Roles decreed by the very alignments of gender organization itself are brought into question by this interaction between the subject and her world. Does the appropriated feminist rhetoric of equality and emancipation mean that women's lives and their perceptions have benefited from feminist struggles? Can the experiences of this change be articulated into the social fabric such that an equitable and just society envisaged by all critical theories including feminism, is made possible?

The community studied here comprises the women who have come alone to the city from outside in order to take up opportunities in the public sphere that the city offers. The self-definitions that have emerged from the consensus among this community are expressed in images of opportunity, empowerment and independence on the one hand. On the other hand, these are accepted to be lacking and articulated as such in the lives of women in general and particularly for non-urban women. Non-urban women who have entered the process of urbanization in circumstances that have brought them into the public sphere were the subjects of the survey: hence whatever this study examines, addresses and attempts to articulate stems primarily from the diverse experiences of this community. Some views that generally apply to women in the globalizing urban milieu under the regime of capitalist patriarchy may emerge: but the study may simultaneously reveal the variety of what we broadly called the 'urban'. The small town and the iron ore mines across Odisha and Bihar where I spent my school years were what we now think of as cosmopolitan since people from all over the country were living together in order to facilitate the industrial production of steel. The structure of such stratified societies that are arranged according to the male earning member's position in the production chain, whether in plant or office or in other places where this hierarchy was operative, has some effect upon gender organization, not fitting seamlessly into the semiotic system that denotes 'woman' in cities. Hence though cities are seen as bigger opportunities, the society within which these opportunities are located demands a lot of negotiation. A different set of negotiations, for similar reasons, will be required of women who come from suburban areas, and another set for those who come from district towns of the same state. In each case, patriarchal gender organization is inflected with the class and caste hierarchy, whether revealed or concealed, following the nature of the space: mofussil, suburbs, village, small town. Thus, the diversity of urban space, a point that we may note in the context of Urban Studies, is accessed in this book through the discourses that form around the idea of 'gender'. By foregrounding the fact that any perspective is gendered, this book directs attention towards an argument made by feminist thinkers: it does not begin from the premise that a perspective is a 'natural' given and has to be lived unquestioningly. There is a crisis that the ideals of freedom and progress espoused by the women's movement have not been realized. This is one of the areas that this book attempts to explore.

The idea of gender we shall work with comes from Elspeth Probyn (1993: 3) who defines it thus: 'gender must be represented as processes that proceed through experience ... ways to talk about individuation without going through the individual and that I can talk about my experience of being in the society without subsuming hers.' This presupposes the fact that the women who have spoken here have experienced a similar situation in their lives in different ways, often referring to one another through direct contact, through transmitted knowledge, even, often, through the survey that was conducted as the basis for this book. Their experiences are not only context-specific but inflected by various other factors. What unites them in one place is the fact that they were all faced, at different stages in their lives, with a particular circumstance: coming into a city to live alone as single women and to participate in the 'public' sphere. They are addressed and positioned in multiple ways by their gender, their home location and their status as 'outsiders'. It becomes necessary then to explore their difference from the hegemonic construction of 'woman' as defined by the domestic sphere. But this difference must be placed in the context of their original location in place, class, ethnicity, language.

It must also simultaneously be placed in the context of their final destination—the city—considering their goals and decisions and negotiations once they arrive. The consequences that these differences relate to women's perception of themselves, the world around them and the relationships they forge with this world and with one another. This forms the material for this book. As is probably already clear, the affective and the material must be intertwined in the very realization of this project. I attempt to map these double coordinates in relation to each other to understand how a processual 'self' is constructed through the experience of the material and the affective. The shorthand used for this process is the word 'selfing'. Understanding this process through the women's own words is the primary aim of this book.[1]

It's actually very sad when you have to leave home to make a life of your own, coz nothing is easy. You make sacrifices, but you also learn a helluva lot. (Trainee ad professional, 23, from Durgapur)

Henri Lefebvre, theorist of space and urban life, commenting upon the life of the *pavillon* dweller of Paris designates it as utopia.

What do those who live in a *pavillon* expect from it? Nothing less than happiness. Many people experience it like that, forgetting the disadvantages, arguing them away. This happiness, in which fiction and reality are as thoroughly mixed as water and wine in a glass, ought to be attained via nature, a healthy and regular life and normalcy all connected in this utopia with the pavillon.... (2003a: 132)

Does the woman who comes to the city from outside really inhabit a dream or a reality; does the city imagined as utopia remain thus when it is inhabited on a daily basis? Lefebvre describes it as a question of signification, linking it to the symbolic and affective appropriation of space (ibid.), a process we will attempt to understand and then interrogate as we are more familiar with the praxis of the women who populate this project. There are many forms of this process recorded here. There are many journeys in one. These range from those initiated by the oldest respondents, almost thirty years ago, to the one that the 16 year old with whom we began is preparing to take in the future. In between, the text weaves through the journeys that all the respondents have taken—the journey of a single girl who comes to the big city from the outside, from a small town, a village, in the same state or from a different one, and begins to live on her own. What hopes and dreams does she harbour that cause her to break the mould of the 'girl'? How does she struggle to fulfil these dreams and hopes? When and why is she happy and what makes her yearn for the safe comfort of home where nothing is to be worried about and all is taken care of, until this unrippling calm becomes deadly boring? And is this an unmixed happiness, where she cannot discern the 'water' from the 'wine', the 'truth' as Lefebvre calls it from the 'fiction'? Such a project seems to want to investigate the nature of 'being', hardly amenable to what sociologists would call ethnographic research. Is this material that can be understood within the rubric of social science research or is it material for some other genre? If social sciences as disciplinary formations provide various kinds of knowledge about different social forms and different aspects of human endeavour in the organization of life called society, the narrative occurs through language and is a means of accessing what it is like to act and live in the situational space of this city.

It is in this context that I now approach the underlying assumptions of ethnography, the idea of research and the nature of what comes to be known, which are assumed to be connected to this form of knowledge. Michel de Certeau, in excavating the notion of ethnography which he calls the science of writing the other, comments:

> The power that writing's expressionism leaves intact is colonial in principle. It is extended without being changed. It is tautological, immunized against both any alterity that might transform it and whatever dares to resist it. It can be taken as the play of the double reproduction which, as history and as orthodoxy, preserves the past and which as mission, conquers space by multiplying the same signs. (1988: 216)

De Certeau (1984) is writing about the Calvinist missionary Jean de Lery's sojourn among the Tupinambous people of coastal Brazil in the sixteenth century. The opposition between savage and civilized, Christian and pagan, the scriptal and the oral are being structured, then, and it is the process of structuring that de Certeau excavates—he is trying to understand how the 'objective' science of ethnology, and its translation into script, that is, ethnography, is being actively produced through such texts as de Lery's *Histoire d'une voyage facit en la terre du Bresil* (History of a voyage made in the land of Brazil, 1578). Is it an exaggeration to use this text to approach the study of single women's practice of living alone in the globalized third world city in the twenty-first century? On the surface it might seem so; if we study closely, as de Certeau helps us to do, the processes by which people are written into the discourse of 'civilization'.

The gendering of 'justice' and 'equality' are ongoing processes: often in our daily interactions, and even in our theoretical engagements, these remain abstract, not substantive but formal. Also, the theory cited above comes from Europe, the colonizing force which fuelled a certain kind of urbanity which influenced the gender organization in the colony. Thus the lived realities of industrial class and locally existing caste hierarchies inflected by colonial and postcolonial modernities influence the way these ideas impact upon daily life and struggles. In other words, the equality we, middle-class women, have gained seems to be the freedom to be equal to middle-class men, and justice is done to a neutral de-gendered subject which, for all its specificity, may be any existent made of flesh and blood. Let us refer back to de Certeau: what is written, the canon, the social norms, the codes by which women and men know/become themselves in particular societies, remains as the norm, which is necessarily patriarchal, but with this difference: it has extended itself to the end of the world as in de Certeau's example, and also to the space of the other. Moss (2004) cautions against the power that accrues to the researcher from her freedom to 'position' the subject of research, criticizing the tendency of the academic to hold on to her/his standpoints even if these go against the transformative situation of research. Ethnography functions on a relation of power, the researcher and the researched are locked in a hierarchical relationship, the former 'studies' the latter in order to inform his own people about what she/he has witnessed first-hand. The academic researcher produces knowledge through a process of translating the findings into her own terms, for the consumption of readers in her own domain. Unless we are willing, as academic researchers to encounter and acknowledge the 'transformative situation' referred to above, ethnology remains, as Foucault describes it, limited to studying 'the structural invariables of cultures rather than the succession of events. It suspends the long chronological discourse by means of which we try to reflect our own culture within itself and instead it reveals synchronous correlations in other cultural forms' (Foucault 1970: 376). This 'long chronological discourse' is the basis of this book, and the attempt is precisely to reflect our own culture: as women across a loosely named but not homogeneous 'middle' class, from varied locations and backgrounds, coming to live in the same city as single women who do not have a family, marital or natal, in the city itself. As anyone who has read thus far must have noticed, this story begins autobiographically. As such the process of writing also must be constantly reviewed, to discern whether the tropes and codes of the city as defined by patriarchy infiltrate into our understanding of our own experience of the city and the processes by which we make sense of them. It is too early to claim for this book a difference from an ethnographical account and what we learn from it. In contrast to 'scientific knowledge', Nelson (2006) proposes experiential knowing, and Sayers (2000) 'testimonial knowledge'. Our aim is to understand how the common perceptions/myths regarding women in patriarchal society articulate with the gains of the women's movement. The starting point in our explorations is the production of what Merleau-Ponty terms 'situational space' (2002: 138) through the interaction between an entity called the 'single' 'woman' and her apparently singular setting, the city of Kolkata. These women have come to live there alone. How they 'inhabit' the city is seen herein as crucial to a conception—and narration—of 'self'.

Lefebvre conceives of 'habitation' as expressed by a 'double system' (2003a: 126) which he describes as both 'palpable and verbal, 'objectal' and semantic'. This means that the affective idea of 'habitation' has two dimensions: the feelings generated by space as well as by the actual material objects that make up the space. Both these are connected and interact in order to produce a 'feeling' and/ or a 'sense' of habitation. In a study such as ours, there is a further dimension: the woman who finds herself in this space feels that she has to 'produce' the sense of habitation through a set of actions, all of which, as respondents have recorded, relate to their construction/ understanding/knowing of their own 'selves'. Sociologists collect quantitative data from which they also try to understand the places, ties and things perceived by the people whose social lives they are researching. In this survey, the data are not quantitative. The affective and the empirical must be interpreted in connection with each other if the researcher is to gain some understanding of the situation. The experiences of the women recorded here are located in their milieu, and not meant to illustrate any pre-existing theory. Rather, attempting to connect their affective experience of the space they inhabit the different dimensions of an urban, 'modern' milieu contributes to experience in contemporary times.

The narratives collected through the questionnaire and discussions connect the functional and affective experiences of habitation. These experiences form the process of negotiating the unknown space in order to make it a dwelling—the process we have called 'selfing'. This moves away from seeking factual or quantitative answers to questions of 'adjustment', 'accommodation', 'friendship' or 'security, as it is social articulation of gains of feminist struggles that we are studying here, the questionnaire was designed to encourage reflection and collect narrative rather than simply numerical data. Connections have been sought between the construction of the 'experience' and its narration by the respondent. Hence, the written responses elicited by the questionnaire allowed the respondents time and space to be alone with the questions, think them through and reply at their own pace.

Respondents themselves were aware of the presence/absence of the 'interviewer' and the peculiar nature of the activity of responding. As one of them, a 28-year-old executive from Ranchi, put it:

> If everyone is frank like I am some important discoveries will be made about girls like us. That will benefit everyone in the long term. But some girls will definitely romance their lives to make it more glamorous as there is no way of verifying what they say.

This raises an important question: can such statements, however factual or tentative they appear, be the raw material on which conclusions may be based? Are they to be taken as constructed narratives of the truth that people desire to share with others? In order to engage with these questions, at this point, we could turn to the theoretical understanding of 'self' offered by cognitive science and the scholars of consciousness such as Daniel Dennett (1991). Dennett wittily calls the idea of a unifying spectacle that forms our 'point of view' the Cartesian theatre. He asserts that there is no 'Oval Office in the brain housing the highest authority' (ibid.: 428). He calls humans 'virtuoso novelists' (ibid.: 114) attributing to them coherence and meaning which are post-facto constructed into a unified self, and express as narratives.

However, a differing view comes from Oatley (2007) who points out

> ... most of us westerners who work in the brain and behavioural sciences tend to think in terms of individual selves, individual minds and individual brains. But if our species is predominantly social and depends for its being on mutuality and joint planning, we need to consider also such interfaces as the interface of language along with its conscious access to what we consider our goals and plans, by which we arrange our lives with others.

According to Velleman (2002) the formation of a conscious unitary self may be modelled on the functional properties of the narrative. This begins with Helmholtz's proposal (1962), foundational to cognitive science, that perception is the unconscious drawing of conclusions by analogy. We are not conscious of the means of drawing conclusions, though we are conscious of the conclusions themselves. Citing Virginia Woolf's narrative technique wherein neural processes are expressed in mental images, Oatley points out that these images have 'as much to do with preoccupations, memories, emotions trains of inward thought as they do with perceptual input' (Oatley 2007: 383). This insight is further buttressed by Vygotsky's position (1962) that the social world becomes internalized as the mind. Taking these critical insights on board, Oatley asserts that consciousness is not 'a post hoc account, but a mobilization of the resources of human culture which become available to each of us' (ibid.: 382). Finally, using the work of George Herbert Mead (1913), who thinks of the consciousness as voices in debate or discussion, Oatley concludes:

> [the] self is not just a kernel of autonomy, Self is self-in-relation-to-other, an amalgam of the implicit theory we inhabit, suffused with the emotions that prompt our lives and are generative of our actions in the social world. (ibid.: 385)

Instead of looking for the truth of experience in first person narratives, we are trying to understand the experiences that produce a sense of self through engagement in and with situational space. An

interactive and processual conception of self is helpful in understanding the activities and thought processes that make up what I have here
described as 'selfing'. The interaction between inhabited space and
the subject that inhabits the formation of a continuous coherent self
forms this process. The coherence, it is argued, is achieved as a result
of this interaction, and the continuity is sometimes preserved and
sometimes surrendered to 'change' also as a result of interaction. As
I have stated at the outset, all of us who were involved in the process
of what, for want of a better term one is forced to call data collection,
are women who have had some experience of the situations that our
respondents have told us about. In that sense, we are all implicated
in the narrative construction of our own and others' 'selves'.

The feminist critique of knowledge which I refer to below, has
served to refigure sociology and its practice as a social science. Firstly,
the experience of women in the world in which they participate from
an assumption of equality and strength bears investigation. The mainstream feminist movement addressed issues that are now being seen
as affecting middle-class lives women's right to equal opportunities in
education and work. This acceptance seems to have created a milieu
in which these rights are taken for granted by younger generations of
middle-class women as well as middle-class society at large. In this
context, we may ask, how have these women's assumption of these
rights changed them and the social milieu in which they function? Is
the natural assumption that women are equal participants in a global
economy, really 'natural', and how has it inflected the nature of the
society in which they live and work? Has society changed through
their participation, such that it is now 'natural' for both middle-class
men and women in a class- and caste-divided society to expect similar
access and opportunities? What has happened to the 'traditional' role
definitions of men and women, the 'traditional' divisions regarding
their spheres of activity? Has society accommodated women despite
these differences and divisions, or because of them, and how have
these accommodations reflected back on the world that we inhabit
today? Hilary Standing (1991), whose research on women joining
the workforce was located in Kolkata as well, argues, 'Any account
of the impact of women's entry into employment must ... examine
the social and historical terms upon which gender enters the labour

market. This must include associated ideological constructs of the genders as specific and different kinds of persons.'

One of the respondents, who was also a resource person, answered the question 'Do you think such surveys have any practical aim or are they an empty academic exercise?' with these words:

Suddenly Indian media, especially the English language media has woken up to the fact that many small town women are migrating to metros for jobs and not marrying. That means they have independent lives. They are real women from middle-class homes living outside patriarchy but still in the mainstream and with a large disposable income. So are they a threat to the foundations of society? Will these women impact urban Indian society with its eyeballs still glued to the telly-Tulsis and -Parvatis to change? Will they cause a ripple effect in smaller towns, kasbas and villages of India—empowering women in general with more choices? But with the dumbing down of the media, there are no answers, only easy to digest stereotypes of a large-income-group where a woman in designer-wear who has no time for a relationship after a sixteen-hour workday and has posted her profile on a matrimonial website or is still waiting for the mythical metrosexual man. And who's the metrosexual man? The high-income-group guy who manicures his fingers and goes to a spa and is not averse to wearing fuchsia. We who are middle-class educated intelligent single women living alone, read or see these hackneyed, supercilious media representations with anger and disdain. We need a polyphonic and real representation immediately (29-year-old advertising professional from Jamshedpur).

The research questions came from experience and participation rather than from observation. It is because my own involvement in these issues begins from a personal plane that I am aware that an 'objective' method of data collection and analysis will be inadequate to understand the complex experience of negotiating the city through the process of constructing a 'self' to meet this challenge. Though respondent and interviewer were totally unknown to each other and were connected only by their status as women who had come to the city from outside and were living here alone, in response to the question

'Do you think people from the city are sympathetic to women who come from outside?' a 36-year-old manager in the hospitality industry responded thus: 'The lady who formulated these questions must have come from outside. I know exactly what you mean.' This research follows a methodology that arises from and culminates in the acknowledgement of the concepts of 'situated knowledge' (Haraway 1988) and 'connected knowing' (Hill Collins 1990), as well as the views of Sayers (2000) and Nelson (2006) reviewed above. Instead of looking for the truth of experience in first person narratives, we are trying to understand the experiences that produce a sense of self through engagement in and with situational space.

Marx's first thesis on Feuerbach, criticizes materialism's inability to take cognizance of practice because it conceptualizes reality as 'an object of contemplation' rather than 'human sensuous activity'. But Marx goes further and says that reality must be seen 'as practice ... not subjectively'. Feminist theories of knowledge have connected human sensuous activity with modes of knowing reality, but Marx's opposition between 'practice' and subjectivity seems puzzling until one recalls that Marx's philosophical position is constructed in the milieu of cast iron oppositions between the excesses of empirical objectivity on the one hand and Romantic Idealism and emotional passion on the other. In forging a dialectic, therefore, Marx turns to actual lived experience, praxis, and bases his philosophical explication on situating this praxis in the actual world. Reality, however, comes to us through sensed thought, amalgamated in experience located in specific social milieu.

The contribution of long years of feminist scholarship has been not only to problematize the 'male' concepts on which the enterprise of knowledge production and circulation is based by demonstrating that it is gendered, but also to propose different modes of production and circulation of knowledge, in order to make visible the 'invisible' female experience that cannot be articulated until these concepts are refigured (Hekman 1993). Harding (1984) took the position that it is futile to suggest concepts like Man of Reason could be opened up to include the Other hitherto excluded, that is, women. This insight is the foundation for positioning the research that this book is based upon.

Firstly, this indicates that there are other possible ways of under-standing and knowing, other modes of acquiring and/or producing knowledge than those designated as legitimate by scientific research into the natural and physical world. But this is not the goal of social science research. We have described the nature of the current project–to understand the formation of a gendered self in the situational space of the city. This is why we turn to ideas of connected knowledge, situated knowing and situational knowing that I have referred to earlier. Patricia Hill Collins (1990) posited that concrete experience is a means of knowing that knowledge does not only come from books. She asserted that empirical proof or authoritative backing, may be two modes of legitimizing or assessing knowledge claims within academia, but they are not the only modes through which the truth of a knowledge claim can be assessed. Based upon the experiences of African-American women who did not have the privilege of institutionalized knowledge acquisition from schools and colleges, Hill Collins also indicated that dialogue, exchange of views and experiences, can be a valid mode of assessing knowledge claims. Thus we see that Marx's emphasis on practice, 'human sensuous activity' is borne out by the theory of knowing that Hill Collins proposes.

There then arises the question whether knowledge is the same as knowing. Women know how to do things or what to use to do them, but can this be called knowledge? There are two possible answers that directly and indirectly address this issue. The first is the classic question that Freud, attempting to diagnose the dilemmas of his famous patient Dora, has asked: what do women want? This in itself indicated the incomplete nature of what he was trying to posit as the science of psychoanalysis. If knowledge was abstract, ungendered and easily available to rational empirical enquiry, why should this question arise at all? What Dora, or any woman, wanted would be no different from what Dick or James would want in the same situation, about which Freud seems to have no questions. And if science follows objective and unfailing 'scientific' methods to produce knowledge regardless of gender, then those methods should also be able to answer the question about Dora's desires conclusively.

Is knowledge then not something absolute, 'finished, closed, whole'? Is it fashioned more like an expensive consumer good that only some can afford to possess by virtue of their social identity, and therefore a weapon for asserting the power of one who possesses it over the one who does not? Is it contingent, incomplete, provisional, and as Gadamer (1981) says contextual and relational? 'It is more to the point therefore to show not that women too can excel in scientific activities but that science is not an absolute gauge of what counts as knowledge' (Hekman 1993: 57). Again, one is reminded of Marx's insistence on human sensuous activity, as opposed to both idealist abstraction as well as pure contemplation. We have suggested that our quest is for understanding, which can integrate the different aspects of the city experience assembled here, and interpret them through the frame of gender.

Different scholars have suggested modes of knowledge acquisition that fall outside the domain of the academic. Some instances of these could be gossip (Belenky et al. 1986), listening (Forester 1989), tacit and intuitive knowing (Polanyi 1985), which provide different kinds of knowledge. We will have occasion to reflect upon these in detail later; at this stage, we mention them to indicate that different means of knowing serve to differentiate kinds of knowing according to mode of acquisition, production and transmission (Sandercock and Forsythe 2000).[2]

Apart from indicating that knowing entails a series of connected activities these writers also focus on sharing this knowledge and its uses. This renders knowledge more functional, whether in concrete or ineffable ways. And that increases the importance of the contribution of these writers to feminist research methodology in enabling the understanding of women's realities in the current context.

This brings us to the issue of women's acquisition of some forms of substantive equality in that particular form of gender organization, i.e., patriarchy, which acknowledges sexual difference through its strict hierarchization. Patriarchy fosters the culture of male dominance and consequent female subjugation in its social, legal and psychic manifestations. We cannot gainsay the fact that capitalist relations of production are most adequately buttressed by this form of social organization. Patriarchal culture values the masculine delineated in a particular formation: whether this is the only possible formation in which masculinity is identifiable and even viable, is unclear because this has been the hegemonic formation available to modern western society which seems in the contemporary period to be regulating non-western theory and some life practices as well. This gender organization was exported to the colonies after initial contact between the West and the rest and later continued to be made available through globalized media in the world outside the West, where it was inflected with existing local gender organization and different forms of existing patriarchal practice to create the context for women's lives. Within this context, other possibilities, whether they are called deviant or alternative or novel, are structured, taking this hegemonic formation as norm. Feminism places itself at a separate perspectival location from which it challenges this particular form of gender organization.[3] Thus, to say this book assumes a feminist position is to acknowledge that concepts like 'freedom' or 'equality' or 'emancipation' are, in their usage within the context of patriarchy, neither gender-neutral nor value-free. So we could legitimately ask on what terms the perceived equality of opportunity and access for women have been achieved. In other words, has this visibility of women in the workplace, and what is directly pertinent to our concerns in this book, in the city, become possible because women have conformed to the masculine standards of labour and citizenship that are taken as gender-neutral and therefore 'human' in an abstract sense? Or has the workplace and the city in particular, and therefore society at large, changed to accommodate women as female, and not abstract, human beings? Halliwell and Mousley (2003) explain the project of critical humanism thus:

> To restore a sense of context to otherwise abstract definitions is …
> [an aim] of critical humanism committed to the idea that people are
> primarily socially embodied and culturally situated beings. To abstract
> the human from historical embodiment is paradoxically to alienate
> human beings from a sense of situation, context and locality. (ibid.: 9)

Gender is crucial to understanding human embodiment and situation: hence the theoretical frame of critical humanism may be gainfully extended through the use of gender as a vantage point to understand change in gender organization and gender relations. If this change has occurred, has it been because women have forced it through their actions and desires, or because these were the minimum changes required by global capital to maintain women as profitable units of the workforce? In other words, has patriarchy also reoriented itself to accommodate women in their new roles as workers in the global consumer-capitalist milieu, so that it is not overtly threatened by women's perception of their changing roles after the right to work outside the home has been socialized not as the fruition of a feminist demand, but as a normal 'civilized' human's fundamental right?

To put it directly in the sphere that this study addresses, women from outside coming to the city in pursuit of education and thereafter following their dreams of a particular kind of life and work, are now part of a very visible reality. How has the city changed to accommodate the women who have come to live in it alone, in material as well as affective terms? Or is it the women who have had to change both their lives and their thinking in terms of the city? Is the city forced to be more gender-sensitive just because it is faced with an influx of women alone? Does it also work in invidious ways to oppress and exploit the woman's solitariness, her insecurity, her sense of being an outsider, playing upon its acceptance of her desire to be an insider? This is the crux of what we have tried to understand in this project.

NOTES

1   Quotations from women who responded to the survey are reproduced exactly as they were written by the respondents, including grammar and spelling. Each quotation from the respondents is followed by the person's occupation, age and the place she comes from.

2   'All of these ways of knowing are inseparable from the subject who is doing the talking, listening or acting ... knowledge therefore is partially autobiographical and ... gender-based. Different kinds of knowledge including scientific and technological must be shared through communication to construct meaning' (Sandercock and Forsyth 2000).

3   B. Parekh. 2006. *Rethinking Multiculturalism Cultural Diversity and Political Theory*, London: Palgrave-Macmillan.

WORKS CITED

Belenky, M. 1986. *Women's Ways of Knowing: The Development of Self, Voice and Mind*, New York: Basic Books.

Blumer, H. 1969. *Symbolic Interactionism: Perspective and Method*, Englewood Cliffs, NJ: Prentice Hall.

Bondi, Liz. 1990. 'Feminism, Postmodernism and Geography: Space for Women?' *Antipodes* 2:22: 156–67.

De Certeau, M. 1988. 'Ethnography: Speech or the Space of the Other. Jean de Lery', in *The Writing of History*, trans. by Tom Conley, New York: Columbia University Press: 209–43.

———. 1984. 'Introduction', *The Practice of Everyday Life*, trans. S. Rendall, Berkeley: University of California Berkeley Press: xi–xxiv.

Dennett, D. 1991. *Consciousness Explained*, Boston: Little, Brown.

Forester, J. 1989. *Planning in the Face of Power*, Berkeley: University of California Press.

Foucault, M. 1970. *The Order of Things: An Archaeology of the Human Sciences*, New York: Pantheon.

Gadamer, H-G. 1981. *Reason in the Age of Science*, trans. by Frederick Lawrence, Cambridge, Ma: MIT Press.

Gilligan, Carol, Janie Ward, and Jill Taylor, eds. 1982. *Mapping the Moral Domain: A Contribution of Women's Thinking to Psychological Theory and Education*, Cambridge, Ma: Harvard University, Centre for the Study of Gender, Education and Human Development.

Halliwell, M., and A. Mousley. 2003. *Critical Humanisms: Humanist/Anti-humanist Dialogues*, Edinburgh: Edinburgh University Press.

Haraway, Donna. 1988. 'Situated Knowledges: The Science Question in Feminism and the Privilege of Partial Perspective,' *Feminist Studies* 14:3 (Fall).

Harding, Sandra. 1984. 'Is Gender a Variable in Conceptions of Rationality?' in C. Gould, ed., *Beyond Domination*, Totowa, NJ: Rowman and Allanheld.

Hekman, Susan. 1993. 'The Feminist Critique of Rationality', in Linda M. Alcoff and Elizabeth Potter, eds, *Feminist Epistemologies*, New York: Routledge: 50–61.

Helmholtz, H. 1962. *Treatise on Psychological Optics*, vol. 3, New York: Dover.

Hill Collins, Patricia. 1990. *Black Feminist Thought: Knowledge, Consciousness and the Politics of Empowerment*, Boston: Unwin Hyman.

Lefebvre, Henri. [1966] 2003a. 'Preface'. *L'habitat pavillonaire*, in S. Elden, E. Lebas and E. Kofman, eds, *Key Writings*, Athlone Contemporary European Thinkers Series, London: Continuum: 121–135.

———. [1975] 2003b. 'The Other Parises', in S. Elden, E. Lebas and E. Kofman, eds, *Key Writings*, Athlone Contemporary European Thinkers Series, London: Continuum: 151–59.

Merleau-Ponty, M. 2002. Phenomenology of Perception, London: Routledge Classics.

Mead, G.H. 1913. 'The Social Self, Philosophy,' *Psychology and Scientific Methods* 10, 374–80.

Moss, Pamela. 2004. 'A Bodily Notion of Research: Power, Difference and Specificity in Feminist Method', in L. Nelson and J. Seagar, eds, *A Companion to Feminist Geography*, London: Wiley Blackwell: 41–59.

Nelson, K. 1996. *Language in Cognitive Development: Emergence of the Mediated Mind*, New York: Cambridge University Press.

Newman, D.M., and E. Grauerholz. 2002. *Sociology of Families*, Newbury Park, Ca: Pine Forge Press.

Oatley, K. 2007. 'Narrative Modes of Consciousness and Selfhood', in D.P. Zelaza, M. Moscovitch and E. Thompson, eds, *The Cambridge Handbook of Consciousness*, Cambridge: Cambridge University Press.

Polanyi, M. 1985. *Personal Knowledge: Towards a Post-Critical Philosophy*, New York: Harper and Row.

Probyn, E. 1993. *Sexing the Self: Gendered Positions in Cultural Studies*, London: Routledge.

Sandercock, L., and A. Forsyth. 2000. 'A Gender Agenda: New Directions for Planning Theory', in R.T. LeGates and F. Stout, eds, *The City Reader*, 2nd ed, New York: Routledge.

Standing, Hilary. 1991. *Dependence and Autonomy: Women's Employment and the Family in Calcutta*, London: Routledge.

Velleman, J.D. 2002. 'The Self as Narrator'. First of the Simon Jerome Lectures in Philosophy, October, University of Toronto, retrieved from www.personal.unich.edu/_velleman/Work/Narrator.html (accessed on 8 November 2007).

Vygotsky, L. 1962. *Thought and Language*, trans E.H.G. Vakar, Cambridge, Ma: M.I.T. Press.

TWO

The City: Relations in Urban Space

Having placed the research question and the theoretical under-pinnings of the methodology used to collect and analyse the data, I move now to the survey itself. The survey covers the complex interactions between the spatial and the affective, linking the city with the woman from outside, forming her relation to the city, which I call the process of 'selfing'. In the survey, this process is located in the city of Kolkata.[1] The city appears in this study as a physical and conceptual space playing a crucial role in the life of single women who come from elsewhere, to live in it by choice. This chapter is grounded in the concept of 'habitus', reserving for later chapters the actual praxis of 'habitation' which is related to it. I shall consider the nature of the 'urban' as it functions in this study across time, in the appropriate place where we address the idea of 'habitation' in more concrete terms. Here we investigate the relations between the single woman who comes from outside this city, and city-as-built-space as well as the city as community, asking how this relationship has changed historically. It is in this context that I want to place the experiences of the women who have participated in the survey and shared their perception of living alone as outsiders in a particular city, i.e., Kolkata.

The number of women interviewed was 300. All except four were single at the time of the survey. Of these, three live elsewhere now. The rest are single women who were living alone in Kolkata and still do so. Some are still single, but are now living in other cities. Two of them came as single women, worked and married in Kolkata and are living here with their husbands or marital families. Most of them—230 to be precise—have filled in questionnaires (see Appendix 1). Others have participated in group discussions. A handful have done both, and another group of women have been instrumental in circulating the survey sheets and conducting the discussions because they themselves were single women from 'outside' living in the city and familiar with the networks through which other such women could be contacted and persuaded to respond, in person or through the questionnaire. I had initially planned a series of group discussions with those who were willing to talk about the experience of coming to the city and living here alone; I felt this would be quite simple, because my earlier experience with a survey on women's responses to the popular media had met with overwhelming enthusiasm; we had held a number of really fruitful and very enjoyable discussions and I made a whole lot of friends in the bargain. This time round, however, I was taught a different lesson, one that has helped me to think a little more subtly about the process that I am trying to study and the insight that all themes do not necessarily demand the same kind of methodological procedure in participatory research. My primary problem with labelling what I have so far done, in this project and in another that is now a book,[2] as 'ethnography' arises out of such understanding as I have been able to come to in the course of the work itself.

In this instance, I was unable to cobble together a group for discussion, because most of the women were too busy with their professional lives; indeed, I ought to have thought of this before, for while the respondents to the popular culture survey were homemakers as well as professionals, those who were the target respondents in this one had to be able to earn enough to support themselves independently in the city, and this meant, invariably, a particular position in their professional hierarchies, which left them with little time to themselves, certainly not enough to meet unknown women and discuss housing/landlady/security/fears and dreams. In fact, one of them put it lucidly, 'I thought this was going to be an anonymous affair, I only had to respond—this meeting business sounds like some sort of AA stuff—I hadn't bargained for that'. This is perhaps something that living alone as women in the city has taught them: despite the rosy picture of purposive associations, networks, commonalities and cooperation, the city has taught women to be wary. This is not exclusive to women alone, but for a woman the cause of the wariness and the possible and unimaginable consequences of relaxation in the city where she lives alone are surely more devastating than it may be for men generally.

Louis Mumford in his seminal study *The City in History* (1961) outlines his concerns by first quoting an inhabitant of one of the pioneering cities of the 'modern' western world: John Stow on Elizabethan London, where he mentions a value particular to the life in the city as 'urbanitas': men congregate in cities for 'honesty' and utility's sake.[3] Instead of asking the obvious question, what about women, let us consider what Stow sees the city as offering: utility, urbanitas, that is, refined behaviour, and the ease of association which is the foundation of what we know today as networking, contacts. As Mumford comments on Stow's description, a city is a collection of primary groups and purposive associations. The first, which consists of family and the neighbourhood, are common to all settled human habitation; but the second is especially characteristic of city life (1937: 94). Mumford's definition of the city, therefore, is 'the city in its complete sense ... is a geographical plexus, an economic organisation, an institutional process, a theatre of social action and an aesthetic symbol of collectivity, unity' (ibid.).

Women's advent alone to the city means their participation in 'the city in its complete sense', which includes all of these aspects of the city Mumford enumerates. It also means that they are now able to consider themselves as capable of such participation and that the city too does not turn them away. Elizabeth Wilson in her book *Sphinx in the City* (1991) reflects upon the relation between women and the city. Rejecting the representations of women as afraid of the city and oppressed within it, she writes of the ways in which women can reclaim the city space. But for that she has first to deconstruct those texts of high modernism in which the man who inhabits the city, the classical *flaneur*, sexualizes the city space, mapping the dangers of sexuality onto the space that women inhabited within the city, that is, the prostitutes' quarters, the so-called 'red-light areas' of city lore and legend. The role of the single woman in modernist city literature was exclusively that of the prostitute; to the extent that any unaccompanied woman was thought to be of this persuasion, a convenient assumption that deterred women from literally 'walking the streets' alone. The city lore thus constructed women into a special class with a particular profession related to their gender and its exploitative masculine use. Wilson's attempt is to deflate the masculine power that modernist theories of city space gave the *flaneur*, leaving women relatively invisible in public urban space, or visible with a stigma attached, therefore denied civic subjectivity and urban sociality.

The present study establishes the visibility of women in the city, and the city's voracious energies that work overtime to accommodate these women because they represent easy money. Ironically, as we will see when discussing accommodation for single women in the city (Chapter 4), often women pay to inhabit the unhabitable, because they must live in the city. Does this mean that the city has made itself gender-friendly, or that it has put on a particularly welcoming face because it sees women's desire to live in the city as an opportunity to make a fast and easy buck? Has the visibility of women in all kinds of spaces in the city and the acceptance of their free movement, changed the city and its attitude to women in any basic way? Or is the exploitation of the woman by the city's shared and 'public' spaces differently inflected now?

Such questions at the outset may simply lead to the conclusion that the relation between the city and the single woman, who does not have the support of family and familiarity to fall back upon, is necessarily fraught with danger and heartache. If that is exclusively so, why do women keep coming to the city? Sharon Zukin (1995) explains that 'real cities are both material constructions with human strengths and weaknesses and symbolic projects ... [and] are also macro-level struggles between major sources of change ... and mid-level negotiations of power'. The women who spoke to us felt the tensions and the attractions of the city in varying measure, and inasmuch as one exceeded the other, they could describe their experiences as 'good' or 'bad'. But even if they turned out to be 'bad', the city did not loosen its hold upon them—their negative feelings about it did not impel them to go away—certainly not to the place they came from.

One of the aims of this book is to understand the nature of habitation in which the social implications of gender play a defining role. As women who came to the city from outside, and have lived here alone for some time, we are prompted to ask ourselves: does this define us as female individuals who have finally breached the traditional divide between the public and the private, thus rendering that barrier a thing of the past? Does the woman's entry into the city on her own, earning and fending for herself, participating in the symbolic project of the modern urban space, on what are generally seen as 'her own terms', represent to her and to the world at large, the final stage in the journey towards self-fulfilment? Is the city really appropriated by women as utopia, in the way in which Lefebvre conceives it to be for men?

Apparently not, as we shall see, and this inability to name the city as utopian, a place of dreams, magical or mythical, seems to be directly related to gender. In Lefebvre's work on urbanity, several gestures are made to what he calls the 'sex' of the inhabitants. He seems to mythologise, in the Barthesian sense, the differences in appropriation and the experience of both urban space and everyday life that are hinged upon gender. So when he states that village life is feminine, and presided over by women while the city is patriarchal, it seems as imaginative as his description of the city as utopian. So, it is not surprising that his characterization of the city as utopian and mythic, involving, a 'constant reference to naturality, that is, the myth of nature, a naturalization of the human' (Lefebvre 2003a: 133), is not borne out by the respondents to this survey, or even by my own experience. This is one of the most telling examples for a woman in the city; unlike the unbridled happiness that Lefebvre associates with the utopian/mythic/natural, this scene produces a sense of desire for belonging that is in the first instance manufactured/achieved rather than natural. Besides, there is an undertow of 'reality' that marks the single woman's experience of being alone in an unknown space which has to be made into home, a reality that utopia does not admit. The single woman 'outsider' is alone here: those who belong here are men, wary of her solitary, unattached presence. She is here because she has chosen to be in this city, not because she has, literally, a birthright to it. To her, this presence signifies an achievement, but with all the struggles and tensions that underlie such achievements by a woman 'outsider' in a male space. Let us again reflect on her presence and its meaning for the time and place in which it occurs. Is the independent and self-directed presence of the woman-outsider in such a space what one would call the death of the gendered woman and the birth of the human being who transcends gender? Is that the goal of feminist struggle that has culminated in the advent of the single woman alone to the city? Is the city that neutral space par excellence, where arises the spectre of an equality that attempts to homogenize difference by subjecting all to the laws governing exchange value?

Beginning his work on cities, Mumford (1961) asks the following questions: What is the city? How did it come into existence? What processes does it further? What functions does it perform? What purposes does it fulfil? We may follow the similar line of enquiry in mapping out the chapters that follow; the responses provided by the women who are actually in the process of living the city may help either to reach certain answers or to sharpen our questions. On the surface, there seems to be a contradictory relation between the woman and the city. It is one of unease and danger. But that apparently does not prevent her from coming to it and fighting tooth and nail to stay on, as many of our respondents have done. At the other extreme, it seems to represent the ultimate utopia, the promised land, which radiates the heavenly light of achievement at the end of a long struggle. In that case, does a move from the small town to a city provide a final solution to all women's problems, economic and social? Out of the 48 women who answered the question: 'Do you see yourself as a city woman?', 25 said they saw themselves as women belonging to the city, while 23 felt they were still outsiders. Sixty women answered the question 'Which place do you see as home?' and 39 saw their present location as home: out of these 39, 22 said they considered the city home, while 17 were more specific and considered their dwellings, whether flat or hostel in the city, their 'home'. The remaining 21 out of the 60 women who answered this question, however, felt that they were outsiders: they still thought of their place of origin as home.

Taken together it would not indicate a state of unmitigated bliss or an unquestioned, unproblematized satisfaction with city life, in material as well as affective aspects. The truth, therefore, lies in a more complicated reality. Does Foucault's notion of the heterotopia encapsulate this reality? According to Foucault (1986), heterotopias are *des espaces autres*, the other spaces, 'the space in which we live, which draws us out of ourselves, in which the erosion of our lives, our time and our history occurs, the space that claws and gnaws at us'. This doesn't indicate a feeling of well-being or satisfaction; quite the contrary. Foucault's examples of these *espaces autres* include two categories: the space inhabited by individuals in stressful conditions, heterotopias of crisis, and those of deviation, where individuals who have been unable to cope with the crisis end up.[4] Foucault in summing up the concept says that either there is a creation of a space of illusion or one that is seen as perfect though this may be far from real. This unreal perfection/real imperfection seems to describe the sense of the city that women from outside who live here alone carry with them, simultaneously or separately.

The city is an illusion that exposes the smallness and triviality of the original home; conversely, when one begins to live in the city and gains acquaintance at first hand with the realities and the trivialities that it must needs harbour, the heterotopia shifts geographical boundaries; then it is the home that takes on the space of compensation, a real and perfect space, no longer an illusion, but no longer accessible; home but not habitable, home because it cannot be inhabited, as the many responses to the question: 'What would you feel if you had to return to your original home for a week/permanently' indicate. Forty-one women answered this question: of them, an overwhelming number, 25, thought they would love to stay in their places of origin for a week's holiday. But four were not certain they wanted to do even that. Only twelve said that they wanted to go back to the place they came from and stay there forever. If the three questions are taken together, in each case, it would show the ambiguity as well as the inexplicable attraction radiated by either the city itself or the life that it almost forces the woman to live. This is that un-named and perhaps un-nameable quality that draws us, outsiders, to meet head-on the challenge of the unknown in the form of the city; and in most cases, success brings with it not only exhilaration and exhaustion but also a further question, a loss and another quest.

The difference between heterotopias and utopias is obvious; the latter are fictional from the moment of their birth in Sir Thomas

More's work, but the former, as conceived by Foucault, exist in reality. As Genocchio (1995: 38) states in his critique of Foucault's idea of heterotopia, they are the 'real existing place of difference that are variably constituted and formed, over and against a homogeneous and shared spatiality, in the very founding of all societies as part of the presupposition of social life'. Should we conclude then that in the twenty-first century, the city is a gendered heterotopia, the symbolic goal of the woman who inhabits a world in which the fruits of the feminist struggle around women's rights to find employment outside the home and be economically self-sufficient, is accepted as a social given? The city then exists in reality, it is not utopia; it is sometimes illusion, at other times compensation, different from the shared spatiality of smaller places in which the woman has grown up. Foucault further elaborates his idea by saying that heterotopias are juxtapositions of several spaces, 'several sites that are in themselves incompatible'. Commenting on this aspect, Edward Soja (1995: 15) says, 'It is this complex juxtaposition and cosmopolitan simultaneity of difference in space that charges the heterotopia with social and cultural meaning and connectivity'.

As we will see from the responses, the city is not uniformly any single entity, giving rise to a similarity of feeling; rather it is an accumulation of several situational spaces, relating work, home, leisure as affective states to roads, flyovers, railway bridges. Some women choose areas to live in based on these considerations, as the survey reveals; others return to some places that are not connected with either their work or their city-home, simply because for them, these are the places which constitute the city, these are the places that encapsulate the inexplicable attraction that draws them and keeps them here. Conversely, other sites within the same city are associated with memories of fear, loss and embarrassment and are thus avoided. Perhaps the city is a metaphor for life itself; perhaps the city represents as a somewhat more tangible reality the intangible capacities revealed through the human being's conscious intentional relation with the world.

It is through the activity of 'selfing' the city, of inhabiting the heterotopia, that one is able to sense that the affective economy does not perfectly fit within the socio-cultural economy. Gender is a frame through which this lack of fit becomes visible. Realizing and negotiating this lack of fit plays a part in understanding that intangibles like an increased sense of confidence, the gradually sharpened ability to perform tasks that seem trivial (like finding a functional laundry service, perhaps) are crucial in ensuring one's own comfort and integrity, emotionally, intellectually and socially. The ability to perform such tasks reflects the increasing ability to develop and operate systems of crisis management and other such apparently minor but extremely important capacities that the city causes one to find within and for oneself. This is not what the woman has come to the city for; it has nothing to do with her work, with successes that she does or does not have there, the social standing or lack of it that satisfies or worries her; but the fact remains that these are things she finds herself able to do, on a continuous and almost daily basis, things that form the fabric of life, which one does not give much thought to until one has to do them, or realizes that one has learnt how. To use the term coined by de Certeau, a 'space-act' forms the basis of the process that I have called 'selfing' in this study. This concept stems from the distinction that is made by the seventh-century polymath, Isidore of Seville, himself an inhabitant of one of the most flourishing of the earliest cities, between the civitas and the urbs. The former is a space defined as a community while the latter is an architecturally conceived or mapped concept of the city. In other words, the former is a city inhabited, and the latter is a city constructed symbolically, as a network of concepts that are supposed to regulate the lives of those who qualify as citizens. De Certeau's idea of space, according to this definition, is a practised place (Conley 2000: 57). He views a space-act as a bodily performance based on an often unconscious choice that citizens of given areas are prone to making in the way they live and literally, the way they work through and about what is in their midst. A space-act transforms the urbs into the civitas, inhabited space. This study proceeds to contextualize such practices of inhabiting and understand them through the frame of gender. We shall utilize the metaphor of 'selfing' at a later stage when the aspects of the actual process are considered including its effects upon the woman herself, her associates in the city and back at home. Our question is, does this process also change the city in any radical way, making it more gender-sensitive and equitable space? Does the apparently equal opportunity for women in the workplace translate into any fundamental change in urban space, material and mental, that can be seen as a transformation in the way society constitutes itself and its spaces?

What is the nature of space-acts? De Certeau puts them within the practice of everyday life. It is to him an investigation of 'the ways in which users—commonly assumed to be passive and guided by established rules—operate' (quoted by Buchanan 2000: 98). While this study tries to understand these operations as actually performed by one group of people, there are certain elements in de Certeau's formulation of a conceptual frame for studying these practices that we cannot but take issue with. To begin with, if our study is to proceed from a gendered perspective, it takes in passive space acts, complying with the established norms, especially under question in our study. Initially, when I was attempting to mould the many conversations with many women into an account of our collective struggle to self the city,[5] I had begun from the understanding that the operations that we perform upon the given space 'organized by the techniques of socio-cultural production', our manoeuvres as 'users' to 'reappropriate' this space constitute what de Certeau (1984: xii) designates as a 'culture'. However, I could not agree with his characterization of these operational combinations constituting culture, since for him, they do not imply a 'return to individuality' (ibid.: xi). In searching for an 'operational logic' for the 'schemata of action', he argues that 'the subjects or the persons who are their authors or vehicles' are not the concern of his theorization (ibid.). But how then are these operations, these actions performed, if not performed by subjects, willing or unwitting, authors or vehicles as he calls them?

De Certeau (quoted in Conley 2000: 57) himself asserts that these are not arbitrary. These belong to an indescribable and immemorial time informed by generations of subjectivity. Hence he implies that, it is possible to think of these operations as less inscribed by specific subjectivities, and more as belonging to the realm of historically learned, subconscious performances of habit, perhaps the imaginative basis of the term 'in-habit'. However, for women who come to the city, there are no 'generations of subjectivity' that inform these operations enabling us to negotiate the city; we do not have access to the 'immemorial' time where, according to de Certeau subjectivity that underlies the practices of the everyday is forged, because no such repository of habit is available to us. Our ancestresses who have 'come before us' are few and far between, and if the age-related difference between respondents is anything to go by, the older women whose conception of the struggles and problems and their solutions could contribute to the task of crafting 'generations of subjectivity' are clearly circumspect about their achievements (see Chapter 8). On the other hand, the establishing of a tradition can only happen with the passing of time, and the willingness to leave behind some signposts and/or traces that can be later formulated into lore, legend or just a data-base.

A part of the survey relates to this effort and the responses to attempts made in this direction which we will consider in detail below. At this point, we may only state that the commentators who argue that it is wrong to think of de Certeau as privileging the ordinary man over the ordinary woman because he is not concerned with subjects at all, but with traditionally 'learned' practices, miss the point. We can extend the idea of space to situational space, wherein subjectivity is constituted by object-relatedness: the city is the name of a multitude of experiences that constitute the subject as a citizen. Such a tradition does not exist for the woman who steps for the first time into spaces that were hitherto barred to her materially or constructed socially in such a fashion that in order to fit into her social role, she had to either avoid them altogether or step into them only in a particular way approved by social codes. Hence such a practice cannot be understood without specific reference to narratives that explain how places acquire the affective dimension and become what de Certeau calls 'spaces' and Merleau Ponty extends as 'situational spaces'.

The absence of a tradition into which the woman coming to the city from outside is socialized is obvious from literature itself. As we are talking of a particular city in this study, we can consider the literature that has largely grown around this city. Kolkata, Kipling's city of dreadful night was the site of the earliest negotiation between two alien cultures, of which one was certain of its superiority and possessed the means to assert it. It participated in India's long march towards globalization by hosting merchants and missionaries from across Europe and becoming the hub of mercantile capital as well as of western culture as opposed to the composite culture earlier spawned by the melding of several strains of Islam and the local varieties of worship that we much later learnt were to be called Hindu. The formulation of modernity, in all its guises and in all its extremity was visible in this city from the middle of the eighteenth century. To this place people had always come from outside, but the influx grew from the time it became the hub of empire. Menial workers came from other states: cooks and gardeners and palanquin bearers and watchmen and sweepers, all from the eastern region where all roads led here because it provided a wealth of opportunity. Bangla literature documents the presence of these people from other states. It also documents the hordes of servants who served the upper class people the stories are about. All these servants come not from other states but from other provinces in Bengal, and would go to their 'desh' periodically, to their own land, to sow or harvest or to marry off or be married, causing much upheaval in the families of their masters. But they are generally men; rarely do we meet women who live thus alone in the city, separated from their homes and relatives unless, they are widows or prostitutes. Like all literatures, Bangla too has its fair share of bildungsromans in which the stock character of the prostitute with a heart of gold plays a pivotal role. Not only in the nineteenth century, also for most of the twentieth, and till date, the woman who comes alone to the city is conspicuous by her absence.

If I were given to binaries, I could say that apparently, men's experiences make literature, while women's make theory. I shall say, instead, that it gives us a chance to look at the human per-spective within a particular context, and therefore, we conclude (provisionally!) that the social sciences which accommodate this theory are the sciences that make space for marginalized groups. In Bangla literature, Sribilash of Rabindranath Tagore's *Chaturanga*, or Apu of Bibhutibhushan Bandyopadhyay's *Aparajito* embody the experiences of the young man who comes to Calcutta from the vil-lage or small town. Men's experiences fill the work of male writers who have themselves often come from outside Kolkata and have romanticized their struggles. Readers of Bangla poetry can easily recall the yearning of Jibanananda Das for the beautiful face of rural Bangla even while he walks the streets of Kolkata lost in a reverie, his subtly cruel picture of the midnight city the fatal lure that prevents him from going back home until it is too late. Das died walking on the grass upon a tramline on the Kolkata streets. For the petty clerk in Rabindranath's poem 'Baansi', the city is place to flee to, flee from the responsibility of marriage, followed, however by the still sadness of love. The tumultuous life of depression and comedy lived in full view by Shibram Chakravarty, who immortalized his mess, those ancient, mildewed bastions of male camaraderie and creativity, adds another dimension to the male outsider inhabiting the city.[6]

These are only a few of the many literary vignettes of the male outsider's experience in the city. The established doyennes of Bangla literature were firmly rooted in the Kolkata soil after the initial family move from erstwhile East Bengal during the formation of Pakistan. Neither Ashapurna Devi, nor Mahasweta Devi nor Nabaneeta Dev Sen or even the younger writers like Bani Basu or Mallika Sengupta seem interested in the stories of women who come from small towns outside Kolkata to seek their destinies. The characters in their work did not do so, because in their times, women did not, either. We have come across a number of women so far whose ages range between 40 and 60, roughly the ages of the generation of women now at the height of their powers in Bangla literature. Our respondents have been here for 20-odd years, but it is only in the last seven or eight years that the phenomenon of the woman from outside Kolkata has entered Bangla literature. How many of us, however, have read Aparajita's *Debolina* or *Chander Gaye Chand*?[7] These novels focus in a more significant way than before, upon some of the experiences of women like our respondents, exploring the growth of the mind, so to speak, of single women from outside who have decided to make the city their home. Now that such women are increasing, the barriers to women's mobility, the entrenched ideas about their roles, limits and goals are in the process of transformation. And so it is time to underscore their visibility and speculate upon its consequences for the fabric of the city, whether through fiction or research.

What disciplinary name should one give this attempt to understand our experiences and communicate their variety as part of a larger process of social transformation? In locating it within a disciplinary formation for academic purposes therefore, we can do no better than invoke Raymond Williams' comment (1989: 52) that 'intellectual questions arise when you draw up intellectual disciplines that form bodies of knowledge in contact with people's life situations and life'. This proceeds from Williams' understanding of Culture Studies:

> You cannot understand an intellectual or artistic project without understanding its formation. Project and formation are different ways of materializing—different ways then, of describing—what is a common disposition of energy and direction ... 'project' and 'forma-tion' are addressing not the relation between two separate entities ... but processes which take on these different material forms in social formations (ibid.: 152) ...

Not only can an artistic process or product, literally understood as 'culture', be explored and understood thus—the project of living in the city, not conventionally artistic—is, as those who have been through it would understand, a creative process of everyday life. Given a set of materials and places, subjects use them in hitherto unexplored ways and within constraints, to fulfil their needs. For those of us who have been doing this for a large part of our adult lives and many of us have arrived here with the onset of legal adult-hood, this is a 'culture' in the conventional sense.

NOTES

1   See Appendices for civic history and history of the suburbs.
2   I. Chanda. 2003. *Packaging Freedom: Feminism and Popular Culture* (Kolkata: Stree).
3   Men are congregated into cities and commonwealths for honesty and utility's sake.... First men by their nearness of convention are withdrawn from barbarous fixity and force to certain mildness of manners.... Good

behaviour is yet called urbanitas ... men by mutual society and compa-
nying together do grow to alliances, commonalities and corporations
(quoted in Mumford 1937).

4   Foucault sums up heterotopias as: either their role is to create a space
of illusion that exposes every real space, all the sites inside of which
human life is partitioned, as still more illusory . . . or else, on the contrary, their role is to create a space that is other, another real space, as
perfect as ours is messy, ill-constructed and jumbled. This later would
be the heterotopia not of illusion but of compensation (1986: 27).

5   M. Foucault, 1970. *The Order of Things: An Archaeology of the Human Sciences*,
New York: Pantheon.

6   Bodhisattva Kar and Subhalaxmi Roy, 'Messing with the Bhadralok:
Towards a Social History of the Mess Houses in Kolkata 1890's–1900's',
Sarai, CSDS, Delhi, fellowship. As far as I was able to find out, a similar
study on women outsiders was based in Hyderabad and conducted by
Shefali Jha and Navaneetha Mokkil 'The Space Between: Women's
Hostels as Urban Spaces', also on a Sarai fellowship.

7   Tilottama Majumdar, *Chander Gaye Chand, Desh puja sankhya*, 2001, and
Aparajita, *Debolina, Desh puja sankhya* 1996, both published by Ananda
Bazaar Patrika group.

Works Cited

Buchanan, I. 2000. 'Introduction. Other People: Ethnography and Social
Practice', in Graham Ward, ed., *The de Certeau Reader*, Malden, Ma:
Wiley-Blackwell: 55–59.

Conley, Tom. 2000. 'Introduction. Other Cities: Cultural Politics, Part 2', in
Graham Ward, ed., *The de Certeau Reader*, Malden, Ma: Wiley-Blackwell.

De Certeau, M. 1984. 'Introduction'. *The Practice of Everyday Life*, trans. by
S. Rendall, Berkeley: University of California Berkeley Press: xi–xxiv.

———. 2000. 'Ethnography: Speech or the Space of the Other', in Graham
Ward, ed., *The de Certeau Reader*, Malden, Ma: Wiley-Blackwell.

———. 2000. 'Walking in the City,' in Graham Ward, ed., *The de Certeau
Reader*, Malden, Ma: Wiley-Blackwell: 101–18.

Foucault, M. 1986. 'Of Other Spaces', *Diacritics* (Spring): 22–27.

Foucault, M. 1970. *The Order of Things*, New York: Vintage. Books.

Genocchio, Benjamin. 1995. 'Discourse, Discontinuity, Difference: The Question of Other Spaces', in S. Watson and K. Gibson, eds, *Postmodern Cities and Spaces*, Oxford: Blackwell: 35–46.

Lefebvre, Henri. 2003a. Preface. *L'habitat pavillonaire*, Paris: Editions du Cru; rpt 2001. Introduction: *À l'etude de l'habitat pavillonaire* in *Du Rural a l'urbain*, Paris: Anthropos; English trans 2003. *Key Writings*, S. Elden, E. Lebas and E. Kofman, eds, Athlone Contemporary European Thinkers Series, London: Continuum: 121–135.

———. 2003b. 'The Other Parises', *Espaces et sociétés* 13, 14 (Oct 1974–Jan 1975): 151–59.

Merleau-Ponty, Maurice. 2002. *Phenomenology of Perception*, London, New York: Routledge.

Mumford, Lewis. [1937] 2000. 'What Is a City?' *Architectural Record* 1937, reprinted in *The City Reader*, edited by R.T. LeGates and F. Stout, 2nd edition, New York: Routledge: 92–96.

———. [1961] 1989. *The City in History*, New York: Harcourt, Brace and World.

Soja, Edward. 1995. 'Heterotopologies: A Remembrance of Other Spaces in the Citadel-LA', in S. Watson and K. Gibson, eds, *Postmodern Cities and Spaces*, Oxford: Blackwell.

Williams, Raymond. 1989. *Politics and Letters*, London: Verso.

Wilson, E. 1991. *The Sphinx in the City*, London: Virago.

Zukin, Sharon. 1995. *The Cultures of Cities*, Oxford: Blackwell: 3–34.

THREE

Inhabiting the City: The Challenges

'The Place de la Concorde does not exist, it is a notion.'—Malaparte[1]

Q: Where did you live when you first came to Calcutta?
A: With myself in a little place in Panditiya Road, a room so small that my bed couldn't get in without my sawing off the legs.
Q: Do you still live there? If not, what made you change your residence?
A: Yes, I have made the room bigger with mirrors.

These citations seem to bear out the words of Rilke, translated by Bachelard (1994: 200) in his work on the poetics of space: 'Space, outside ourselves, invades and ravishes things'. The reader will notice in the citations the variations of a theme. To 'achieve' the entity of some other being, advises Rilke,

Invest it with inner space, this space
That has its being in you (ibid.).

Both poet and philosopher conceptualize space as an incomplete, always-in-process becoming through the creative endeavour of 'habitation' undertaken by the human being. Habitation is an act of spatialization (Lefebvre 2003a), through which the self constitutes itself through relation to its world. As Heidegger (1971) wrote famously: Man *dwells* and does not just occur, like some mineral on the surface of earth. The Akan-speakers of Ghana, who count among their number the ancient Ashanti nation, have no word for being without a spatial referent that does not specifically qualify this condition. So in Ashanti, *ho* (there) is necessarily added to *wo* (to be) (Berry 1975). To be is to be somewhere; being is a spatial experience. Hence the concept of 'dwelling', being-in-space, is a human condition perpetually actualized as an everyday lived practice. For the purpose of this study, the word 'selfing' denotes this process of being-in-space. In this chapter, we shall consider the praxis and poiesis[2] of 'selfing', and in the later chapters, place within this frame narratives about ways of dwelling/being in urban space, shared by the survey respondents.

Before we embark upon this exploration, a moment on the verb 'selfing', coined for the specific purpose of this project. We have, in Chapter 1, considered the implications of the noun 'selfhood' and its relations with narrative. There, with the help of cognitive science, we have seen how the 'self' is amenable to narrativization. However, here, it is the activity named by the verb that we are concerned with: is narrativization the only way in which the self can be enacted, made active, given agency? On a superfluous level, the word 'selfing' derives from the Hindi word '*apna-na*', rooted in the word *apna* that can be translated as one's own. Exploring the processes of making one's own forms the core of our explorations; but perhaps finally we can move from the confines of the 'selfing' of a particular city, and wonder where the being of the modern 'emancipated' woman situated in an urban space structured by the ebbs and flows of global capital, might find a dwelling that creatively enhances becoming: not a place of rest or refuge so much as a space, geographical and metaphysical, that forms the context of her project of the future. Bachelard (1994) conceived of such a dwelling, as 'one of the strongest forces for integrating man's thoughts, his memories and dreams.... It keeps man safe through earthly and bodily storms.... It is body and soul'. But Lefebvre (2003a) sees this as a traditional patriarchal dwelling. *Demuere* in French refers to dwelling, and Lefebvre interprets this as a place where man's ego, his memories and dreams may find integration, wholeness and peace. But is 'man' to be taken literally? Do the conditions in which man's ego finds wholeness and peace through dwelling apply uniformly to all human beings? Or are we instituting one standard without accounting for differences of affect and socialization? With these questions in view, we turn to the business of making sense of the concept and the processes of selfing, applying our understanding to the actual experiences of our respondents.

To begin, then, with the notion of place. According to Lefebvre, 'moveable and immovable property constitutes habitation, embracing and signifying social relations' (ibid.: 124–25). He points out that in everyday life systems of signs comprising objects used as habitation require a constant translation into ordinary language. This is possible through 'a legitimate process of abstraction of relationships with nature and the material world (technology and poiesis)' (Lefebvre 2003b: 27). Since this remark is based on research in France, the question that we may ask is, is this place shared by men and women? Are women 'allowed' to enter it as equals, or is there a particular space within the house which is gendered male, and another gendered female?

Everyday life is hence a site for multiple confrontations between the natural (which Lefebvre sees as a part of all social constructions) and the artificial, constructed by detachment from nature and opposed to nature and also between the private and the public (Lefebvre 2003a: 100). The intertwining of the public and the private is manifestly more crucial for women, confined as they have been by hegemonic notions of femininity, to the so-called private sphere. And, indeed, theorists of postmodern culture, like Featherstone (1995), have identified it thus, differentiating between the 'heroic' extraordinary life described as male, and the everyday world, mundane, trivial yet crucial for the maintenance and reproduction of the stuff of life itself, which is the space of the feminine. But this division is not as neat as it would seem. Feminist social theory has shown that the private is constructed by, and constructive of, the public, and feminist work in geography has applied this insight to the study of space (Raju and Lahiri-Dutt 2011). The advent of single unattached and unchaperoned women to the city seems to be a rather violent assertion of this. It is what risk theorists like Tulloch and Lupton (2003) would call a border crossing: simply put, a movement from the known into the unknown world, whether physically or emotionally or both, thus creating a situation with the potential for risk. The women who come to the city from outside have to search for and construct their private space in an unknown and alien environment, emphatically gesturing towards the constructed nature of the private/public divide. Women in the city construct this differently, as they are 'protected' within the family space. But women who come from outside have to forge both the 'home' and the 'world' in an alien environment which is often different from what they are used to in their place of origin. This differentiates their efforts from those of women who live in the city by birth and are not outsiders here, and this difference is felt in the processes of everyday life by women who are 'outsiders'. Their responses will show that this difference also creates a dynamic of gendering the home space distinctively different from that studied by Mohan (2011). The acts of publicly earmarking a private space, that is, looking for a house to inhabit on one's own, or negotiating public spaces from the position of an 'outsider' assumes added significance when performed by single women, whom the mainstream is still unused to encountering in certain roles in the public space.

It appears as if the mundane, quotidian daily-maintenance activities of the 'everyday' are performed by these women in full public view: searching for accommodation, interviewing and being interviewed by prospective landlords, dealing with the nitty-gritties of daily existence. These are activities that women who come from outside the city and live alone in it, perform for themselves, simply because there is no one else to do them. Women who 'belong' to the city perform some or all of these actions, but are not compelled to suffer all or any of the consequences of these actions in an individual capacity. To the question: Are Calcutta people sympathetic to women like you, a 46-year-old university teacher replied, 'In my experience most of them have no idea what it means to look for a house and move house.' This particular respondent remembered that on the day her divorce came through, a number of single women who lived in established family homes in Kolkata had called her up to welcome her into the world of singletons. Her response was that since they lived with families at home, they could have no idea what exactly the word 'single' might mean, literally and metaphorically. This incident occurred when she had been living alone in the city for almost fifteen years, having come here when she was a student at college.

The first encounter that a single woman from outside has with the city is inevitably an extreme one. And ironically, the women themselves realize the violent intensity of the encounter only when they are well within its confines. In the first instance, it appears that a textbook case of the silenced female in patriarchy is enacted by women who have come to the city on their own. In doing so, they may well feel that the mould of the silenced woman is exactly the one that they are attempting to break out of. Thus the decision to break out of the circle of the accepted, institutionalized female role is generally a common experience that our respondents have expressed. The actual activity of doing this, however, apparently creates a situation of conflict between the 'natural' and the 'artificial' that Lefebvre (2003b) describes. Consider these experiences:

> Finding my way around the city on my own and often landing up at the same place from where I had started is an experience that I associate with the first stages of my acquaintance with the city. But then perhaps I did not know how to ask for help (51-year-old university teacher from Giridih has been in Kolkata since she was 16).

> I was very introverted so even when I got into the bus, I couldn't call the conductor for the ticket.' This was nervousness. One day when my stop had come, I had not called the conductor, I stood up and he was behind many people, I decided to overcome my fear and call him to purchase the ticket. This was a memorable incident I cited at my group discussion and personal interview when I went for my MBA admission in 2000 as my first public speaking.... I spoke up for the first time ... when there were lots of strangers around. If I had always spoken up before, I would have been treated better by my family and friends (29-year-old sales executive from Dhanbad).

> I remember I wanted to go to College Street to collect admission forms from Presidency College and boarded the ubiquitous mini-bus from Jodhpur Park ... I got on one, got a seat and patiently sat through many many stops with my ears all pricked up to hear the conductor shout for 'College Street', but the trip seemed to carry on and on and on. A knot was beginning to churn in my stomach. It seemed to me everybody in the bus was staring at me anxiously, yet I continued sitting through carrying that smug look of confidence on my face as if I knew where I was going. Ultimately I landed up

somewhere in the Airport area. When the bus drew to a halt at the terminus I got down very casually after paying the conductor and looked around for the next bus that would take me out of the terminus ... after getting up and down a couple of buses and walking some more, I reached the college only to find that no more forms were being given out for the stream that I wanted to apply for (34-year-old artist and project freelancer from Agartala).

Taking the gains of feminist struggle for women's emancipation from the level of economic self-sufficiency to the level of empowerment and capability may well be the contemporary concern of the women's movement in societies like ours. Differentiated processes of modernization, inflected by class and language-access will translate into varied access to opportunities for social and economic mobility, for men and definitely for women. This is the reality which our respondents, single women relocating to the city and attempting to make it their home, are engaged in negotiating on an almost moment to moment basis. Through this engagement they come to 'appropriate' the alien 'given' as part of their lives: a process without which survival in the alien environment is impossible. And if we remember that entering the alien environment was the result of a choice opened up through feminist struggle, we will be able to appreciate that the culmination of the struggle would be to appropriate the city and effect a socialization of the victories gained by the struggle itself; which in Lefebvre's terms would amount to a naturalization of what patriarchal norm designates as artificial with respect to women. Only then is it possible to experience the fruits of the struggle for emancipation and empowerment of women, resulting in what, again to use Lefebvre's terms, would constitute 'social development'.

These reminiscences are crucial to our understanding of the process of a gendered selfing of the city, a process that can be described by what Lefebvre calls 'appropriation', which 'is the goal, the direction, the purpose of social life.... Without appropriation, there can be economic and technical growth, but social development ... remains nil' (Lefebvre 2003a: 130). The first memories of the city that we have recorded above can be read from this perspective for each of them in very specific and individual ways recounts an experience of disempowerment, that is on reflection the beginning of a journey towards self-confidence that we may constitute as a crucial step out of the feeling of powerlessness. The project freelancer from Agartala who took the wrong bus and landed up at the airport instead of College Street explained why this incident was memorable for her:

> Before I came to Kolkata I had lived a sheltered, close knit, familiar and comfortable life. Then all of a sudden, there I was alone, all by myself, completely at sea and inexperienced. I had to brace this transformation straightaway without feeling browbeaten. I didn't feel lost though because I was conscious of having to deal with the situation I put myself in. I was determined to do things differently than the usual practice back home. I was confident I could do it; the whole transition was an event I was experiencing without help or company. I did not want to feel intimidated under the circumstances. The independence and being responsible for my own self was sometimes unsettling. The whole experience/feeling was akin to that of a grown-up fledgling taking flight from its nest and was now among a million others in the sky, learning to fly.

The realization that help has to be asked for and the subsequent decision about how to request this help, or whether to ask for it at all, the sense that help is not something one can take for granted in a situation of strangers are all tentative steps towards appropriating an alien space. Help comes only from certain types of people, and for the stranger trying to enter a new environment, this choice of helpful 'insiders' often inflects the whole experience of settling down. A 56-year-old university teacher who came to the city from Burnpur, first to study in 1964 and then returned after higher studies in 1979 to work, summed it up thus

> People in the city helped me settle down [provided important information], but [they] never ran around on my behalf as they would in a small town.

The sense of realizing that one is alone is traumatic as well as therapeutic as the artist from Agartala pointed out so poetically. A number of respondents recalled being conscious of the fact that they had no one to fall back upon, a threatening and dreadful situation. But most of them also felt that this was therapeutic: it taught them the value of themselves as individuals who would henceforth have to learn to interact with others on that basis. Two comments might be cited here. One young woman working in advertising, reluctant to give her age ('does it matter?') and her place of origin ('a place in another planet, another time zone'), in reply to the question 'What has Calcutta given you that you could not have got anywhere else?' answered 'It has given me myself to celebrate and calibrate in memory'. Even if we take this, for the present, as poetic excess (and we shall have occasion to follow this particular story at some length later), the gift of self is something that most women claim to have received from the city. They may put it in different ways, calling it 'independence', 'confidence' or even 'struggle', but the fact remains that they have transformed the city into intimate affective ground. A 31 year old from Giridih, now settled on the east coast of the United States, spent seven years in Kolkata after an engineering degree from the Indian Institute of Technology in Kharagpur, working in a multinational company. She is now a homemaker in another continent, but

> It's surprising that I remember every bit of the places I used to go to. I remember all the main milestones from Bally to Salt Lake (my workplace). I remember my people like the dhobi or the grocer, faces of the waiters at Azad Hind Dhaba, in fact little things like what the tequila shots at Someplace Else used to be like, the music they played also affect me very greatly. I remember all the nooks and crannies of New Market. So I think it's very difficult to get Calcutta out of your system.

Our friend the artist from Agartala has been living in Delhi since 2001.

> Right now I do not know which place to call home…. But I know that whenever I go to Kolkata it feels as if I have come home. My formative years have been spent in Kolkata and most of my friends, near and dear ones are in the city…. I am familiar with the pulse of

Kolkata more than any other place even where I grew up. If I ever
I call any place home, it will in all likelihood be Kolkata. No matter
where I have been and seen and get better facilities and advantages
of a metropolis, there is only one place I feel relaxed to let my hair
down and feet up.

And this is because the city is enmeshed with the discovery of a self
not possible in other circumstances. As a 45-year-old educationist
put it, 'Whenever I write a letter to a married friend, I have to put
c/o. But here there is no c/o....' This sense of self is catalysed by the
city; the process of appropriation seems to have been enabling and
it is narrated as such. In other words, the respondent was conscious
of her actions resulting in a realization and a consequent sense of
fulfilment that she could name.

The idea of the narrativized self that we gleaned from cognitive
science (see Chapter 1) orchestrated with Lefebvre's idea of poiesis
(2000c) can describe how the single woman outsider to the city,
appropriates urban space and urbanity as part of her lifeworld. We
are trying to understand how this space and its real and imagined,
social and psychological dimensions shape this process that I would
call the creation of a self. For example, learning to ask for help is an
acquired skill whose inherent quality may be debated upon, but a skill
that is necessary if one is to find one's place and survive in an alien
environment. And the acquisition of the skill must start with realizing that one does not have it. That the ability to speak for oneself
is instrumental in being 'treated ... better by family and friends' is
not a happy thought if one is concerned with human relationships in
the idealist sense; but the realization that this trait is crucial to living
everyday life if you are not 'c/o anyone but yourself', as one of the
respondents pointed out, can only be acquired through experience.
The city provides this experience by offering situations which can be
dealt with only on these terms. Once confronted with these situations,
as we will see again and again throughout this study, we come upon
resources within ourselves that we had no awareness of possessing.
Thus remaining calm, pretending to know where one is headed even
when one is lost, masking one's vulnerability with a show of 'smug
confidence' may not be the best strategy, but it is precious because it

is an unprompted independent action taken when one has assessed a designated situation. Again, whether it is the best strategy or not, will depend on the person taking the action and her assessment of the situation. Even if it is not the best path to take, it remains precious and memorable, because of its novelty; its novelty as a situation in which one has not thought of finding oneself, it is true, but more than that, the novelty of dealing with it and the awesome weight of taking responsibility for one's success or failure to do so. The artist from Agartala sums it up thus

> When one is an outsider the person faces a lot of issues ... identity crisis ... you don't belong to the city, you are from elsewhere, your family is not with you, you don't know the city well or what lurks around the corner, you feel lost or are extra sensitive. Well easily or not it can certainly be solved. All it takes is some time and of course the ways and measures you need to undertake to make life easier for your own good.

Combining representations on the one hand with modes of behaviour on the other, de Certeau also aims to study space from the point of view of how this space is 'made' or 'used' (quoted in Buchanan 2000: 99). He too defines this 'making' as poiesis, whose chief characteristic is its lack of visibility. Ian Buchanan comments on this activity as a hidden production because it takes place in fields already defined and occupied by large production systems, which according to the logics of scale, swamp the non-systemic with their outputs, leaving no space where this other production could actually exhibit itself (ibid.), earlier marked as a creative act. Thus the minute everyday activities of 'selfing' are often lost on all but those who have to decide consciously to act thus, and then, having decided, take the requisite action. Even more frustrating for the researcher is the fact that this is a creative act which does not manifest itself in products, but to quote de Certeau, 'rather through its ways of using products imposed by dominant economic order' (ibid.). The city is one such product par excellence, imposed by this order, and capable of sucking the woman into its womb, a space that can be both threatening and sheltering, full of both promise and despair.

What it finally culminates in is a personalized geography: space individualized through memory suffused with meaning, enacted as habitus. Appadurai (1995) thinks about locality in the performative: far from being unproblematic and immediate. Habitus, in his view, is the figural effect of cultural-social *production*. If we follow this view, then the city is performed in everyday life, and it is through such performances that it is produced, made, used, 'self-ed'. And in this process, as Lefebvre points out, 'the city was both the scene and the issue at stake' (Lefebvre 2000c: 154). Taking exception to historians' descriptions of political struggles as though they were waged on and in abstract space, Lefebvre demarcates 'three Parises' central to his theorizing of a single city, each a living theatre of change and affected unchangeably by it. As we progress further into this study, we shall look at the changes that have occurred in the face of the city and perhaps in its heart, to accommodate the single women from outside the city who live and work here alone. We shall investigate the inflections that the city has made in its mind and body because they have arrived at its doorstep and come in. The process of entering and staying, that we have called selfing, is also a process reflected in the city itself. Where these women live and how, where they feel safe and why, how they travel and how they spend their leisure are dictated by the city's own division of space. Yet this division is also inflected by the women themselves, as they settle in the city, even in the minutest of ways, the city has to change its structures, its forms of organization so that these women can enter. But how does this occur? This is the process that this project has set out to study. Fawcett et al (1984) have identified three types of female migration: the kind that is generally considered in this study is of the first enumerated type, which the authors describe as being undertaken by middle-and upper-class women for improving their educational credentials and also to get suitable employment, in a quest for social advancement, as well as to enhance their status in the marriage market. As K. Shanthi (2006) points out, in the Indian context, 'Among the semi-literate, young girls migrating to towns/cities to work in export processing units, garments industries, electronic assembling industries and food processing is continuously on the rise in recent years.' Most of the women from the rural areas who responded to this study were in the medical sector, doing skilled and semi-skilled jobs. But there are two respondents, women from Jharkhand who could fit into the second category of female migration, that is, 'relay migration' that entailed women coming from rural families with land holdings to work as domestic help to augment family income.

To introduce some degree of order into analysis of urban phenomena, Lefebvre (2000b) uses the linked notions of levels and dimensions. On the space-time axis, the levels reached by economic and social units are rural, industrial and urban. Considering the final, that is, urban level, the levels that can be identified are the global level (made up of the most general and thus the most abstract relationships, for example, the capital markets, the politics of space); the second is the mixed mediating or intermediary level, or the specifically urban level, and the third level is the private, the level of habitation. We shall consider all these levels in the course of our acquaintance with various stories of selfing the city. But given the age-range of the respondents to the survey and the extended period that some of them have spent in the city, this process of selfing seems at various crucial points to occur in concert with the history of change in the cityscape itself: a point that is important to help us understand the process of habitation and the process of 'self' constitution across time. Since gender forms the frame of this study, these changes will help us to understand the inflexions in the discourse of gender and emancipation.

Firstly let us rehearse the space itself, a difficult task to say the least because the timespan that we are here dealing with goes back at least to the early 1960s when the oldest women who came to the city were teenagers. As a 53-year-old doctor from Silchar explained,

> Then it was very rare for girls from middle-class families to go to Calcutta to study. I was only 19 years old. My father [had] a very progressive outlook that boys and girls have equal right to study. He also knew that I wanted to do something. Even today, I am a veteran but I feel like a young girl when I remember my father's words. I also feel proud when I remember them.

We might also conclude that the incidence of women working in cities away from home has only now begun to increase. This was not the case twenty years ago. As a 42-year-old educationist from Chandannagar explained,

> My father had a deep reverence for higher education for women. When I completed my Higher Secondary with high First division, my father said I should go to study in Calcutta. He was a very forward thinking man with enlightened views.

The words used here, 'progressive' and 'enlightened', reflect the milieu which women who came to the city aspired for, and the milieu from which they came: they were, as these respondents point out, not many of them, but their goals were clearly related to certain beliefs that their families espoused, or beliefs that the women themselves caused their families to accept. As time passed however, and more women came to the city in pursuit of courses of study and careers, the frontier-mentality of 'progress' and 'enlightenment' metamorphosed into a form of acceptance: women could, after all, leave home for reasons other than matrimony. This metamorphosis was realized as much in terms of space as it was in terms of mentalities of those families who were first 'enlightened' and 'progressive' enough to send their daughters out to study and work, and then gradually took this course of action as natural if they lived in smaller towns and semi-rural areas where education and opportunities for women were fewer. In 1991, the growth of the urban population of Calcutta was 22 percent as against a 28 percent overall population growth. The Calcutta Urban Agglomeration and the area under what was then called the Calcutta Metropolitan Council rose by 30 percent in the decade ending with 1991. Though jobs for women in old colonial industries declined, the sex ratio in the city increased from 50 women to every 100 men at the beginning of the twentieth century, to 80 women for every 100 men in the last decade of the twentieth century[3] in this period, Kolkata itself metamorphosed from an industrial into a post-industrial city. Appendix 2 attempts to encapsulate that change with certain specific areas in focus, as this process enables us to understand the nature of the space into which the respondents to this survey came and the changing nature of that space which they inhabit.

J. Lovering describes this change as a 'Simple Story' from the point of view of the UK, once known as the 'workshop of the world',[4] where industries have disappeared as a result of technological change, and consumer goods industries have shifted to areas with cheap labour, fuelling growth of multinational capital. India was an important destination of these industries. This was facilitated once the ideology of market protection changed in India and controls on the market were eased in the early 1990s (see Table 3.1). Opening up to globalization with its vast reserves of cheap labour, and later with its almost equally vast reserves of educated English speakers who were lapped up by the Business Processes Outsourcing sector, India's cities changed in character. The most striking change was elsewhere, but Kolkata, the oldest of the colonial urban centres and the hub of the eastern region, also underwent some change. Considering the process of the city's transformation as capitalism itself changes its shape and becomes globalized, Edward Soja (1995) has explored this process around what he calls the geographies of restructuring. Since Soja's example is Los Angeles, we here consider only those aspects of his analyses of restructuring that hold true for a 'third world' city, specifically, Kolkata. For example, a changed urban geography 'arises from the restructuring of the economic base of urbanization, from fundamental changes in the organization and technology of industrial production and the attendant urban social and spatial division of labour'. Particularly helpful for us in understanding Kolkata's urban reorganization in the current time is the insight that restructuring can also be described as a combined process of deindustrialization and reindustrialization or in postmodern terminology, a deconstruction (of the earlier city)

Table 3.1 Growth of cities and population projections

	1991	2001	2010
Bombay	9,925,891	11,978,450	13,830,884
Delhi	7,206,704	9,879,172	12,565,901
Bangalore	2,908,018	4,301,326	5,438,065
Calcutta	4,399,819	4,572,876	5,138,208

Source: World Gazetteer http://www.world-gazetteer.com

and the beginnings of a reconstruction of 'a new regime of urban industrial' (ibid.).

This change has accelerated in the last few years, but has been much slower than elsewhere. The presence of a Leftist government in the state since the late 1970s may have prevented the closure of local industries on the scale as large as that in the Mumbai cotton mills through the weakening of a once strong trade union movement, but this has not been completely avoided (see Chapter 8). The closure of industries and the economic stagnation that followed was ascribed to union activities of the workers, with or without Left support. This led to a stagnation that was addressed, ironically, through the unplanned acquisition of cultivable land for showcase industrial projects. This acquisition exposed the contradictions within the structures of governance based upon Left ideology through which the state was ruled for thirty-odd years until 2011. We may note that the data used here is from the earlier period—we do not know whether women who now come to the city from the outside are better off because the state has a woman at the helm. More pertinent to our concerns is the development of Salt Lake Sector V (see Figure A2.8). This area comprising a planned space of 100 ha is an industrial sector dedicated to Information Technology, developed in the late 1990s. It is part of the satellite city on the eastern fringes, where women have found work in professions other than the ones traditionally seen as fitting for women. These industries are characterized by their position within what is known as 'the secondary circuit of capital'. Explaining the process of deindustrialization, David Byrne (2001: 64) identifies three crucial processes of the global capitalist system: increased productivity in the manufacturing of commodities which means fewer people make more, the freedom of movement of industrial capital so that industrial jobs can be outsourced where cheap labour is available, and finally, the freedom of movement of financial capital and the emergence of a global system of speculation based on purely financial instruments. Hence, at least in the short term, production is less important than circulation for the capitalist system. Thus, land speculation; old industrial sites are more profitably used in other ways. This change in what Appadurai (1995) would call the 'scape' change, which represents the character of social structures in a world of movement and formations. This is the city that must be understood as the 'city' that women have entered, negotiated and inhabited over the period under consideration. As Byrne (2001: 73) points out, locality is the 'product of human interactions of everyday life in which we construct our social world on the matrix of the natural world and of the equally real, in the case of the built environment, equally material social world which is the product of previous human action in history'.

This forms the context of some everyday life-activities performed by women from outside the city who have come here on their own. One of our respondents, a 51-year-old academic who has been here since she left school, described her experience of visiting College Street coffee house, that paradise of intellectual high culture, in the early 1970s, when she was a newcomer dazzled by the city.

> Going to the College Street Coffee House is an experience of immense significance, liberating yet one that is decidedly unsettling—you know you do not belong when you go there with other women like yourself, your desire to look, to stare, to take it all in like a cultural tourist before cultural tourism was invented—you cannot be at ease, isn't that so-and-so, and did you see X or Y, famous people, men—men who belong. Whenever I have gone with women like me, women who have come from outside, even if they are studying at Calcutta University, even if they know a couple of famous men at the tables earmarked as 'theirs', when I have gone with men from my own city, and we have sat with men who are from Calcutta, those who also have their 'own' table, the two experiences have been completely different.

This conversation occurred while sitting in the College Street Coffee House within a year of my moving to Kolkata, more than twenty years ago; but every word is clearly etched in my mind. Perhaps this survey began from that scene: two women from small towns, sitting at a spot representative, almost emblematic, of the history of the city we had chosen to live in, and immediately aware of our position as outsiders, literally as well as through our gender. The College Street Coffee House is nothing if not an iconic monument which can be counted among those that Lefebvre (2000a: 152) suggests act both as useful landmarks and as symbols, 'paradoxically concrete within an invading abstraction, the abstraction of anonymous places and impersonal comings and goings'. And the first thing that struck us as we sat there was that this was a male space, certainly so in the early 1990s, and we were women sitting there with each other. Here we were, women from 'outside', sitting at the defining spot of the city, and, yes, we did know a couple of men who had their own earmarked tables, though they were wary of us that day because we were unaccompanied.

We may discern here the way in which the physical spaces offered by the city are 'appropriated' by the *citoyenne*/female citizen, for her own use. We have begun with the assumption that 'use' of space is both affective and material, given the condition of the women who are subjects of this study, the 'users' themselves. These users are not born into a home in the city, which sets them apart from the women studied by Paul (2011) with respect to access to and use of various kinds of public spaces. Women who come from outside must leave behind those homes which appear to be theirs by birth, to seek out a similar or intensely and deliberately dissimilar space which they may call by the same name, in an alien city. And this construction is not to be inhabited by mere physicality; as all dwellings, this space in the alien city too acquires the affective impulses of 'home'. Whether this is actively sought by the women, whether the process is a conscious one or whether we, as women from outside staying alone in the city, suddenly discover that it has happened without much conscious endeavour on our part, are questions central to the process of 'selfing'.

From the monumentality of College Street Coffee House, we now move into the street, undertake an activity that is, literally, the most pedestrian: walking in the city, also a form of introduction and appropriation. It is difficult to understand how a simple act like walking can be seen thus. After all, have we not all walked from here to there even in the smallest of towns or suburbs that we have left behind us? What is so special about the mundane activity of walking that we here mark it out as worthy of comment? To this there can be two different responses. The more functional answer is that learning the geography of the city is one of the first steps towards finding one's locus within it. As a woman who came to the city from a small town, my own memories of the city include learning how to tell bus routes from bus numbers as well as exploring lanes and bye lanes with friends who were all hostel-mates from other cities. But on the more affective level, for the woman who comes to the city from outside the city has to be found, and the acts of finding the city and locating oneself within it have to be performed. The semantic level of words uttered and the semiological level of signs that the words represent, that is, the concrete 'monumental' spaces that the walker 'discovers' for herself, are two systems that, in synchrony, produce a narrative of space.

Walking here is seen as an act that simultaneously produces the city as well as the *citoyenne*—and this is the crux of the process that we have named 'selfing'. Commenting on the relationships between spatial practices and signifying practices, de Certeau (2000: 1) identifies three nuclei on which such relationships may be based: the believable, the memorable and the primitive. One of our respondents answered the question 'What has Kolkata given you that you could not have got anywhere else?' with a memory of walking in the city:

> I remember feeling thrilled that I was in a big city and there was no one to stop me and ask me if my parents knew where I was going. I walked all around Park Circus and around Chor Bazar. Would spend hours inside the Park Street cemetery carefully watched by Makdoom, the caretaker from Samastipur, who thoroughly disapproved of my coming there alone.... I think it was in Calcutta that I first began exploring a city quite freely (46-year-old university teacher from Burnpur).

Part of this also formed her first memories of the city. De Certeau calls this perambulatory rhetorics of the urban system, just as what the act of speaking is for language, in other words, a process of appropriation (ibid.: 106). This is a process of discovering one's ability to speak/move/manufacture meaning and memory; a process that integrates the myriad sensations of the world into experiences, constituting the self and its relation to the world. As a 29-year-old advertising professional from Jamshedpur said,

Long walks with close friends are always entertaining and even profound. I have always had my most philosophical discussions on the roads of Calcutta, even while sweating like a pig…. I buy a lot of books from the pavements, mostly second hand, so browsing for books is another entertainment.

The city, because it is the space where this act is performed, becomes a personal locus; it provides both geographical and affective space. The specific act of walking is located on the intermediate, or mediating or intermediary level as defined by Lefebvre (Lefebvre 2000b: 137). And for many women who come from smaller towns or suburbs, this median space is threatening as well as challenging. It is not controlled by a higher authority and is not even a space in which one can be completely alone, the space of dwelling, a private space. It is a space outside these two extremes, and thus one in which it is necessary for the individual citoyenne to make at least a gesture towards the environment, whether in its material or affective forms. This might well be a gesture of rejection, but it demands a minimum recognition of the space as lived in a practice that is crucial to one's daily living. Lefebvre explains that this space takes 'in our minds … a form related to the site (immediate surroundings) and the situation (broader surroundings)' … characteristic of the social 'real' (ibid.: 137–38).

> Any experience or feeling you remember from your first days in the city?
> A corpse lying unattended on the roadside (university teacher, 51 from Giridih).

> When I was going to college in the morning, I saw many children, about 3 years old, being taken to school by their parents. In the village no one goes to school at that age (19-year-old student from a village in Medinipur).

This urban reality is always to be constructed through interaction with others—even experiences of rejection, of neglect and callousness come home to one with greater force when one is in an alien environment, just as experiences of the positive kind do.

Within the median space of the street, a private is thus constructed that is continuously inflected by the public: it is as if through the sights and sounds, the experiences and interactions that walking in an alien environment open us up to, the city itself is sending out certain signals, hailing the walker. For the single woman who is trying to find her own space, physically and emotionally within the city, these experiences, or at least the ones that are remembered, often occur from the first days of their stay. These are the experiences that remain as memories which define one's impression of the city, sending out a silently eloquent message about what to expect in this space.

Any experience or feeling you remember from the first days in the city?

It was my first day in the city and I asked this smartly sari-clad lady the direction of a place and she curtly said, 'Sorry I am busy'! (28-year-old university teacher from Nagaland).

On the fourth to fifth day after moving into Brabourne hostel ... a bunch of hosteliers including me went out shopping.... We were going to Gariahat and we decided to walk to avoid the crowded buses ... we were around seven girls and we were trying to cross the road on Park Circus crossing.... By the time I was crossing and I was in the middle of a wide, wide road (Circus Avenue), the traffic was released and suddenly I saw automobiles of all shapes and sizes come hurtling towards me. I got so paranoid that I just stopped in the middle of the street and started crying.... When I looked up after a minute, I saw people, traffic police, the bus drivers, cabbies and my friends, etc., screaming at me, sympathetically though, to cross. The traffic was put on hold once more just so that I could cross, I was embarrassed but happy to be alive and I felt relieved that cities are not all about survival and ruthlessness (27-year-old programme coordinator in a non-profit organization, from Ranchi).

Many women talking about the experience of living in their home-towns, have said 'In Dhanbad [or Gaya or Patna or in their mofussil town] women don't go out on the street alone' or 'It is not safe for women to go out alone' or 'It is not possible for a woman to stay out alone after (a certain time)'. Sil (2011) has studied the lives of women in a 'globalizing' town but Bardhaman, where her research is based is not yet a metropolis. So, does the metropolitan city then provide safety which enables women to do what they would not be able to do in a smaller city or in towns? Is the median space of the street or public areas in the metropolis replete with considerate progressive and urbane citizens who have been educated by feminist struggles to make public space as much women's property as men's? Has, in fact, a resistance to the global ideology of capitalist patriarchy occurred on the streets of Kolkata, most visibly because a number of single women from outside the city have found here a safe place to play out their dreams and aspirations?

A 22-year-old postgraduate from Habra, South 24-Parganas, who is currently looking for a job, remembers an experience within the university, which occurred when she had already spent about three years on campus. A rock band had come to play and as she was entering the auditorium in the melee, she was pushed by a volunteer, a male student who was junior to her. She turned around, took him by the collar and landed a punch on his nose

> To protect oneself from beasts, one must become bestial perhaps, sometimes … the boy did not know where to run—I had exposed the animal within him in front of so many people. But I was very satisfied—I had been able to protect myself.

The emphasis placed on voice and consequently, the breaking of silence as an emancipatory process, has long been central to the methodology of feminist research in the humanities and social sciences. Kamala Visweswaran (1994: 50) affirms the centrality of speech while also emphasizing the process of voicing. As she points out, who says what to whom, why, when and where, and in what language, has an effect upon what is being said, and what is heard as well. 'Locating the temporality of speech' as she terms it, 'we gain another lens on the construction of subjectivity.' She urges us to take note of the circumstances 'when and why do women talk to assess 'the strictures placed on their speech, the avenues of creativity they have appropriated, the degrees of freedom they possess' (ibid.: 51). Thus for us, perhaps placed in similar situations ourselves, the Dhanbad MNC executive's first 'public speaking' experience in asking the bus conductor for her ticket in front of so many strangers may not be such an obviously dramatic realization. But we might recall that she too felt speaking up earlier would have earned her the respect due to her from her friends and family members. This kind of self-assertion in overt or covert ways, seems in general to be 'natural'; but as the women who live alone in the city have found, these are momentous to the process of self-construction; crucial, because in a public space, they establish the individual to others and, most importantly, to the self. For our purposes, it is also important to note that these incidents are of significance because they occur, not in a restricted private space or in a faceless institutional space, but in what Lefebvre has called the median space. In the street or in an auditorium, it is safe to merge with the crowd, but necessary for a woman in particular, to maintain her private space, for the sheer imperative of 'safety', a gendered concept that we will have occasion to consider at length later (see Chapter 7). In all the cases that we have referred to above, and in many more that we will be considering in the course of this study, we shall find that in such circumstances, self-assertion may be seen as a part of as well as a deterrent to self-preservation. Self-assertion is an imperative, for who will speak up for the single woman in the city if she herself does not do so? On the other hand, is it right to draw attention to oneself by protesting, speaking out, standing up? This is the crux of the daily struggle that characterizes living in the city for women who come from outside. Perhaps these women outsiders represent the unarticulated dilemma of all women venturing into public space, but their experiences are underlined with the added awareness that they often do not have the support that women who have families in the city to fall back upon, may take for granted. And so the most innocuous of activities become fraught with significance and sometimes with anxiety, at other times with pure exhilaration of minute but tangible achievements.

So, is a woman walker safe in the city? And if she is, is it because she has taken steps to protect herself, or is it because the city, as a functioning mechanism, as an ideology of the urban, has articulated itself to accommodate her? De Certeau says: 'Walking, which now pursues and now invites pursuit, creates a mobile organicity of the environment, a succession of *phatic topoi*'. As a woman who wonders whether it would be safe to take a taxi from City Centre in Salt Lake to Jadavpur, an hour's ride through empty streets, at ten in the night, this fine nonchalance about 'inviting pursuit' is disturbing to say the least. The function of walking, is, truly, an effort to set up communication, but on whose terms, and under what circumstances? A number of women have commented on the safety of the neighbourhood, the *para* as it is called in Bangla, but here we are concerned with perambulations beyond that space, and we are not yet considering the unspoken conditions that are inherent in the protection that the 'para' gives to the woman living on her own in a city. Always beneath the surface of the social scaffolding, which appears to condone the employment, economic and social mobility of women, lies the ambiguity about protection, the possibility of pursuit, the problem of safety. Why should the 19-year-old woman walking in the crowded market area of Jadavpur, just across the road from her university face this experience?

Would these issues have arisen at all, had these women, following the dictates of patriarchy, not ventured out on the streets unescorted or unprotected by a solid male presence? In Lefebvre's words, the 'second' level where the activity of walking occurs, is, as we have seen, an intermediary between 'society, State, powers and knowledges on the global scale, institutions, ideologies and on the other, habitation. If the global seeks to govern the local, if generality aspires to absorb particularities, then the middle level may act as the terrain for attack and defence, for struggle (Lefebvre 2000b: 141). The street is indeed the space of resistance against the general attempting to absorb the particularities, but this resistance is enacted in the interstices of the general patriarchal mindscape of the city by women who have ventured to inhabit this space. For the unconcerned (male) walker, may be accommodated by such (male) theoretical interventions in generalized terms. But the gendered nature of this theory is in direct relation to the gendered nature of the object which has given rise to the theory, and the context within which the theory is functional: the patriarchal city in the moment of global capital. Women are invited to come to the city, allowed, as it were, their space in the city; but on what terms?

Let us return for a moment to Foucault's critique of ethnology (1970: 376–77) as a 'western' science. Demonstrating the validity of his claims by locating ethnology in the history of its foundational moment, Foucault nevertheless finds a use for it when applied at ground level to study the workings of those Foucauldian grand narratives, that is, biology, economics, philology and linguistics that have thus far been perceived as dominating the human sciences from a very great height. Foucault sees located ethnology as a mode of reintroducing historicity using sets of questions that can determine, through an investigation of the symbolic systems employed, the prescribed rules, and functional norms chosen and laid down, what sort of historical development each culture is susceptible of, thus revealing 'the foundation of that historical flow within which the different human sciences assume their validity and can be applied to a given culture and upon a given synchronological area' (ibid.: 377–78). Our attempt is to uncover the 'norms' of gender realized, expressed and lived through symbolic systems which underlie gendering in a specific neocolonial urban space. Foucault's list does not include gender, which has been shown to impinge upon all the other grand narratives even if by the very fact of its absence. Neither does Foucault make any gestures towards the position of the ethnographer as a located subject. Feminist philosophers have reconsidered theories of knowledge and research, which will form a conceptual frame for our understanding of the experiences narrated by our respondents. As Code (1993) points out

> prompted by a conviction that gender must be put in place as a primary analytic category, I start by assuming that it is impossible to sustain the pre-assumption of gender-neutrality that is central to standard epistemologies.... But gender is not an enclosed category, for it always interwoven with such other socio-political-historical locations as class, race, and ethnicity, to mention a few (20).

One of the main aims of this study is to discern the consequences of making gender a category open to the dynamic social forces active in space and time, what Code might call locations. I have selected a city as a particular location, and attempted to discern how gender is being reinscribed within specific urban situations. The women who inhabit the city and this survey are both actively engaged in negotiating with these locational dynamics, as well as instrumental in creating them. These intermeshed practices are what Lefebvre would call both poiesis and praxis. They form the poetry of new styles of being and living while engaging with the phenomenal and material world as it is given to the agent. This exercise appears important because it throws up multi-dimensional engagements that can be termed feminist praxis. In other words, these questions, in the current time, forge a series of issues that should figure on our agenda as feminists at a particular historical conjuncture. The range of such questions encompasses the lives of many women. They include such questions as has the city accommodated some women alone and unchaperoned, and allowed them to inhabit the spaces that it offers for 'public' and 'private' habitation? What has it expected of these women in particular, and all women in general, in return? Have these women for whom a home in the city has to be publicly constructed through interactions with strangers and in alien spaces, found the city responsive to their struggles, their efforts and desires? What impact does the metropolitan Indian city have on the process of gendered self-fashioning? And, more pertinently, will the city change because female citizens from within and outside the city have changed?

NOTES

[1] Quoted by de Certeau (2000).

[2] According to Lefebvre, 'poiesis is [that] human activity [which] appropriates nature [physics] around and within the human being (its own nature, sense, sensibility and sensory perception, needs and desire)'; see Lefebvre (2003a).

[3] Figures from Annapurna Shaw, ed. 2007. *Indian Cities in Transition* (New Delhi: Orient Longman).

[4] See J. Lovering. 1999. 'New Regionalism Criticised', mimeo: 68, University of Wales, cited by D. Byrne (2001): 51.

WORKS CITED

Appadurai, Arjun. 1995. 'The Production of Locality', in Richard Fardon, ed., *Counterworks: Managing the Diversity of Knowledge*, London: Routledge: 204–24.

Bachelard, Gaston. 1994. *The Poetics of Space*, trans. Maria Jolas, Boston, Ma: Beacon Books.

Berry. 1975. *Akan Speakers of Ghana: An Introduction to Akan*, Evanston, Ill: Northwestern University Press.

Byrne, D. 2001. *Understanding the Urban*, New York: Palgrave Macmillan: 51.

Code, Lorraine. 1993. 'Taking Subjectivity into Account', in Linda Alcoff and Elizabeth Potter, eds., *Feminist Epistemologies*, New York: Routledge.

De Certeau, M. 2000. 'Ethnography: Speech or the Space of the Other, Jean de Lery', in Graham Ward, ed., *The de Certeau Reader*, Malden, Ma: Wiley-Blackwell.

Fawcett, J.T., S. Khoo, and P.C. Smith. 1984. *Women in the Cities of Asia: Migration and Urban Adaptation*, Boulder, Co: Westview Press.

Featherstone, M. 1995. *Undoing Culture: Globalisation, Postmodernism and Identity*, London: SAGE Publications.

Foucault, Michel. 1970. *The Order of Things: An Archaeology of the Human Sciences*, London: Tavistock.

Heidegger, Martin. 1971. 'Building, Dwelling, Thinking', in *Poetry, Language, Thought*, trans Albert Hofstader, New York: Harper and Row.

Lefebvre, Henri. 2003a rpt. [1967]. 'Myths in Everyday Life', in S. Elden, E. Lebas and E. Kofman, eds, *Key Writings*, Athlone Contemporary European Thinkers Series, London: Continuum: 100–06.

———. 2003b. 'Prolegomenas', in S. Elden, E. Lebas and E. Kofman, eds, *Key Writings*, Athlone Contemporary European Thinkers Series, London: Continuum: 22–30.

———. 2003c. 'Preface to the New Edition', *The Production of Space* in S. Elden, E. Lebas and E. Kofman, eds, *Key Writings*, Athlone Contemporary European Thinkers Series. London: Continuum: 136–50.

Mohan, Taneesha. D. 2011. 'Interrogating Temporal and Spatial Negotiations: Home as the Gendered Site for Working Women in Delhi', in S. Raju and K. Lahiri-Dutt, eds, *Doing Gender Doing Geography: Emerging Research in India*, New Delhi: Routledge: 157–78.

Raju, Saraswati, and Kuntala Lahiri-Dutt. 2011. *Doing Gender, Doing Geography*, New Delhi: Routledge.

Shanthi, K. 2006. 'Female Labour Migration in India: Insights from NSSO Data', Working Paper 4, Madras School of Economics www/mse.ac.in/pub/santhi-wp.pdf accessed 8.10.2016.

Shaw, Annapurna. 2007. *Indian Cities in Transition*, Hyderabad: Orient Longman.

Sil, Tanushree, 2011. 'Creating New Places: Women and Livelihoods in the Globalising Town of Burdwan, West Bengal', in S. Raju and K. Lahiri-Dutt, eds, *Doing Gender, Doing Geography: Emerging Research in India*, New Delhi: Routledge: 110–30.

Soja, Edward, 1995. 'Postmodern Urbanization: The Six Restructurings of Los Angeles', in S. Watson and K. Gibson, eds, *Postmodern Cities and Spaces*, Oxford: Blackwell: 125–37.

Tulloch, J., and J. Lupton. 2003. *Risk and Everyday Life*, London: SAGE Publications.

Visweswaran, Kamala. 1994. *Fictions of Feminist Ethnography*, Minneapolis, MN: University of Minneapolis Press.

FOUR

A Room in the City: Constructing a Private Space

It's hard to find the right kind of set-up always, when you come from a different one. Obviously in the city where you are not born or grown up, your life is going to have to start from scratch and it can be a daunting ask for many (34-year-old artist and project freelancer, Agartala).

Q: Any experience/feeling that you had when you first came here?
A: Felt like Mr. Biswas in Naipaul (18-year-old student of English from Bhopal).

The most difficult thing is to find a home for oneself. Any woman who is alone and wants to rent a house will find herself in difficulty.... The way to solve it is to lie with as much cleverness as you can when necessary (25-year-old student from Murshidabad).

In the neighbourhood, interactions with shopkeepers, the gas vendor, the cable TV man, plumber, etc., are enough to convince me that as long as I am the sweet dumb woman, dependent on their mercy and giving them my business, they will be okay with me and cheat me just a little. Otherwise there'll be complete war and after an age no one likes *para* boys looking at you in lusty admiration when you are in a pair of very comfortable and decent jeans (28-year-old advertising professional from Jamshedpur, currently living south of Jadavpur in a rented place with a flatmate).

A woman arrives in the city. Where has she come from and where is she headed? These are the first questions that she becomes aware of in relation to her 'self', for on these is predicated the most obvious necessity that she must acquire before anything else: a place to stay. When the advertising professional talks about her current living conditions, myriad dimensions of the act of finding a house in the city and settling into it unfold before our gaze. One of the most obvious of these is that the outsider living in your house/room/neighbourhood is a woman, and she is alone, without male protection. This chapter places the 'affective' connection with space, locality and habitation (see also Chapter 3) at the foundation of a discussion about some inescapable realities that women who come to the city from outside have to negotiate. These are not exactly seen as 'problems' by people who live within the city; if they are perceived as such by those who move into the city as a family, their nature will be different from the way in which they are perceived by single women coming to the city alone.

This chapter and Chapters 5, 6, 7 and 8 form the core of the experiences that the respondents to the survey and women like them, have undergone. There is a simple premise for structuring these chapters in this way. Very little attempt has been made at tabulating and analysing the response-data available according to sociological categories, namely, the kind of accommodation inhabited or the kind of employment or course chosen. Such classification of data does not necessarily illuminate the nuances of the process that is our fundamental concern: one of the main pitfalls of such categorization could be a tendency to 'manage' the data to arrive at an unnecessarily mechanical analysis. Our aim is not primarily statistical enumeration, and we do not proceed from the assumption that all members of a particular class will act in similar ways or that they act thus because they belong to such a class. Sayer (2000) advocates a realist rather than a mechanical or relativist analysis for the social sciences. He criticizes the Grand Narratives or Grand Analyses, as 'they neglected to tell stories and instead just absorbed empirical material into their pre-existing categories and frameworks' (Sayer 1981). Critical Realism is differentiated from Empirical Realism through the establishment of three separate categories, which Sayer enumerates as the 'empirical', the 'real' and the 'actual'. The empirical is the data derived from the senses, but it cannot be the sole basis for knowing and understanding the 'real' because as Roy Bhasker (1975) points out, knowledge has two dimensions, transitive and intransitive. The objects of science, that is, physical or social phenomena, are intransitive, while theories of discourse or media and resources through which science is transmitted, are transitive. This is because the 'real' exists even outside our sensing of it, that is, it exists regardless of our empirical knowledge of it at any given moment within a particular context. Critical Realism conceives of an emergent world, where the interaction of two or more features of any given structure would cause new phenomena to emerge, which are not in any way reducible to the causal elements (Sayer 2000). The realist account, in the social sciences leads to the view that causal mechanisms generate structures that are complex products of interactions between the 'social' and the 'natural'. Since they cannot be attributed to singular or collective human agency alone, though made and operated by humans, they are still perceived as 'caused' (Byrne 2001: 10). Data presented in tabular form serves to show certain facts at a glance: interpretation suiting our purposes is possible only when various aspects of the data, that is, a number of tables, not necessarily evenly matched, are taken in conjunction with the narratives out of which the tables are constructed. The narratives cannot be merely substituted by the tables. As Sayer (2000: 17) cautions, there is a 'possibility that powers may exist unexercised and what has happened or been known to have happened does not exhaust what could happen or could have happened'. Hence, 'meaning has to be understood, it cannot be enumerated or counted and hence there is always a hermeneutic or interpretive dimension to the social sciences'. This may be explained by the fact that the systems we are here discussing are complex, and the interaction between systems yields emergent properties which cannot be derived from those of its components. These are evolutionary systems, in which the whole is greater than the sum of its parts, making the systems irreversible (Byrne 2001: 11). The use of empirical data in this study has been made keeping these ideas in view, and must be read or used in a similar fashion.

Detailed maps of different parts of Kolkata are included in Appendix 2. As the reader will see, different areas figure prominently in the text as places where the women live or aspire to live. The ambience and culture of these areas, in all their subtle differentiations, have a visible impact upon the process that we are trying to study.

So, these maps are referred to in the relevant places in the text, in the hope that the bearings of these places, their interconnections and their relative distance from the other parts of the city will help the reader to better understand the views and opinions held by the respondents about the city and about living in it. Similarly, there are maps showing the eastern fringes where the Information Technology industry has been accommodated in Sector V at Salt Lake. Since many of the women work there, and some live there as well, their relative distance from the workplace and the place where they live becomes a factor in their experience of the city. As we have noted in the introduction, conveyance to and from the workplace is a crucial factor in the selection of places to live. The roads marked in the map of the city and the areas referred to (Figures A2.2 to A2.8) may be read together in order to understand the choices of accommodation in specific cases. The statements made by the women about different parts of the city as workplaces or places of residence cannot be elucidated by a map alone: but at least the bearings of the areas may be discerned, contributing, however marginally, to a semblance of understanding an 'unknown' city.

Let us turn to the set of questions on accommodation available for young single women living alone in the city. The reader might wonder why we use the adjective 'young'; what about the old? As Table 4.1 tells us, older women who have been in the city for a while and travelled up the hierarchy in their workplace, have been able to make arrangements for themselves that are permanent, even though, as we shall see, they too had to go through the experience of finding a suitable place to live when they first came here. As a 36-year-old media professional from north Bengal, explains, 'Thankfully I am now in a better position to articulate my terms and live according to them than before.'

Another consideration worked with older women who came to the city, say, thirty years ago; at that time, the idea of women living alone did not occur even to the women themselves. I speak from experience as I myself lived, in the late 1970s, in a hostel where there were working women as well as students and none of my hostel-mates who held good jobs ever talked of getting a place of their own until they got married. If they did move out of the hostel,

Table 4.1 Where do you live in the city?

Total Respondents (English medium: 90; Bangla medium: 30)						
Occupation language of response:	Hostel	Own flat/ house	Paying guest	Relatives	Rented accommodation	Others
English:						
Working	21	8	14	4	8	4
Studying	Open hostel 19[1]; univ/ college hostel: 2		8	1		1
Bangla: Working	5			3	2	3
Studying	Open[2]: 5 univ/ college hostel: 3	1			8	

Source: The Survey (Appendix 1).

as some did, it was when a younger brother or sister came to the city to stay and then a family unit was set up. Recently, a woman from Mirik, who had studied in Kolkata since 2004, and lived in PG accommodation for that time, moved too, to a rented place quite far from the university where she is now registered for an MPhil degree, because her brother has now joined her. He is in the first year of a Bachelor's degree course in the same university. She is currently in the process of setting up house for the two of them. Apparently, the thirty intervening years have changed some things, but not all. So 'young' is a considered adjective in this case, and one that defines this conjuncture.

The other reason is chilling. Just before we started this survey in 2004, while many of my friends from outside the city who later became resource persons in this project were discussing the idea amongst ourselves, one of the oldest working women's hostels in the Jodhpur Park area decided to ask boarders above a certain age to vacate their rooms.[3] One of my friends had just left that same hostel and she still had contacts there and that is how we came to hear of this. It turned traumatic for many of the residents who had not planned for this contingency; they were caught in a dilemma. They were single women, independent and no longer young, unused to the ways of staying in typical homes; many of them had no strong links with those homes and had developed their independent space. But this very space was now being threatened; where would they go? It was almost like the dilemma faced by young women who first come to the city; only the energy, enthusiasm and hope with which the younger women meet this challenge could not be expected from women who had spent their whole lives struggling with daily trivia in order to keep themselves independent especially in a milieu which was even more hostile to single women from outside the city than it is now. Indeed, these women could well be called pioneers of the process that we were setting out to investigate, and even before the investigation had begun, we were cruelly made aware of the insecurity that might await the subject of our study when another woman in her position, but much younger with better prospects, lays claim to her space. For the hostel also could not be blamed: how could they allow a limited number of seats to be occupied for years on end by some women, while more and more women were coming to the city in search of jobs?

Our friend who had lived with some of the women who had almost become permanent residents, remembered their tantrums and demands upon the hostel superintendent; long residence had given them some unwritten rights over space that they thought of as their home. These rights did not always receive adequate acknowledgement from the younger women who came to stay there later, leading to clashes and conflicts that would never have occurred had they not been forced into a situation of competition produced by their lives as single women outsiders in the city. On the other hand, this same friend remembered the care and consideration these older women showed her, a younger woman with a job in the city and hence forced to live outside the home environment. She remembered them taking her out for sightseeing trips during the Pujas, sharing food, and generally looking out for her. The hostel was not entirely wrong in asking the long-time residents to vacate their seats, because it was not meant to be a permanent home; on the other hand, where would the older women go at the stage in their lives when most were on the verge of retirement?

This was a crude way of understanding the ideological apparatus that works to regulate the lives of women wherever they are found outside the niches that patriarchal society has designated as 'safe' for them. There could have been no more disturbing thought than contemplating the sudden onrush of insecurity that women who had spent a lifetime coping with diversity had now to confront and win over. The media professional from north Bengal, who came here to study, then married and divorced, is now back in the city as a working woman, single and not so young, according to her own assessment. She puts it bluntly

> I feel Calcutta is safer when a girl is young because of the inherent chivalry shown towards the young girl. Everybody protects and pampers her. As one approaches middle age people become very ruthless. I am speaking from the sexual angle also. I know this is different from the perceived notion of Calcutta, but I am speaking from personal experience.

As we have seen in Chapters 2 and 3, dwelling is here not confined to its literal meaning. It is seen rather as a continuous process, and to it we have connected the process by which one inhabits a space and fashions a being that is marked both by the place and the process of inhabiting. This is the core of the activity we have defined as 'selfing' (see Chapter 3) which we shall explore throughout this study. Looking for accommodation is often, as we shall see from the experiences our respondents recount, contingent upon where the individual woman comes from and what her goals, professional and personal, are, overtly and covertly.

We will consider these questions from the material and the affective points of view. This is because the experience of hunting for a place to live in for the woman-outsider, alone in the city, is an activity with many emotional implications. A 28-year-old respondent from

what she describes as a 'tribal Christian' family in Ranchi recounts
her experience of house hunting in Kolkata

> I spent three months running scared, searching for an affordable PG.
> No Bengali took me in, but they will celebrate Christmas. I don't
> understand it. I went to a house in Belgachia.[4] The whole family
> interviewed me. They commented about my looks in front of me in
> Bengali, thinking I won't understand. The head of the family even
> asked me whether I thought conversions were right or wrong. I was
> very angry but I kept quiet because I needed this place badly. My
> sister faced many problems too when she came.

A similar experience can be attributed to the women who come to
Kolkata from the Northeast: they too are visibly different and are
exposed to the crudest exhibition of the outsider syndrome. As a
25-year-old teacher from Darjeeling, from the Lepcha community,
remembered, 'It was hell, the weather. No place to stay. The crowd.
People staring at you ... even though I come from one of the districts
of West Bengal, people tease us and stare at us making us feel alien.'
The artist from Agartala, who comes actually from Manipur, says

> When I landed up in Kolkata, I was an instant outsider I was
> Northeastern [read chinky-eyed] and back then [in 1989], our num-
> bers were few, and people generally stared a lot, as if we were a dif-
> ferent species of human being. I was always on my guard. I didn't
> want to be taken for a ride one way or the other. I could speak the
> language a little. I would speak the language everywhere in Kolkata,
> be it with bus conductors or rikshawallahs or shopkeepers, after a
> few months I could articulate the language, and then it wasn't so
> difficult to behave like a local.

These are however only the most obvious and obviously jarring
instances of being made conscious of one's status as an outsider, alone
in the city. Many of the comments are gendered, substantiating a version
of the complex problems that the MNC executive from Ranchi points
out. Thus finally finding a house and settling there depends on many
factors, which we will consider one by one in the following sub-sections.

WHERE DO YOU LIVE?

To begin with we can consider the options available and the preferences that some respondents have shown.

'Where did you stay when you first came? Do you still live there?
If not, why did you change?' 'Are you happy with your present living
conditions? Why?' These were the questions related to accommodation in the survey sheet.

Among the women who replied in detail are some who have come
to work; others had come to study and continued staying on with jobs.
The age range begins abruptly in the middle of the twenties because
the postgraduate degree and/or professional courses are completed
by the time a woman is 23. Then the woman enters the job market.
In the 22–35 age group, the places to stay are pretty evenly distributed
across the types available: paying guest accommodations, open and
mixed hostels like the Nari Seva Sangha in Jodhpur Park in south
Calcutta or the Salvation Army at Dharamtala, in central Calcutta,[5]
where both working women and students can stay (as these are working women, they cannot stay in other kinds of hostels), rented flats
shared among friends or separately rented. Hostels often impose all
kinds of rules, but it is not as if paying guest accommodations are
completely free of interference or constraints.

Some respondents have had experiences that can only be called
strange: owners of PG accommodation lay down the law about
clothes, ask that mobiles should not be used. Some women who have
had to bear with such questions and comments feel that these are
initial hiccups that can be sorted out with time; on the other hand,
many are unhappy with their current arrangements. The incidence
of dissatisfaction goes down as the age range goes up, indicating that
the women who have been in the city longer, or have better jobs and
more experience and so are able to bargain better, do not settle for
whatever they are offered and have either the power or the ability
to choose accommodation that is generally satisfying. Also, as the
age increases, the incidence of paying guest accommodation goes
down, and the number of house-owners increases, too. However,
we did not attempt to keep uniformity in any way between ages,
localities or professions. Hence, those who conducted the survey,

women between 20 and 30, themselves distributed the sheets to their peers and friends who spread them further, and the bulk of our respondents belong to the 25–30 age group. The findings from our sample must be read keeping this fact in mind before any blanket conclusions can be drawn.

LOOKING FOR A 'HOME'

Some respondents above 30 did come earlier; a woman who is now 35 and has been living here for five or six years, came to the city when she finished her education. One who is 51 and has been living here since she was 16 has been here for 35 years. Such women have now found an optimum level of comfort, as much as can be expected in a place where there is no family establishment. Other women also have aspirations of setting up such establishments. A 26-year-old sales executive from Dhanbad, who came to Kolkata after her parents separated, says, 'I would like to get my own pad in Cal so that my mom can come and stay with me even when I am married, I want to have a place that I and my mom own legally, so I'm working towards that'. A 28-year-old accountant from Patna plans to bring her sister to the city for higher education once the latter finishes her Intermediate, because 'in Patna the atmosphere is not free'. The MNC executive from Ranchi has already helped her sister to settle down to study here. A 33-year-old computer professional from Bhubaneswar is planning to educate her niece. These are instances of selfing that follow a pattern of economic and social mobility and will create family units of a different sort. The 51-year-old doctor from Silchar remembers that when she came to Kolkata at 19, to study,

> My father blessed me [and] said that I am the eldest daughter of the family, after Father I am responsible for the welfare of my five brothers and sisters. So I have to prove that I have courage and he is not making a blunder. I have always discharged my responsibilities and honoured my father's memory.

This has extended to concern about the welfare of a married brother in the same profession as herself.

> I live at Lake Town in my own house.... The only problem is that I want to expand my house further so that my youngest brother (also a doctor) who is now in Burdwan practicing there can come and stay here with family. I also want a joint chamber in my residence.

The university teacher from Giridih pointed out that 'families in frames', that is, the typical couple family, is the norm, and couples prefer couples, but the number of all-women families or instances where single women have become the nucleus of a family set up are not completely absent. In fact, in Bangla literature, there are quite a few examples of the strong paternal aunt, the pishima, widowed at a young age and back in her father's and then her brother's household as the centre of the domestic structure. Ashapurna Devi's story 'Baluchori' revolves around Mandira who loses her parents at a young age and is left with three siblings and, luckily, an ancestral house. She puts the latter to good use in order to provide for them, thus giving an example of a household headed by a single woman. In our survey, the older women have wisely provided for themselves if they have remained single.

Some of the younger women too have taken advantage of expanding opportunities in their place of work: rising salaries, easy equated monthly instalments, wise investments, in a nutshell, the gifts of the city, which they have accepted with alacrity, have enabled them to do what took a lifetime for the older women. The youngest house owner in our survey was the 28-year-old finance executive from Ranchi, who bought her own flat in 2003 in Kasba.[6] This has now developed into a new neighbourhood that borders the road connecting the upscale area of Gariahat in the south to the Eastern Metropolitan Bypass. It is reached by crossing a flyover which goes over the tracks on which local trains ply between Sealdah Station and the southern suburbs of the city. The woman who bought her own house there said that she did so 'because I thought that with a housing loan it was a more attractive proposition as well as an investment better than a rented apartment'. At the end of the day, they have a home to return to. The

36-year-old media professional from north Bengal puts it clearly, 'I married right after college, and had a difficult marriage. I divorced in 1990. So I am single for more than 14 years. This flat is my lifetime achievement award'. The 50-year-old school teacher sums it up thus

> My home is my flat. I am very house-proud and would like my home to reflect my taste. As I am in sole charge of the establishment, I do the work of both husband and wife to maintain it well. When I invite my friends and relatives, everyone compliments me on my aesthetic taste.

Other women who have been able to buy houses for themselves have similar feelings:

> My home is my flat. It is my own purchase. I feel responsible about it I and also happy about it (computer professional from Bhubaneswar, aged 32).

> I was fortunate to get a permanent job in a nationalized bank in 1982. I therefore purchased a plot of land near Salt Lake and in 1985. I was the proud owner of a single storey house that is now a double storey house (45-year-old senior public sector undertaking officer, Murshidabad).

> My home is my flat. I have done everything myself, from the decorations to plants. My parents have stayed here; my brother got married from my flat in 2000. So it has many happy memories also (44-year-old gynaecologist from Burdwan).

> I stayed (in my maternal uncle's house) for ten years. Then the joint family house was sold. I had made an arrangement with my cousin brother and the promoter to buy one flat for myself (42-year-old educationist from Chandannagar).

There must be the attendant burden of maintenance and taxes, but none of them have mentioned these as problems, perhaps allowing us to conclude that if the primary problem that women from outside have indicated is finding a place to stay, then the ultimate solution is certainly owning one's own house in a city where once you did not have even a room of your own.

The women who have been able to make a home for themselves in the city have a sense of achievement, even if that achievement is still expressed in terms that are comprehensible to society, and not on the woman's own terms; as Hekman (1993: 53) pointed out, 'women are inarticulate because the language they use is derivative of male definitions of reality'. I would argue that this is not the inability to articulate one's thoughts; it is rather the articulation of one's experiences in terms of the experiences undergone by those of another 'genre' as Luce Irigaray (1991) would term it. These experiences are considered 'normal' by society for this order of being, but 'abnormal' for oneself. It is because of this construction of 'abnormality' that no words exist to identify the difference in felt experience, and one must always articulate one's feelings and experiences in terms borrowed from the other. The gynaecologist from Bardhaman in reply to the question 'Is there anything that Kolkata has given you which you could not have got anywhere else?' replied, 'I think freedom. I am a professional with my own flat and car. This is like being a man'. Houses and cars and professions have been identified for so long with men that even women who have achieved them on their own merits, think that it is normal for a man, and man-like for a woman.

HOSTELS

This may, however, be seen as the end of a very long and arduous journey. Not everyone wants a home in the city that they have for the present adopted as their own; not all are sure that they want to remain here in future; and not many are in a position to find the ultimate solution just yet. So in the meantime, we might consider the different options that are available to the women who come to the city from outside. As a 33-year-old journalist from Bhubaneswar explained, 'Even though there are hundreds of accommodation and PGs available, one can land up at the wrong place where you don't like the food (if you are a PG) or maybe there are hundreds of rules and regulations.' The easiest option for women who come to study is of course the hostel attached to the institution. The common problems there are of various kinds. The pettiness and triviality that may well characterize personal relations when people are forced to live together create some of these problems: 'political issues should not be brought into personal issues' (21-year-old student, Jalpaiguri) a 'vengeful mentality' ought to be avoided (23-year-old from Ranaghat) and, on the flip side, 'I have learnt how to get even with others' (printing engineering student from Murshidabad, 21). A 21-year-old woman from Dhanbad looks at the pros and cons of hostel life: 'Though my hostel has a very lively atmosphere, I am still on the search for a private space. Here freedom is there but lots of suspicion (almost monitoring every action) and behind the back pinching is too much.' Besides, as an 18-year-old student from Siliguri explained, 'Being a woman staying alone I have to abide by many compulsions which are not just.' Why do hostels attached to educational institutions, and the working women's hostel insist on rules that sometimes verge on the irrational? Take, for instance, a women's hostel where both students and working women live; some of the women have been there for almost ten years, and at least one is in her sixties. This hostel is in Jodhpur Park.[7] The rule in this hostel is that the women have to be in by 9 o'clock. What happens after that? The Superintendent of the hostel says that after that, she waits for fifteen minutes before calling up the boarder's guardians to inform them that she has not returned, and that the gates are being closed. She remembers a recent incident when a girl called up from Sealdah Station at 9:30 pm and said she would have to stay out until 10 pm on work. The Superintendent says she had no choice but to ask the girl to arrange alternate accommodation for the night.

The irony of this situation is difficult to overlook; the women who live here all agree that this kind of hostel is much more secure than the messing or paying guest arrangements that are available, precisely because it is run by an established institution and one is not dependant on the whims of individual householders, but regulated by a set of rules made by a committee. Yet this very place forces a woman to look for alternate accommodation because her work keeps her out until after the hostel's designated curfew. How does one square such rules with the thrust towards corporatization and the odd working hours that globalization demands of men and women? If society has sanctioned the recruitment of women by the Business Processes Outsourcing industry that works according to time zones different from ours, why are these same women being forced into situations where they cannot get safe accommodation merely because society's definition of safety for women demands that they be indoors by certain hours of the night? The contradiction between the 'local' and the 'global', in this case appears in a form which could be comic, had it not involved the livelihoods and the security of women who have no 'family' home to fall back upon in their place of work. The city apparently provides opportunities, but not the conditions which will enable women to take these opportunities.

Is It Safe? What Time Do Gates Close?

Most hostelites whom we talked to, whether in open hostels or hostels attached to educational institutions, agreed that such rules were for their own good; 'discipline' was the word they used to justify them. On the other hand, a number of them, especially those coming from smaller towns in West Bengal, said that they had no idea of the larger city beyond their place of work or their college; they even felt, in some cases, that they were in the city at the wrong time, that they would have been able to take better advantage of the opportunities offered by it if they had come when they were slightly older. From this emerges quite starkly, the central concern of this study: that women are being socialized to want certain things that the first wave of the feminist movement has taught them is justified, and natural for women to demand. Economic independence is one of them. But the conditions that make this independence valuable, even usable, do not exist, as they have not been part of socialization; we have concentrated on the goals rather than processes, and the consequences of this emphasis are clearly reflected in the experiences of the women who have chosen to live and work alone in an alien city. More precisely, as the nature of the work that women have come to the city to do has changed in concert with the change in the economy of the city itself, such incidents cause us to reflect upon the kind of change that we have accepted as progress.

Irigaray raises a salient question about the relation between technological society and women by pointing out that while it is easier for women to enter, given the belief that they are patient and obedient and hence make better machine minders, capable of more delicate and precise gestures, women need to think through and modify the conditions of such societies. She likens the effect of this society upon women as 'the transposition of the family into the State' (1991: 195–96). Investigating women in 'new generation' jobs in India six years after this survey was concluded, Raju's findings (2013) echo what the women in the BPO and IT sectors told us about their problems in finding accommodation, bearing out Irigaray's warning about the patriarchal family extending itself into the industry and the state. This issue raised from the experiences of these women, therefore, still confronts the women's movement. Their predicament is neither new nor surprising, given the fact that women living alone outside their homes in 'alien' environments have always been objects of speculation and suspicion, if not outright hostility. The articulation of their experiences convey even more strongly to us now that despite our gains in equal opportunity for employment and the freedom of movement, crucial steps that will make these gains operative, meaningful and finally acceptable as gains, are still to be taken.

PGs (Paying Guest Accommodation)

Returning to the places where single women from outside can live in the city, among the 'hundreds of accommodation', the paying guest option seems the most popular though it also appears to be the most hazardous. The computer professional from Bhubaneswar has been in Kolkata since 1990, doing an engineering degree. She has now bought her own flat, but she first came to stay with her grandparents and then moved out as 'there was a double generation gap. I had moved out to stay as a PG in Rashbehari.[8] I thought hostels were dirty.' In response to the question 'Has Kolkata given you anything that you could not have got anywhere else?' Her answer is, 'Cheap student PG. My friends who were in Mumbai/Pune/Bangalore were spending 6,000 a month and compared to that I only needed 3,500.' When asked 'Do you know any more women like yourself who have come from outside? What problems do such women face in the city?' she replied, 'Many problems. One friend even faced attempted rape. Women in PGs and rented houses face daily harassment.' This harassment is par for the course, as it involves living cheek by jowl with a completely unknown family and having to depend on this family for everything. As a 27-year-old programme coordinator from Ranchi sums it up

> I stay in a paying guest accommodation in Gol Park and I'm not very happy with the arrangement because paying guest accos.[9] in Kolkata are usually run by middle-aged/old homemakers who are snoopy, interfering and covertly money minded. These women try to extract as much money from the PGs by providing the poorest of facilities under veneer of superficial sentimentality ... moving into another PG is not a solution because most PGs are the same (they don't have a legal status, there's no paper work b/w the two parties and hence the PG is always at a disadvantage) and I can assert this from my own experience.

This is corroborated by another 29-year-old woman from Jamshedpur who has been working in advertising, 'PGs are not legalized; the income is tax-free; girls have no say and security. In rented places, brokers might swindle you, landlords are omnipotent.' She lived in a PG in Hindustan Road as a student, close enough to Gol Park, and remembers, 'Hindustan Road was a posh place, but there were no amenities in the PG, besides they suddenly brought in a male PG to stay in the landlord's room when 4 girls were already staying there. The landlady would do anything for money.' She lived for a while in the same PG in Gol Park that the programme coordinator from

Ranchi has described above, and she too remembers the Gol Park PG thus, 'In Gol Park the landlady was a frankly money-minded vicious lady underneath the posh South Calcutta polish, the food portions were unbearably small.' A 21-year-old student form Balurghat changed PG accommodation from Annapurna, near Jadavpur, to another one in Bapujinagar, also close to this area because 'the landlady in the previous one used to behave very badly whenever we used extra water. The problem of water is there in this new PG place as well; that still remains.' Evidently, it was not the water problem but the human one of being treated properly that made her change residence. Perhaps also the deeper southern location of Annapurna which is part of the 'colony' (see Appendix 3) area settled by erstwhile refugees and outside the purview of the Calcutta Metropolitan Development Authority, made it less attractive than Gol Park which is the more sophisticated and up-market part of south Calcutta. This upscale south Calcutta area is one among those inhabited by people who settled here after coming from East Bengal, before partition and independence and much before the formation of Bangladesh. These areas comprise large old houses often complete with gardens, adequate civic amenities and some of the oldest apartment buildings are in this part of the city. The 'colony', on the other hand, is further south (see Figure A2.3 and Appendix 3) and comprises small plots of uninhabited land taken over by refugee settlers from East Pakistan and then Bangladesh, located beyond the southern borders of the city as it stood at partition. The ownership of these lands was gradually regularized through the efforts of various Left parties. The history of the establishment of 'colonies' is given in Appendix 3 and discussed below. The location of the PG accommodation often, though not always, serves as a pointer to the needs and desires of the guest who chooses to stay where she is comfortable; on the other hand, given the ambience and the location, what she needs or desires may elude her until she earns enough or comes from a family that can afford to pay the rents here.

A 26-year-old computer professional from Malda lives in Salt Lake,[10] close to her workplace. Salt Lake was developed as a planned satellite township on reclaimed land to take the pressure off the central business and residential areas of Kolkata, in the early 1970s. It is now connected to the rest of the city by the Eastern Metropolitan bypass, which skirts the city and its busy arterial roads, and makes the journey to Sector V, where the IT industry and the BPO firms have been located, slightly simpler. Naturally, women who are in this profession look for places there, which are cheap in comparison with accommodation within the city, especially in the up-market south and central parts. However,

> My landlady doesn't give food. I want home cooked food because this situation is bad for my health. I am also spending too much money on food. I am saving money on conveyance because office is walking distance but that money is going on buying food. My skin is also getting bad. I have repeatedly asked my landlady to provide me with food or make some cooking arrangement for myself. She has not said yes. I am really trying to explain this to her that how can a working girl like me go out to work for 8 hours with an empty stomach and come back the same way. The only proper food I eat is the office lunch.

A 19-year-old student from Jamshedpur first stayed with her relatives in Howrah, which is an hour and a half's journey from her college in south Calcutta. Many people do undertake this journey daily, taking the local train to Howrah Station from suburban towns, and then using the public transport system to commute to their destinations across the city. This woman, however, found that 'local trains scared me, boarding a train at Howrah can easily be passed off as nightmares, it is crushing;' so she shifted to a PG close to her college in south Calcutta, but 'I am not happy with my living conditions. The first requisite would be a little more privacy. Better food, less interference in other people's business by the landlady.' A 27-year-old designer from Siliguri shifted to a PG near Kalighat Metro station[11] to save travel expenses. Kalighat is an old temple locality in south Calcutta, older than the Gariahat-Gol Park area, with older houses and closely knit but not as well-planned and apparently more conservative, 'backward' neighbourhoods. Its main attraction is that it is located on the Metro route that now stretches from Dum Dum in the north to Garia in the south. Access to the Metro makes the journey to work in central Calcutta much faster and more comfortable, the Metro service being one form of public transport that works adequately in the city. However, she feels dissatisfied with her living conditions because

> I am paying 4k for a single seater acco which is too much 4 me but I can't say anything. I bot a comp recently + uploaded costly software so I can wrk from home/carry back assignments, but I can't use it as these guys here don't believe running a comp costs as much as a tubelight (electricity bills) so I suffered heavy loss buying expensive branded stuff.

'Adjustment'

All these women recount accommodation problems that stem from their preferences regarding localities, ambience and amenities. It appears that despite their original choices guided by what seemed practical concerns, unaccounted for factors that now compromise their choices have surfaced and have to be dealt with. But problems are not limited to these alone. A variety of problems graduate from what has generally been dismissed lightly as adjustment issues to a number of situations that most probably would not be seen as problems but for those who have faced similar incidents and can appreciate the nebulous but threatening nature of the event.

> My landlord's son's a bit nervy. I mean he likes chatting up if I am like working on the computer at night, he'll suddenly pop up and say hi let's chat and all that but my landlady's a perfect sweetheart and I can't tell aunty that ur son's being a creep. She'll be so hurt (24-year-old BPO employee from Dhanbad).

The MNC executive from Ranchi, a 'tribal' Christian woman living now with a non-Christian family, said, 'One day while watching the news my landlady made an offensive comment about SC/ST reservation. It could have led to a fight but I had early office next day so I didn't rise to the bait. That really made me think about my position.'

It is naïve to think, as both these incidents show, that such experiences lead automatically to an immediate upheaval and action for change on the part of the woman involved. The BPO employee from Dhanbad too knows that she must stay in this PG despite her landlady's 'nervy' son; she came first as a student and stayed in the college hostel, and then in the final year, shifted here, to Paddapukur Road, which is on one of the main thoroughfares that takes you from south Calcutta to the central office areas. Apart from the convenient location, she had chosen a paying guest option over hostels or messes for a specific purpose 'actually I was preparing for Univ exams + competitive exams so I had to live alone'. A 26-year-old sales executive from Dhanbad stayed first in her maternal uncle's place in Bowbazar[12] which is in the heart of central Calcutta, close to Calcutta University as well as the old office area. These were areas that grew around the Park Street Esplanade neighbourhoods whose earliest inhabitants were the British, the Anglo-Indian functionaries of the empire and those Bengalis who rose into prominence during British rule: lawyers, industrialists, and so on. She then moved to a PG in Lake Gardens[13] which is a newly developed area in the southern parts. Then she shifted

> To a new PG in Southern Avenue ... because earlier it was on room-sharing basis. Now I have to carry work home from office, so lights on creates disturbance for other girls. When you work you also need more privacy than students. So I took this single room PG in response to a newspaper ad.

Southern Avenue is also one of the most beautiful and greenest areas in Calcutta, a wide tree-filled road that borders the Dhakuria Lakes, a set of water bodies off Gol Park. The road is bordered on the other side by older spacious highrises and old ornate homes, parks and playing fields where a number of coaching clubs for football and cricket thrive. So, not only the room, but the people and the surroundings, everything must synchronize for the woman; only then will staying in a particular accommodation be viable. And since those who own these places are well aware of this intricate balance, they are at an advantage. As the MNC executive from Ranchi points out

> If you are from a minority community, I am wondering if any place is safe for a woman alone? I am exploited by my landlord with exorbitant rent, but I am powerless.... House owners rejected me after knowing my last name. Finding a house in Kolkata is like finding a husband through arranged marriage. I faced so many rejections and then got this after a very heavy price! (monthly dowry).

The advertising professional from Jamshedpur has a complaint; 'People in Calcutta should respect girls more. Here society hasn't advanced so much; people think there are no professions for girls except teaching and medicine. It becomes very difficult to explain to uncles and aunties what I am doing.' The hospitality industry manager shifted out of a PG residence and took a flat in Garia[14] which is in the far south. It would take at least an hour to reach the upscale Gariahat area from here, there being a single arterial road that connects these two places, which has been widened in phases over the last decade. However, south of Gariahat up to Garia and beyond are the refugee colonies, which are outside the purview of the Metropolitan Development Authority (see Appendix 3). The area beyond Jadavpur, was, at the time of the survey, in the district of South 24-Parganas. From Garia it would take a couple of hours at peak time to reach the central Calcutta office areas, and another half an hour to Calcutta University. The extension of the Metro overground to Garia, inaugurated in mid-2009, decreases time and increases comfort, but when the survey was conducted, this was not yet the case. Our respondent was compelled to take a flat on rent because she felt she was too old to share accommodation in a PG with younger women. This area, despite the commuting problems and the inadequate civic amenities, was chosen because of the low rents: living alone meant that she would have to pay the entire amount on her own. The low rents, of course, are the result of precisely such contingencies. And the people of the area are a far cry from the more progressive inner city areas, where the neighbourhood culture thrives still, everyone knows and keeps tabs on everyone else, and single women, especially if they are staying alone, are a natural anomaly. She says,

> Initially when I was new there were officious people who were curious about my timings, but in my profession you are trained and ready to handle all sorts of people. So I made it a point to clear the air first. I showed my landlord my ID, CV, my position, my passport, my visa papers.... I wanted to be very sure that everyone knew exactly who I am and what I do, because I wanted peace and privacy when I came back from work, no matter what time of the day or night.

Even women, who do not face this problem, know why. It is not because of the broadminded people of the locality, more often than not. As the journalist from Bhadreswar explains, 'Right from the para (neighbourhood) shopkeepers to the landlady and colleagues I found most people very accommodating and helpful. But I wonder if I would have been given the same help if I would have been in the hospitality services or if I did not have the "press" tag.'

'I Don't Like It But . . .'

Finding a home in the city is such an intricate and harrowing process that not many want to go through it again, but that is only one of the reasons why immediate and drastic action is not to be taken if untoward incidents do occur. What guarantee is there that the next place you arrive at does not hold even murkier realities behind its smiling exterior, especially since you are a paying proposition? One of the respondents recounted a story of her friend, a senior in her college who came from Asansol. She was staying in a PG in Ballygunge Phari[15] in a flat paying 4,000 rupees as rent, because Ballygunge Police Station is also an upscale area with large old houses and apartment buildings dating to the time when flats were not pigeon holes. Besides, it is one of the nodal points on bus routes that connect the southern part of Calcutta to the rest of the city. But

Suddenly her landlady tells her she can sleep in the landlady's room as [my friend's] room is going to be occupied by [the landlady's] son who is visiting her from Delhi. Her room was actually the son's room. There was no other space. The landlady knew that her son would visit now and then, and she didn't have alternative place for her PG, but she kept a PG anyway for easy money. Now this girl went frantically looking for a place. Finally she went home for fifteen days and this guy left for Delhi she came back to the same PG. Her parents fought with the landlady to accept 2000 bucks for that month, but she lost fifteen days of college.

Packing your bags the moment something goes wrong is not the answer because you have nowhere to take them to, a situation that only women alone in the city will know the full import of. Thus comes the old and ambiguous command: adjust. And as we shall see, the city demands 'adjustment' from the single woman from outside in various forms. The artist from Agartala looks at it quite philosophically

As a woman I look at it this way ... girls grow up, get married and go away to their husbands' homes someday and soon you adjust. One is an outsider there too, but it all changes once you live alone and fine-tune your life. Although, the orientation is different for a real 'outsider' who does not have a real family to belong to, I think the perspective is pretty much the same.

The acceptance of this situation does not mean that the woman who lives here, because she must put up with the problems that are certainly not trivial in the quotidian context, does not know how she is compromising her sense of self-worth. As a 24-year-old home tutor from Kanthi, Murshidabad, says in response to whether she is satisfied with her living conditions, 'I have no other options, so the question of satisfaction or dissatisfaction does not arise'. In response to the question 'Do you know any other women like yourself who have come from outside the city? What problems do such women have to face in the city?' she replies, 'My hostel is an example of this. Thinking continuously about where and how the next problem will come from and having to live with this thought all the time is the biggest problem of all.' Another 21-year-old student from Nabadwip, who at the time of the survey had been in Kolkata for five years, says, 'The place I am currently in is my fifth home so far.... Uncertainty has become my only certainty. I wish for certainty, a positive certainty.'

'Nomads'

This keeps the possibility of a nomadic existence always open, either out of choice or out of compulsion. The manager from the hospitality industry went away from the city for three years during which she did an MBA in Delhi. When she came back to work, she stayed in a PG in Beltala, a quiet area off the more noisy, glamorous Gariahat in the south. But the moment she could afford it, she shifted to a rented place of her own in Garia, which is deeper in the south as we have seen, and much further away from her place of work than her PG was; she is 36, and as she says, 'I cannot live with college goers'. A 23-year-old trainee in advertising from Durgapur came here in 1999. She stayed first at the home of her father's friend in Dhakuria, then 'I shifted to a private hostel near Park Circus.[16] Then I got very scared of the locality and shifted to Tolly (Tollygunge).[17] This was all in one month.' Park Circus is off central Calcutta, and one of the most cosmopolitan areas in Kolkata: though there is no dearth of Bengalis the number of people from all communities and religions living there is visibly large: one wonders whether this is the reason for her being 'scared'. She shifted to Tollygunge, which is parallel to Garia in the south, but with the advantage of being connected to central and north Calcutta by the metro. Tollygunge was the terminal metro station before the line was extended eastwards to Garia. But apparently, things did not settle there; she continues,

After this horrible time, I went to Salt Lake, seeing an ad in the paper. Place was good, but I had to come to Sovabazar and catch the Metro to Park Street [St Xavier's College]. So my money used to run out fast, my health became very bad, hair fell as water had lots of iron. I had malaria five times. I used to look like a ghost. Then my friend in Panchanantala told me to shift to her place. So luckily everything fell in place.

A 27-year-old marketing executive from Ranchi stayed first at Sinthee More in North Calcutta,[18] but 'I did not like the area. I wanted to migrate to south Calcutta which has a more modern outlook. So I shifted to a PG in Dhakuria. But here the pricing was excessive compared to amenities. So I decided to share a flat with 3 other girls in mess system in Garia ... the main negative point is conveyance. Travelling to work takes minimum 1.5 hours every day, so 3 hours are spent on the road.' The other side of this is comforting, though. The positive factors about her present living arrangements are important, indeed, as anyone who has lived in PG accommodation will appreciate: 'It is more economical. We have installed TV, fridge, geyser. We have a cook and her husband has a laundry system. So there is every comfort'. But not everyone is so lucky. Some women have not found their niche even after many changes. The advertising professional from Jamshedpur tells us:

I stayed in Gol Park[19] with my relatives for the first six months, then I went to Behala (further south) to stay with some more relatives for the next two-three months, then again to Bansdroni [closer to Tollygunge]for the next few months. I went about shuttling for a year like a refugee. It felt pretty scary lugging my bags from place to place. In my second year [of college] I took up as a PG in Hindustan Road (in the heart of the posh Gariahat locality), in 1998 I went to Bagha Jatin [fifteen minutes away from Garia] as a PG in 2002, I went again as a PG to Gol Park, and in 2004 I moved to Santoshpur [across the railway tracks from Jadavpur] in a shared rented apartment.

Tales from the 'Paying Guest'

The experience of leading a nomadic life is different for different people. For the artist from Agartala, the connections were simply made and the places she lived in turned out to be comfortable. So she remembers it thus

> After my admission in college, I wasn't sure where and what I should look for in accommodation until one of my college friends offered me a PG accommodation at her place in Regent Estate. I lived there for three years until I completed my graduation. I was very happy there and the living conditions were good. No complaints. After those three years I shifted to another PG accommodation with a family in Jodhpur Park. I had to shift from my friend's place because her parents were adding another storey to their house and the room where I was put up that was on the terrace had to be demolished. How could I stand in the way of progress? I did not want to stay in a rented place because it was too much of a bother to set up an entire household. Moreover I wasn't ready to live all by myself or look for a partner to share the place. I was particularly looking to get a room at the working women's hostel in Jodhpur Park which would happen only if there was a vacancy. A cousin of mine who was doing his PhD at JU helped me with this next PG accommodation. Although I lived with them for the next few months, they became my extended family. I moved out despite the wonderful time I was having. I felt it would be better that way because PG was expensive and hostel was cheaper. Besides I had just got into a job and needed to save some money to take care of my needs than to keep asking my parents for money.

This respondent was fortunate in her choice: Regent Estate is in the Tollygunge area and has the advantages of communication that we have pointed out earlier. Jodhpur Park is the most upscale area south of Gariahat and on the arterial road connecting Gariahat with Garia, Raja S.C. Mullick Road,[20] on which Jadavpur University is situated, just two stops down from Jodhpur Park. She stayed in 'progressive' upper-class localities, where interference and curiosity apparently did not become problems. Now she is able to analyse the differences between one PG accommodation and another, and her experience gives us an insight into the varieties of attitudes people who run PG accommodations might have to their guests, regardless of where their houses are located:

> The nature of the treatment varied from family to family. Like, for instance, when I stayed as a PG at my friend's, I became a PG first and friend later. They never ever mistreated me though, and everything went on fine because I did not do anything to offend them or cause any problem. Period. The second family was a different story. When I began to live with them I was my reserved self initially but that lasted only for a few days. Being the people they were, pleasant, good-natured and unpretentious, it didn't take them long to get comfortable. Incidentally I was the first and last PG they ever boarded…. Occasionally, they would be concerned without being intrusive. They were very considerate and took great care of me, at the same time gave me space and respect. This family is my second home and are a part of my life.

Many other women also talk of their landladies with respect and affection. For example, a 29-year-old journalist from Bhadreswar in Hooghly, says

> My landlady is very helpful. At a time when I did not have a cell phone, she would send the cordless to my room. She understood I would be groggy in the morning since my job hours are at night and so find it difficult to go and attend the call in the drawing room. She would also make sure that the maid took my clothes for ironing and little things like that go a long way to show that you are cared for.

> I am a vegetarian so my landlady who is a Bengali has learnt some recipes from my mom when she came over last year, especially for me (25-year-old marketing executive from Patna).

> Our Garia landlady is not educated but very broadminded about the four girls staying in her home. She only found a cook for us (marketing executive from Ranchi, aged 27).

> When we had exams my landlady who was older than my grandma would personally see to it that we got light food to eat, fruits, milk.

Even when we didn't have a phone in the PG, the kirana guy on the first floor would receive our calls and messages and we had a monthly system with the STD booth (finance executive from Ranchi).

My landlord stays in the same building as I do. If I have any problems hunting for an electrician, milkman, doctor or if I need any help, the family is always very helpful. Once while going to office I discovered that there was some problem with the fuse and only my flat did not have electricity. While going to office I talked to the landlady about it but did not expect her to do anything. But when I returned home after a gruelling night shift, the fuse had been fixed and repaired. They had made sure we didn't come back to a dark home (journalist from Bhubaneswar).

Bus conductors and traffic policeman and shopkeepers help genuinely with directions. Some even went to the extent of drawing small but accurate maps, also knowing that I was an outsider, gave me a list of dos and don'ts (student, Durgapur).

'As Women ... We Have to Adjust'

As a 27-year-old relationship manager for a multinational financial group who has come to Kolkata from Chandannagar says about the paying guest arrangement: 'Feeling of security is absent sometimes.... I feel lonely after work going to a PG, however polite they are, they are not your family.' What is to be done?

'What do you think is the most difficult part of city life for the outsider? Can this difficulty be easily solved?' is thus responded to by a 23-year-old part-time lecturer and project assistant from Balurghat: 'Adjustment, especially for those who come from small towns, suburbs or villages'. The issue of adjustment, it appears, is crucial, as it always seems to be with respect to women. A 22 year old who has finished her studies and is looking for a job here comes from a small place called Habra in the South 24-Parganas refused to be overawed by Kolkata's status. Asked what was the most difficult thing for a woman who has come to the city from outside, she replied, '[The most difficult thing] is to adjust oneself to the city. But that doesn't mean one has to give up one's self (*vyaktitva*), one's self-respect and one's goal and only compromise'. In Bangla, the word for 'compromise' is *meney neoa*, and the word for 'adjust' is *maniye neoa*. The contrast between the two acts is explained by her when she replies to the next question: How it is possible to overcome this difficulty? She replies:

> There is a solution, but it is not simple. Because everyone does not have equal capacity for assimilation. Just like she who comes must assimilate herself, those whom she has come amongst must also be open to assimilation. Because humans live in societies and no society can progress without exchange. Thinking that everything about the other is bad and everything about the self is good is an indication of stupidity. She who keeps her self intact can rise to higher things; she who loses her self is unable to struggle for existence.

But we must also note the different interpretations of the word 'adjust'. The technical writer from Chandannagar says, 'I think some problems here and there are ok, but there are some girls who are kleptos or pathological liars or violent or basically lesbians so it is impossible to live with them, but apart from that we all learn to adjust bit by bit, if everyone has come from different families there are bound to be clashes within certain limits.' The experiences of our respondents provide some unique insights into the boundary situations on the issue of adjustment because these women who come from outside are virtually playing blind, without safety nets of comforting families or alternate arrangements to fall back upon. Adjustment is crucial, but the terms that are dictated for it to be successful are not always acceptable either from the emotional or the functional point of view.

Assuming of course that the terms will always be dictated by the powerful, and it is the responsibility of the powerless to conform to those terms, the most important question is inevitably this: To what extent should a woman compromise with her sense of 'self' in order to adjust? A student from Nabadwip says, 'I spend my time worrying. What is the worst that can happen? I must prepare myself. Yet I feel pain. Which means I am not prepared enough.' It appears that she is in search of a limit which will define her as a person, beyond which she herself will draw the line at further changing and adjustment, the boundary that will mark her self out, in her own experience.

It is, I submit, a social threshold that ascertains this limit; a threshold beyond which the woman's (or the man's—but that threshold is rarely socially challenged with such covert violence as the woman's) sense of self cannot be compromised without disrupting her very personality. This apparently psychic limit functions in relation to society. There is a difference between a personality change and this disruption. In the former case, the violence is either not acutely felt, or contained and channelized in forms acceptable both personally and socially. In the latter case, however, I call this disruption because the manifestations of this violation cannot be contained or channelized into socially as well as personally acceptable forms. All our respondents seem to have gone through various levels of stress related to finding and keeping accommodation to their minimum satisfaction. There is no doubt that the experience has changed them, as the very experience of living in Kolkata itself has. However, no one has reported instances of disruption despite the fact that many of them may feel the threat of such trauma lurking at the edges of their daily lives. This innocuous apparently trivial experience which the advertising professional from Jamshedpur recounts, can speak volumes in this regard.

I had jaundice when I was in the PG, this was my third time so I knew the symptoms fairly well. But my landlady was convinced that it was flu, so even when I was running temperature of 103 degrees, I was given rice mashed with salt and butter. Finally I got myself tested with a bilirubin count of 4.9! My father, owing to some problem at home, could only come to take me back after a week, so I had to stay on at my PG. even when my bilirubin count shot up to 5.9, I cleaned my own vomit and washed myself. My landlady bitterly resented having to prepare 'different' food for me and even embezzled money that I handed out for medicines and blood tests. My best friend at my PG, incidentally a girl from my hometown, was my mainstay then; she even cleaned up my vomit at night when I was too weak to. Two of my roommates who are also very very close friends, have had jaundice at different times (both with bilirubin counts of 1.6) and they and I witnessed the same apathy of the respective landladies.

Our friend, the trainee advertising professional from Durgapur, remembers that before she ended up at her friend's place, 'My first landlady was a Dracula. She used to give me less food because she wanted to help me diet.' The advertising professional from Jamshedpur, after moving like a refugee in her first few years, now shares a rented flat with a friend. Is she satisfied?

I am happy within certain limits…. We can clean the bathroom properly, we can eat proper helpings of food, we can enjoy the conveniences of a fridge and TV. But again, the landlord's family is a problem. They don't take our problems seriously, in fact even when a snake had entered the bathroom, they thought we had conjured it up out of our imaginations even when we were extremely scared and drenching the whole place with carbolic acid. There is too much of zamindari, too much of hierarchy. Even the servants behave as if they are doing us a favour when in fact we are paying them. It is not a posh place, so the feudal spirit lingers on, and we are perceived as oddities in the rather lower middle-class background.

THE PHILOSOPHY AND PRACTICE OF 'ADJUSTMENT'

Is it possible to ask women to adjust to these situations only because they are not in a position to bargain or reject? But again, the most disturbing thing about 'adjustment' as a social operation is that the issues are avowedly trivial, when they are referred to in conciliatory conversations; yet if they are so trivial, why should they become life and death situations to women, and quite literally at that? This is a question that feminist social ethics must focus on as a pressing area of concern. The irony is that society has 'allowed' women to come thus far, from their safe homes, in search of self-fulfilment in tangible and intangible ways, but will not accommodate their needs and necessities.

They are the ones who will have to 'adjust' to society's limitations, shrinking themselves into the cramped confines of its restrictive structures, so that the veneer of normalcy is not disrupted in any way. Capitalist patriarchy can provide jobs for women and boast of its progressive nature, but true to its nature, as it does with men, it sees them as working bodies, or even dissociated, alienated body-parts that labour. To think of the labourer as human is disruptive of the logic of capital itself; it is not possible to produce a surplus if the entire human being is to be paid a wage. Labourers, to be profitably employed, can only be perceived as alienated body parts, and wages must be tailored to suit the worth of individual body parts only. In the case of male labourers, this lack was fulfilled by the unwaged labour of women. Housewives, mothers, girlfriends daughters, sisters, all were implicated in the capitalist system to contribute directly to the reproduction of labour power whose costs were not incurred by the capitalist himself. As the organization of capital became more and more complex, these relations too became complex leading to fissures and contradictions. Changes in social organization of gender and gender roles were articulated to contain these complex fissures and contradictions.

Women, however, taking on the role of men in the salary sector, have produced an apparently irresolvable contradiction. If they are to remain in this space created for them by global capital, someone must take on the gender-role of social reproduction of labour power for it to be available at the beginning of another day's work. Since those who were designated to perform this role, that is, women themselves are now in need of this service, will it become a waged activity? Will the state take this into its area of operation, or will it simply ignore the reality hoping that either it will go away or that women will with their infinite inventiveness, solve the problem themselves? One way of solving the problem is to get 'reliable household help' as the 29-year-old media professional from Jamshedpur puts it. So if the patriarchal social structure of capital is to be maintained even in times of globalization, class must function to fill in the gaps created by the contradictions brought to the surface by gender. If women have moved out of the boundaries of home that early industrial capital designated for them as 'their' place, then either their empty place is to be filled by women of a lower class or consumer goods that mechanize housework. The former option is possible in areas where cheap labour is still available: the systematization of services by agencies providing household help and the regulation of such help is still in its formative stages in India, and not very common in Calcutta. The latter option, I shall argue in later chapters, is capital's own way of absorbing within it the demands made by feminists regarding the double burden of work that women had to shoulder. It became necessary when women's right to employment became a part of those 'natural' rights that middle-class and upper middle-class women today take for granted. This, I shall argue, is the basis of capitalist consumerist patriarchy, to which we shall return at a later stage.

'Adjustments' among 'Outsiders'

The quest for the perfect living space and conditions may be elusive: a house does not mean a home, a roommate does not necessarily translate into a friend, even though, since both of you are living in similar conditions, it is to be assumed that since both of you come from outside you may face the same problems. 'Adjustment', however, does not actually begin and end with city people demanding that outsiders adjust. It includes 'adjustments' between outsiders themselves. Women who come from different backgrounds, different professions with different mentalities also expect 'adjustment' from one another. A 27-year-old designer from Siliguri says, 'I'm from media and my roomies r all typical 9–5 sorts so massive probs, adjustmt probs, everything. But I hv a screen around me so I dnt feel anything. I'm hr to wrk & if sum1 has a prob, she's welcum.' Another 27 year old who comes from Chandannagar has lived first in a relative's house in Bansdroni, in south Calcutta, and then in a PG in Sector V in Salt Lake, which is at the other end of town. Having lived in Kolkata since she began to study for the Higher Secondary examinations, she now has completed her MBA and is working as relationship manager in a multinational financial group. She sums up her dream of the perfect home in the city thus: 'I want to rent a flat and have 2–3 professional women of the same rank as flatmates so that we can employ a cook and other servants and lead a more comfortable life.' Note the emphasis on 'of equal rank', the requirement that board should be controlled by the women themselves and that there should be no dependence on the house owner, as there is in PG accommodation. Her desires also corroborate our earlier speculations about class papering over the fissures created by extensions in gender roles: employing a number of servants will provide proper organization. It is her experience that has taught her the nature of what should be desired in terms of accommodation in the city.

Yet this very basic demand is often the root of immense difficulty and sometimes of unbearable trauma. Do women who come from outside realize that even the barest minimum that they ask for is denied them by the city and do they resent this? Apparently not, for, as a 24-year-old nurse from Contai in Medinipur said, 'I think no girl should step out of her parents' home if she is only concerned about the difficulties she might encounter. She might face hostile circumstances every day and have no one to vent out her feelings.' So the question 'Are you satisfied with your present living conditions?' yielded different responses which could translate into both yes and no: in some cases the room was fine, but the distance to work seemed a problem; in others, the roommates did not see eye to eye as they came from different professions. The computer professional from Malda explains, 'I share my room with a married lady and as she doesn't work in IT, so her habits are different from me, so there is some tension'. In other cases, it is the background of the roommates that is so varied that it becomes difficult to live peaceably together. According to the advertising professional from Jamshedpur, 'In PGs Bangla-medium rural types both resent and grudgingly admire the English-medium types they come in contact with as room-mates, which is pretty rare also as these two classes normally belong to distinct economic layers. I was an exception I stayed for 4 years in a predominantly lower middle-class 'cheap' PG as my parents had retired. In college and university hostels where specimens of every socioeconomic strata stay together, sometimes problems are pretty fierce, with violent quarrels, non-cooperation, I haven't witnessed those things but have heard first hand accounts that were pretty disturbing.' She reports that in the PGs there is a 'class war':

> English-medium *vs.* Vernac; Town *vs.* Suburbs: Most girls from suburbs or villages of WB come to Calcutta, considering themselves very lucky to have had such enlightened parents. I know a girl from Tamluk, she was the first girl of her school and is a lowly paid clerk in a private firm in Calcutta. That is their tragedy. They become 'too good' for the suburbs and 'not good enough' for Calcutta. Because they can afford to only stay in cramped 'messes' starting from Sulekha and Bagha Jatin to Garia and beyond, they have virtually no contact with their English-speaking, better-off counterparts from towns and cities who mostly live in clusters of posh South Cal PGs. the Vernacs call the Mems characterless, the Mems don't acknowledge their presence. There could have been a strong mutually beneficial network but for this class war.

'Adjusting' to 'Others'

And that returns us finally to the issue of class which has been concealed thus far in this narrative under the rubric of home. When the survey started, previous experience in doing such surveys had led me to believe that responses in two languages would inevitably separate into at least two different sets of experiences that would indicate different geographical and economic location. The survey itself has further inflected this assumption by demarcating the different areas of the city which are markers of living conditions and lifestyles, with one area being inhabited and another being aspired for. This, in itself, is not unusual, but in this case there are further considerations that lead to certain complexities in sensing the field. A 46-year-old university teacher says that when people hear that she lives in the south of Jadavpur, they wonder how an educated person like her can live in a colony area. The obvious reason for living here is that rents are low as these areas, as we see below, were not within the ambit of the municipality and had the barest minimum of civic amenities, most of the houses being built on lands occupied or gifted to refugees from erstwhile East Pakistan or later, Bangladesh. Thus, complicated ownership issues often lead to innovations being stalled, new structures being erected illegally, and possession cases not being open to legal redress as the plots are illegally held anyway. Such problems seem extraneous but sometimes directly affect the lives of the women from outside who choose to live in these areas. But why go into these knotted-up complications, why live here in the first place? Why did the 29-year-old advertising professional from Jamshedpur choose to live in a PG accommodation in a 'colony' in Bagha Jatin? She explains that she had to do so because both her parents were retired and she had to live on slender means, a condition available in the 'colony area' messes.

Some of the women, who lived in the same accommodation and were accessed through a different resource person, answered the questionnaire in Bangla. The narratives of their experiences can be used as source material to discern the difference in their expectations and difficulties in the city, differently conceived and narrated not because of the language alone, but because of the different world within which that language is used to name and communicate realities. If we just take Ranchi or Jamshedpur as places from where the woman comes, her own idea of her origins may be expressed thus

In Ranchi every woman is graduate or MA or has done nursing or any professional course, here I am speaking of my tribal Christian community. I am a third generation working woman in my family, my grandmother was a teacher, my mother also, my two aunts are doctors. But in Kolkata they have diversity in jobs, only they should have the will to try out something new. Everyone finds work in Ranchi or Jamshedpur Steel city, but now I have ventured thus far and now my sister also, so it's for a good cause.

The advertising scene is not very well developed in Jamshedpur, and anyway it is not a place for humanities-inclined people to flourish, so obviously, Calcutta has helped me in my occupation. The variety of jobs in Jamshedpur is limited to engineering, medical and education. But here a woman can aspire to become a copywriter or a television anchor or an event manager. There are more options especially if you can speak English and look presentable.

In contrast, those who come from the suburbs of the city or the rural areas or other small towns in Bengal, mainly tell their stories in Bangla, and also have a different story to tell:

> I had no choice. I had to come to Kolkata or stay in Malda. I am a Bengali and my parents, esp. my father, felt I would be safe and secured in Kolkata (computer professional, 24).

'NON-BENGALIS'

Located as it is, in the eastern part of India, Calcutta becomes the desirable destination of many women from this region and the Northeast; their parents too are more comfortable with the idea of their daughters going somewhere easily accessible: 'My parents didn't let me go to Pune. I was totally ziddi about leaving Dhanbad after +2 so they said, ok go to Cal' (age 24, BPO employee from Dhanbad). The accountant from Patna felt her main problem was the language problem; 'I speak Bengali now but it's hard'. A finance executive from Ranchi who came to Kolkata to study at St. Xavier's College, and then found a job and a husband in the city, feels

> like an outsider. Because I have stayed outside WB, I am not knowledgeable about Bengali culture, even St Xavier's was very cosmopolitan then. I went to Bombay [to do an MBA] then. What I dislike about Kolkata is that if you don't know the typical Kolkata culture you will be dismissed even if you know other things. I mean I may not know much about local bands but we have always heard a lot of Rabindrasangeet at home and I sing it also because I have learnt it for 5 years. But no one will take my views on Rabindrasangeet seriously, just because I am not Bengali enough. This is very irritating.

'If someone is a non-Bong, people are so patronizing. Kolkata is not a cosmopolitan city,' says a technical writer, 24 years old, from Bangalore. But a media executive from Shillong who started her career in Bangalore says, 'Bangalore where I used to work earlier, people are more self-centred. Kolkata has warmth and own-ness not found anywhere else'. Cultural differences are obvious in the way the city functions, a fact that one would not have realized had we not started the survey. Most of us involved in giving out and collecting response sheets were Bengalis from other parts of the country. Our problems loomed large enough for us to ignore what those who did not share our cultural habits must be facing. They are called upon to 'adjust' to everything, from patriarchal, class-divided social organization, from linguistic and culinary chauvinism to religious fundamentalism. A relationship manager from Chennai, 33 years old, is currently posted in Kolkata:

> Food is a big problem for vegetarians. It is my biggest problem. You don't get sour curds in the market … more Indian multicuisine restaurants should open up and not all catering to those north of the Vindhyas.

Some women find that their most useful survival skill is the language that they have taken pains to pick up. In reply to the question 'Indicate if there are things you want changed about your own conditions or about the city/people which will make it easier for women like you to live and work here,' the journalist from Bhubaneswar replied:

> Language. I've seen if one knows Bengali most things are done easily. People like outsiders who can speak their language, even if they know Hindi. I was very lucky to pick it up fast, even though I spoke in broken Bengali. Speaking with the vegetablewala, newspaperwala, cablewala … Bengali makes it easier. People have been helpful but it takes some time to get used to an outsider who doesn't speak Bengali.

What if one is more comfortable in another language? The advertising professional from Jamshedpur analyses her experience, coming from a decidedly cosmopolitan town where she went to an English-medium school

> First there was the language problem. In college my classmates spoke only in Bangla, and although I was a behenji as far as clothes were concerned, I was most comfortable in English and Hindi ... Cultural Shock. In Calcutta, people see you as a complete package: caste, religion, address, father's job, etc., and social hierarchies are very strongly entrenched. Your identity as a professional is never enough.

She is not the only one who has this experience. Another computer professional from Bhubaneswar remembers, in her first few days feeling

> Very unhappy and lost ... I didn't speak a lot of Bengali at home, so there was a cultural shock. Other Bengalis made fun of me thinking I was an Oriya. I always had Oriya friends so it was a great shock.

The media professional from North Bengal explains it thus:

> People who are born and brought up in Kolkata have an insular and peculiar attitude to life. They have strange superiority complexes. They judge people by their father and grandfather, sometimes even on the merit of caste, ghoti-bangal equations, addresses (north Calcutta or south Calcutta). So they are people I have learnt to leave alone.

Two women, one a 28-year-old media professional and the other a 26-year-old content writer, have both been living in the city for some time, coming originally to study and continuing to work. The woman working in media is not a Bengali, the content writer is. Both of them come from Jamshedpur, and they have the same experience about language and culture. The content writer says, 'I am proud to be a Bengali but Calcutta people always force Bangla culture on outsiders. This in my opinion is wrong.' The media professional says, 'People here r very friendly but you have to know their language to gel well. & u have to praise Kolkata'. But the marketing executive from Patna feels, 'Now that I know how to speak Bengali, I feel Kolkata is really my home.' The hospitality industry manager has considered this carefully as she has spent some time away from Kolkata, in Delhi working, and is now back in Kolkata on work. She uses her experience in both cities to analyse the changing face of the city and its people:

> It is easy to be friendly in Kolkata but perhaps it is not easy to make friends. But I suppose that is true of most big cities. But since I do interact with very many people, more than the average working person, I can say that the profile of the Calcuttan has changed. He has become more focused, global and therefore perhaps more hardened, and there was a basic middle-class idealism that was there but which is now gone or on its way out.

Women from different backgrounds, therefore, access the city differently and in their own ways. But how much it affects them is related to what resources, personal and familial, they have brought with them to their struggle in the city. Thus the English language can be helpful in places, but in cases it creates a division, as well. As the 29 year old from Jamshedpur also pointed out:

> In Bagha Jatin after four years, the cultural differences were getting too much. and I finished my studies and started working in a high pressure job [in an ad agency] and it was too much to come home after 12 hours of work to witness yet another all-girl brawl or back stabbing incident and be forced to take sides.

This woman from Jamshedpur feels that though she is happy in her rented flat with a good-hearted roommate, she would 'like to shift to a more educated + less interfering neighbourhood and household soon.' But a 34-year-old executive from the same city could, if they met, tell her a different story. She has been here longer. She lived first at the Sri Shikshayatan hostel during her student days and then shifted

> With other friends as a paying guest in a good South Calcutta locality and I could hear the gossip of mothers who thought their sons were to be kept away from girls like us who did not have any rules and

did not have any guardians and whose parents were 'least bothered' about what their daughters were doing in the big city.

How language and culture, both markers of class, are used to exclude/include vary according to situation; in some cases it is Bangla that sets the woman apart and marks her as an outsider; in others, it is her lack of knowledge of that very same language and its nesting culture. In a city, too, the majority language and culture perform a hegemonic role. Those who are willing to conform to it (like the woman who learned Bangla) signal their willingness to succumb to the dictates of the city itself, and are absorbed hospitably. Those who are more insistent on preserving their difference, whose threshold of compromise does not include the adoption of the norms and values of another culture, are, and remain, 'outsiders'. The limitations of Kolkata have been translated into their own strength by some women: A 30-year-old working woman from Gosaba, on the edge of the Sundarbans, felt that since Kolkata was the capital of the state, it offered her more opportunities.

THE 'PARA' OR NEIGHBOURHOOD

And nothing brings this home to one more than the para, the area in which the woman comes to live. In fact, where you are able to afford accommodation is also an important factor in your process of accommodation to the city. Whether it has been smooth or whether you remember the first days with horror depends as much on where your PG is located as it does upon the kind of people you live with there. This too is a class-based experience. Some women naturally do not sense the tone of a particular neighbourhood before they take up residence in a PG located there. But then they face situations which are also 'natural' for these areas, but not seen as such by the woman herself because she comes from a class background that is different from the one in which her para is located. What does she do then? Some women 'adjust', explaining it thus:

For girls the most important thing is where she stays, where she works and her attitude, dress and conduct. I have not faced any problem even when I wear jeans, because I wear salwar kurta the next day or a sari, so that people can see I wear everything and I am not an ultramod girl (Durgapur).

My landlady had problems with me in jeans+sweatshirt in office, she would say how cum u wear jeans in office, can't make her understand it's not an old-fashioned kind, it's media so it's a different track altogether (27-year-old designer from Siliguri).

The process of adjustment can apparently be summed up in a nutshell as 'to wear or not to wear jeans'. The world at large, at least in Kolkata, seems to designate the worth of a woman not only by her clothes, but also by what clothes exactly. As the executive from Jamshedpur puts it, Kolkata is safe 'provided girls know how to behave and what to wear'. Women themselves feel that for their own convenience, some clothes cannot be worn in some localities: 'In my Bagha Jatin[21] PG I was the only one to speak English so I had to compensate for this vice I had to forfeit the right to wear jeans' (advertising professional from Jamshedpur). And in their own interests, they do not overstep the norms.

Clothes are relatively easy to regulate and change. As a friend pointed out, clothes are also the first indication of 'change', superficially, at least. It seems important to look 'modern' and westernized but what about the ambience of the locality itself? In conservative neighbourhoods like the erstwhile refugee colony of Bagha Jatin, says the advertising professional from Jamshedpur:

I hid my Mills and Boon books because the cozy twosome cover pictures were termed objectionable by the Medinipur types. When my English-speaking friends telephoned, my roommates stopped whatever they were doing and gaped at my conversation. My greeting a person Hi was an event. When I brought to my PG a Dominos' pizza and fruit beer from office (in the initial days of joining an ad agency) I myself realized how incongruous I looked.

Thus localities for accommodation carry their own baggage; the designer from Siliguri is very emphatic when she says, 'sum places of Cal give me d creeps. esp. north Cal. I can stay at north Cal, pgs near metro at ½ prices but I won't cos its so bad. d way they see women is ridiculous like dark ages.' A marketing executive from Ranchi says that Kolkata is very safe compared to Ranchi, 'where no girl goes out alone after 7 pm. I return home late from work but no one has said anything. But still south Calcutta is safer than north Calcutta'. But the way in which living arrangements are organized is also dependent upon the economics of the accommodation itself. In the areas in the south of the city, as we have noted earlier, are the colonies inhabited mostly by those who came from erstwhile East Pakistan at partition in the 1950s and later after the creation of Bangladesh. These were set up on land either occupied and then regularized or what in local parlance is known as 'gifted land'. These areas were, when I came to the city in the 1980s, outside the metropolitan area of Kolkata. Amenities like water lines and sewerage were necessarily absent; however various constituents of the ruling Left Front had organized in these areas and led the struggle for land rights and in some cases civic amenities, so these areas formed a large vote bank which the Left parties had used to come to power and continued to nurture. There is another characteristic of these areas since they were originally outside city limits, they were home to a number of industries (see Appendix 3): Sulekha Ink, Krishna Glass, Dabur Chemicals to name a few. In the last twenty years all of these have systematically closed down. The land, in the initial stages had been easily acquired and built upon; the closing down of the factories did lead to some trauma, and in many cases those who were now out of jobs supplemented their income through a form of accommodation peculiar to Kolkata and made current by men coming from the suburbs and rural areas in the late nineteenth and early twentieth centuries: the mess. This was probably a throwback to the times of the Writers', the administrative clerks in the British imperial administration, when Kolkata was the first city of the empire as well as an industrial and commercial hub, where young men from outside the city stayed to avail of the opportunities for employment that the city offered. These classical, 'male' messes were mostly in north Calcutta, which was the residential area of the 'natives' in old Calcutta; the office neighbourhood or office para was (and apart from the Information Technology sector, still is) in what we now call central Kolkata. The mess was a house of bachelors, not a hostel because the men are not students. Stories of great talent, especially literary and artistic talent being nurtured in these places are legion. Some men spent their entire working lives in messes, never bothering to try and set up home for their families in the city; some never even bothered to marry and leave.

THE 'MESS'

The new version of these messes located south of Jadavpur, are based around the university and beyond cater to women. The number of seats available in hostels has been far outstripped by the number of women who are coming to the city to study. The messes in and beyond the Jadavpur area are mostly meant to take on this population. Messes are technically not for students only; you cannot turn out a woman once she finishes her course of study. But, of course, as residents of messes have told us, you can, since these arrangements are totally arbitrary and there are no regulating rules except the owners' whim. So if a particular mess-owner does feel that he wants only students, he or she is perfectly able to insist that all boarders be students. And this is only one instance of the power of the whim that regulates the economy and the culture of the mess, which becomes one of the central factors, either positive or negative, in the life of a woman who comes to the city from outside and takes up residence in a mess.

Are the messes located in and beyond Jadavpur similar to the ones that were set up for men in north Calcutta beginning from the late nineteenth century? One obvious difference is the gender of the boarders and basic assumptions about needs and natures related to this difference. The other is the fact that there are no mess houses or mess bari in the Jadavpur area yet, as there were entire buildings devoted to housing men under this arrangement in the north Calcutta areas. Rather, the messes for women occupy a floor or a substantial part of the house belonging to the owner. The owner lives in the same building but is entirely separate in domestic arrangements. These messes are supposed to be less formal and more comfortable than hostels. Given the Spartan conditions in which boarders in hostels of reputed women's colleges live, this may well have been true in the initial stages when messes were first set up. But as the idea became popular and as the influx of women wanting a place in the city increased, these considerations took second place to two apparently more important concerns: firstly, the limitations of the large mass-utility structure of a hostel were less attractive than what is regularly advertised as the 'cosy, homely' atmosphere of the mess. Secondly, the prevailing norm for accommodating women from outside the city who were not students was the working women's hostel, where the basic functional assumption was that women naturally needed regulation. Hence they also needed the rules and discipline of a hostel, letting them stay in relatively independent circumstances as men did was not acceptable. The youngest respondent among the working women who answered our questionnaire was a 21-year-old classical dancer and dance teacher from Manipur. She initially lived in a hostel when she came to the city. Her experience was that 'it was like a jail'. She decided to leave its safe confines for increased independence because otherwise, her aim in coming to Kolkata, that is, making headway in her chosen profession as a classical dancer, could not be fulfilled. Now this is where the Jadavpur area messes that cater to women offer attractive options. So the mix that they seem to stand for is more freedom along with a veneer of extended family comforts. Our informant whom we have quoted below insisted that his was a different kind of arrangement; there were proper beds instead planks hammered together, known in Bangla as chouki, steel almirahs, dining table, study table, platform for the trunks. This list makes one wonder at the state of other 'ordinary' messes. Our informant told us that when he had initially started his mess, girls came over from one of the other messes nearby because the rooms they lived in on the ground floor were water logged, you had to cook upon the bed, there was no place to keep computers, and one day they found a mole in the rice pot. It is difficult to attest to the truth of this statement, but there have been a number of stories about the lack of hygiene and the unhealthy conditions in messes, too. For example, the 29-year-old advertising professional remembers that in her mess at Bagha Jatin, 'There were eight girls to a single bathroom-cum-toilet'. Another 27-year-old Tally Operator from Jadugoda in Jharkhand says she changed her mess in Bagha Jatin due to 'water problems'.

One of the mess owners whom we spoke to once used to work for a corporate office that insisted on transferring him from Kolkata. He says he had aged parents and had just started building a house in the south of Jadavpur area, so he refused the transfer and gave up his job. He explained the economics of mess-owning thus:

> If I rent a place, the maximum rent that I will get in this area is 2500. A person who can afford to pay more rent will actually take a home loan and buy a flat—even if he does stay here, it will only be for a very short time. He will prefer to pay monthly to make an asset for himself, rather than spend it on rent. Now I have 11 girls, and including electricity, I charge 2000, it is profitable. Of course there is some misuse of electricity—when I go up sometimes, with the gas cylinder, for instance, I see that all rooms have all lights and fans running, if they had to pay separately for electricity they would be careful, but apart from that I think it is successful.

'PROTECTING' THE FEMALE 'OUTSIDER'

Messes are not free from regulations, of course. Our informant told us that he had started a women's mess because women were (naturally) easier to handle—more of a homely atmosphere would prevail, than if the inmates were men—'you never know what they have done when they come back, there is always the problem of drink, and possibility of commotion and chaos'. Mess owners who house women are not short of thinking of themselves as guardians to the women who stay in their houses. The one who spoke to us looked upon this job of running a mess for women in his house as an onerous responsibility.

Their parents are keeping them here because they trust me. I have told them that wherever they go, they must tell me…. If they have to go somewhere I give them the directions, keep watch that no one disturbs them. Suppose the gas finishes at night—now I will bring it in the morning. I have made a mess for lodging, I don't provide food, but I realized that these girls all come from outside, how will they know what to do, and I have seen that whenever women from the mess go to vendors, they charge extra, if you say I live in that house (where everyone in the locality knows that there is a mess) they will ask for more money. I have fixed a woman to do the cooking, this woman comes in the afternoon, now had it been an unknown person, she might have pilfered things while the girls are out. I tell them which shop is the cheapest, I have had to provide phone facility—everyone has mobiles, but parents call after ten o' clock on the landline to check whether they have really come home or not. Just a few days ago one of them had an eye problem, I was the one who arranged for the initial treatment until her parents arrived.

To what extent this is borne out by actual fact, of course, only our respondents can tell us. In Chapter 7, we will consider an incident that happened one evening at this very mess when the girls chatting on the terrace met a couple of local men who were hiding atop the water tank. As we will see, this incident was assessed differently by both parties. The girls looked upon this as a security problem, whereas the landlord himself looked upon it as an over-reaction on their part, because he was certain that nothing could happen in his locality. As for the home part of the homely comforts, as the mother of our 29-year-old advertising executive from Jamshedpur summed it up

My mother once said that my stay in a PG equipped me fully for my marriage in a large joint family where the landlady is the proxy omnipotent mother-in-law [*sasuri*], her daughter is a pampered and powerful sister-in-law [*nanad*] and my roommates are all proxy sisters-in-law [*jaa*], competitive and squabbling. That is a profound statement, which has proved true everywhere, from Bagha Jatin to Golpark.

Suffice for us to note at this point, that this unique form of accommodation for women from outside living alone in the city is a cross between the hostel and the paying guest arrangement. A single household does not generally take in more than one PG; if there is a room large enough, the number may go up to three. But beyond that, the arrangement becomes what ought to be called a mess, because messes by definition cater to a large number of boarders, though perhaps not as large as a hostel. Neither is it connected to an institution and regulated by that institution as a hostel would be. The other salient feature of a mess is that it is not within the confines of the owner's own family, as a paying guest accommodation by definition is. The economics of the mess is predicated on this separation. Families who had acquired land in the south Calcutta areas we have referred to earlier have of late either been adding a floor extra to accommodate women, or constricting their own living space into a single floor so that they might leave one free to start a mess. Our respondent felt that the popularity of his mess was due to three reasons: there were two balconies, a terrace (which actually became quite a source of controversy, as we have indicated above), the house was easily accessible as it was near the main road, and there were two bathrooms for 11 inmates. He said that he had even included two kitchens, 'if there were problems among the girls and they wanted to eat separately from one another.' But in general, the construction of mess-floors in already existing houses is obviously an entirely ad hoc arrangement; as we have noted earlier, civic amenities in these areas have only recently begun to be made available. Sewerage and water supply lines are gradually being regularized, and roads are slowly being widened. But women have been living in mess arrangements in these areas for the last fifteen years as, from the service provider's point of view, the returns on investment and the infrastructural costs are lucrative enough. There is what appears to be an inexhaustible demand, and therefore, the supply increases daily; anyone who has a room to spare in these areas can now translate this into a paying proposition by putting up a notice. Notices abound at local train stations, photocopy shops, on posts and pillars and trees outside the entire length of the road that fronts the Jadavpur University. Though the largest number of boarders are apparently directly or indirectly connected to the university, the idea that north Calcutta is unsafe or medieval in outlook makes the south Calcutta messes even more attractive as options for women. The manager from Chandannagar says, 'I personally think Cal guys both men and women are not my type because of their attitudes. Some pretend to be intellectually very profound but it is not so becos they live with their parents and neighbours so it affects them even if they are working in an MNC. Their attitudes are totally different from us or south Cal people.' A 30-year-old teacher from Jamshedpur stayed first near Hedua[22] in North Calcutta, but 'it was not a place where a person can stay for long'.

Mess owners are aware of their advantages. All reports from the boarders in messes in the Jadavpur area suggest that one of the ways of maintaining this advantage is by preventing the women from getting together to form a united body to press their demands. However, our informant argued that though the women were not in general united, when it came to what he called 'attacking the landlord', they all spoke with one voice.

> When the [Kolkata] corporation does not provide enough water, what can I do? Girls need more water, but in this case I am helpless; 10–12 of them come to me in a body and they are 100 percent professional. They don't come to negotiate; they want whatever they want now. They will not adjust with the landlord, why is there no water, get a water-carrier. If I had rented out the place to a family, this would not have been the case—here I am also facing the same problem, let us adjust, let us use a little less water, but no.

The relationship manager from Chandannagar also says

> Landlords are suspicious whether there is anything fishy going on between roommates. If there is a fight, landlords follow the divide and rule policy for their convenience. If there is a friendly relationship between the girls then the landlords will often try to create a misunderstanding between them. The landlord and family are usually very petty inside.

The content writer from Jamshedpur also agrees that

> Landlords try to keep the girls in control. I have stayed for five years
> in two PG digs. Landlords keep a close eye on the girls to check
> their habits, what time they come and what time they go. They also
> suspect whether there is any politics between the girls. If two girls
> have fought over an issue my landlady would ask me directly what
> is wrong. Although I am not concerned in the fight.

> The time tested policy of dividing to rule works well, and is often
> used. I have heard of only one instance in the last four years that I
> have been involved in this project of a number of women leaving a
> mess together and moving to another place, where the mess-owner
> has a separate flat for the boarders. The problem arose apparently
> with one of the women, who is a respondent to this survey—she felt
> the mess-owner was taking sides with those who had lived there for
> a longer time even though these women were in the wrong. She left
> the place, and then those who were newer boarders also followed.

The politics of living cheek-by-jowl with women, often under the
power of another set of older women, is not always a pleasant experience. The sheer variety of problems shows how difficult the activity
of sharing space can be. 'Presently I am sharing my room with one
girl who will stay for just 2–3 days more; she was here for a month.
She is from Rishra and Haldia Engineering College and doesn't speak
English very well so we didn't speak much…. I am not uncomfortable about adjusting but I want to stay in a single seater' (27-year-old
technical writer from a pharmaceuticals company).

The relationship manager from Chandannagar said

> At first I didn't like the idea of sharing my privacy with anyone; it's
> very stressful, especially for working women. But I like it now as
> one can chat and kill time if one isn't going out on a weekend. But
> there are some specimens who are very noisy and always drinking
> or smoking or whatever, so in that case is very difficult to adjust. I
> had one roommate who was very vulgar in her speaking with her
> boyfriend over phone and I could hear every word because she

spoke very loudly also. This was disgusting and I was relieved when she went away soon.

The content writer from Jamshedpur shares her current PG with students. Her biggest problem is she says, 'They don't manage their money well, so they borrow from me.' Other sorts of issues also crop up—'Sometimes I am tired and my room-mate has the music on too loud—I tell her about it right then, so it doesn't become a big issue. Earlier we have faced similar difficulties with the land line, some girls would keep the line engaged and others' calls won't come.' Or, as the BPO employee from Dhanbad remembers from her first days in the hostel of a very reputed girls' college in the city

> When I came here I was like shucks, I can't manage living alone in this place. I cried my eyes out. This was when I was not even eighteen so I was a baby only. Then my roomie borrowed 50 bucks from me and didn't return only. But I couldn't ask her.

The problems arising from the differences in background are the ones that most women are wary of, though they do anticipate the possibility of trouble on this front and are prepared to either 'adjust' or to take measures to prevent them. Sometimes, however, there is no way out but to shift. A project fellow had stayed in Kolkata for a while before she went to Kanpur to study, and then returned to Kolkata again to do her PhD. She shared a mess with some other working women whom she knew through her juniors in college. The other two women worked in an NGO. The rule was that whoever came home early from work would do the marketing and the cooking. Invariably, the girls who worked in the NGO came late, while the woman we spoke to arrived early from her job at the university. So she was the one who managed the entire household. Ultimately, she decided to leave the mess and return to the university hostel.

> I couldn't study while doing all the household chores. I did learn how to run a household independently, but I used to remain alienated from the others there. It might seem elitist if I put it like this, but I had no conversation with my roommates; all they talked of was

movies, clothes friends and what's happening in their office. I had a functional relation with them.

This woman seems lucky that she had an option of shifting out to the university hostel. Not all women are so fortunate. A school teacher who now lives in a mess says that she used to enjoy the communal living earlier, when she first came, but now she feels restricted. She had wanted to stay alone, but could not afford it. In such circumstances, women decide to take certain measures that will somehow neutralize the lack of compatibility with the other women with whom they are living in close proximity. One of these measures is to withdraw. A number of women have decided that the way to keep out of trouble is put up a 'wall', be an 'introvert', 'don't talk too much'. The advertising professional from Jamshedpur dealt with this in this way. 'I have always tried to maintain a low profile in the PGs because I know my temper can be bad once provoked. But there have been times when I have fought hard. And the consequences have been pretty awful at times.' She sums up the landlord-PG relation thus:

> I have stayed in posh PGs also and apart from the language question in both types of PGs, there are similar problems. Someone is a spy-cum-chamcha of the landlady and becomes the favourite bahu and gets extra snacks, someone monopolizes the phone, someone habitually doesn't pay up when there's sharing of an evening egg roll or tarka ruti or something, someone is a shrew who screams over everything, someone is a klepto, two girls have boyfriends but are always touching each other or giggling or sitting together with glum intensity.

THE 'ETHICS' OF ACCOMMODATION

This seems ironical. Women come to the city in pursuit of their own dreams, given the standard roles they are supposed to fulfil within patriarchal gender organization, this primary step is itself a transgression, at least, in some strata of society, located both in their homes and in their destinations. So their being in the city is itself an unusual enterprise, which forces them to leave the secure confines of their standard roles. But once they have taken this step, they retreat into the gamut of feminine roles available for them within patriarchal gender organization, perhaps using these known roles as shields to keep them safe from the expected dangers of the city itself. The woman's reserve is apparently construed as her biggest defence, as it is supposed to signal her 'personality'; the jeans syndrome might well be an outward and more dramatic manifestation of this. If you wear jeans you are a particular type of woman, and this is the type who will not keep a chilled silence around herself but go out and enjoy herself. The implied judgement is that both these are related; one an indication of the other, and this is not an acceptable image for women. Women who come to the city from outside, after crossing the barriers that prevent them from leaving home and staying alone and 'unprotected' in an unfamiliar place, need not really succumb to all the dictates of gender roles after this initial step. But they do so because they feel that this decreases the problems they face in continuous flow, every single day, in order to live in the city they have chosen to come to.

The definition of the private in this context may well be that this is a space within which you can do as you choose, but when that space is shared, the rights to privacy are distributed, and by that process necessarily curtailed. Living together can be conceived of in several ways. One of the resource persons of this survey spent her first five years in the city at the Jadavpur University hostel, living in the same room with another woman from her hometown whom she had known since school. She was known in her college days as someone who kept totally to herself and did not speak much at all. At the end of her postgraduate course, she shifted out into one of the Jadavpur area messes while she was working on this survey. She felt that living space awakens feelings of territoriality, and relations of dominance and violence must necessarily accompany these feelings.

For me, however, the idea of doing this survey arose from memories of the experience of sharing rather than from memories of protection of territorial rights. As a Higher Secondary student in an open hostel where there were students from all kinds of courses as well as working women, I lived with women of different ages and different capabilities, varied opportunities and needs. At sixteen I was not really aware that I was adjusting; it seemed to be an adventure rather than a burden, and in retrospect, it taught me some measure of tolerance, to be given and received. I certainly did not think of violence in relation to living in shared space at that point, and not even until it was pointed out to me by the woman I mentioned above.

It is possible that I was fortunate in my experiences. But even on reflection now, after the entire process of the survey has crystallized into narrative shape, it seems to me that the ethics of accommodation can well be derived from the experiences of the women we have come in contact with and from our own experiences as women who come to the city from outside. It is true that if we link the sense of territoriality to space, then lived space is bound to become infused with violence. Property cannot but induce feelings of protection and rights to occupation. However, is it necessary to take this as a 'normal' situation, rather than conceptualizing it as a situation arising out of capitalist patriarchal social organization? If the organization of social relations did not follow the linked hierarchies put in place to sustain both capital and patriarchy, then would space have been necessarily enacted or lived as violent? I would propose an ethics of accommodation (rather than 'adjustment') as an alternative. Women have been asked to adjust and accommodate from time immemorial. As we have seen, this is a demand from patriarchy to further its own ends and keep women in the places designated for them by the hierarchy of patriarchal gender organization. Hence these adjustments have never been on the terms women have chosen. What if women were to come to these adjustments on their own terms? What if these adjustments were mutual rather than made by a single party only, would they be called adjustments then? This is the condition I conceive of as accommodation: linking one's dwelling/habitation to the people who also dwell in that space. From geographical to psychic space, human beings in society strive not to be alone. But their efforts may well be defeated by their own attempts at establishing an exclusionary alienation from those who share their space by mistaking this alienation for individualism. Is it not more pertinent to attempt to chart novel ways of engagement rather than slip back into the role definition of women crafted by patriarchy in order to remain safe? Is there not something lacking in a society in which women's being tight-lipped, staid and serious will ensure her safety? On the other hand, what skills for self-protection does gendering teach women, apart from maintaining an icy reserve? Safety has emerged as an issue due to the increased visibility of women in 'public' space. In truth, this is not an issue limited to the public space, but one that intrudes into private space as well. To question why does not shift the emphasis from its importance to women, and especially to those who live alone in the city without family support to depend upon. From this arises the imperative that we strive, as women who have the support of one another in the city, to reconceptualize the way in which we live and experience private space to emphasize sharing. If I have an area into which I do not allow infringements, then surely, the same is true for you as well? If I am possessive about this area, then I assume that you too must be. If I expect that you respect this space that my self has demarcated as exclusive to it, then surely I am called upon to understand a similar demarcation that you have made for yourself? No definition of self, no psychic demarcation of its existence is possible without cognisance of the space of the other. Discussing a boundary situation in the process of understanding, like the practice of human sacrifice in some cultures, Wittgenstein (1971) asks, 'What makes human sacrifice something deep and sinister anyway?' and answers: 'This deep and sinister aspect is not obvious just from learning the history of the external action, but we impute (or ascribe) it from experience in ourselves.'

I am proposing this form of understanding, imputing it from experience in ourselves, for the praxis and poiesis of inhabiting our most private and intimate spaces. One might argue that we cannot understand everyone or everything, that we have ethical judgements that we carry with us into situations, that we cannot empathize with all experiences because everyone cannot have the entire range of experience possible. All of these are valid arguments to be addressed from specific contexts, which might indicate the way to be taken. All our ethical baggage is crafted to suit a particular socio-historical organization of gender and structures of relations flowing from this organization. Our coming to the city was predicated upon the fact that we have aspired to extend the range of experience thus far unavailable to us. There is nothing apart from the socially accepted rules and definitions of relationships and gender to prevent us from redrawing these boundaries to suit our own transgressions.

Q: Indicate if there are things you want changed about your own conditions or about the city/people which will make it easier for women like you to live and work here.
A: Yes I want to live in Cal. I am very, very happy here. I think we should just stretch Calcutta instead of complaining about the city. Stretch it whichever way we want it to. Calcutta is very flexible. And let's give a damn to people who don't understand us.

Given the fact that we, as women who have come to the city from outside, have to construct our most private spaces afresh ourselves, what prevents us from attempting to structure it differently from the accepted norms that constrict our living with others? What stops us from refiguring the contours of the lived in such a way that we are able to live together, without feeling either alone or swamped by demands and responsibilities that burden the self and force it into positions of compromise? These are the questions that this project has thrown up and these are the questions that we would like to bring onto the agenda of feminist thought and practice in contemporary globalizing urbanizing India.

NOTES

[1] Open hostels in Kolkata parlance refer to those where working women and students can stay, as opposed to working women's hostels or hostels which admit only students, mostly affiliated to educational institutions.
[2] All the places mentioned in the interviews and in any other portions of the text may be found in the relevant maps in Appendix 2; these are enumerated serially and referenced by map number immediately following a reference to the place in the text. When places are mentioned in responses, i.e., when they are parts of actual conversation, the relevant

details about the maps which will help to identify the places are given in the endnotes so as not to interrupt the flow of the conversation.

3   For Jodhpur Park, see Figures A2.2 and A2.3.

4   See Figure A2.6.

5   See Figures A2.5 and A2.6. See also Figure A2.1 for city history and division into administrative units. The data in these maps are correct for the time of the survey—since then, the Metro has been extended, and some areas earlier in the South 24 Parganas district have been included in the metropolitan area.

6   See Figure A2.4.

7   See Figures A2.3 and A2.4 in Appendix 2, and also the relative distance of the area from Sealdah Station in Figure A2.2.

8   See Figure A2.3; see also Figure A2.2 for relative distance from Central Calcutta.

9   Short for accommodation. As stated earlier, written responses to the questionnaire have been retained verbatim.

10   See Figure A2.8.

11   See Figure A2.2 for distances travelled.

12   See Figures A2.5 and A2.6.

13   See Figures A2.3 and A2.4.

14   See Figures A2.2 to A2.4.

15   See Figures A2.2 and A2.3.

16   See Figures A2.2 and A2.3 for relative distances and for the location of Park Circus, see Figures A2.3 and A2.5. See also Figure A2.3 for the location of Dhakuria.

17   For Tollygunge, see Figure A2.5.

18   See Figures A2.2 and A2.4 for the location of Garia and A2.6 for Sinthee. The cases referred to in note 13 above and in the present note give an idea of the range over which women are willing to move to get the most desirable accommodation adequate in all respects.

19   See Figures A2.3 for Gol Park, A2.4 for Tollygunge and Behala Garia; the range over which women are willing to move for suitable accommodation may be discerned from Figure A2.2.

20   See Figure A2.8 for Salt Lake and A2.2 for relative distances.

21   For Bagha Jatin and 'colony' areas like Annapurna, Krishna Glass and Dabur, see Figure A2.4. See also Appendix 3 for their history.

22   For Hedua, see Figure A2.6.

WORKS CITED

Bhasker, Roy. 1975. *A Realist Theory of Science*, London: Taylor and Francis.

Bryne, D. 2001. *Understanding the Urban*, New York: Palgrave Macmillan.

Hekman, Susan. 1993. 'The Feminist Critique of Rationality', in L. Alcoff and E. Potter, eds, *Feminist Epistemologies*, New York: Routledge: 50–61.

Irigaray, L. 1991. 'Women Amongst Themselves: Creating a Woman-to-Woman Sociality', in Whitford, M. ed., *The Irigaray Reader*, trans. D. Macey, Oxford: Blackwell: 1997.

Raju, S. 2013. 'Women in India's New Generation Jobs', *Economic and Political Weekly* 58, 36 (September 7).

Sayer, Andrew. 2000. *Realism and Social Science*, London: SAGE Publications.

———. 1981. 'Abstraction: A Realist Interpretation', *Radical Philosophy* 28: 6–15.

Wittgenstein, Ludwig. 1971. 'Remarks on Frazer's *Golden Bough*', trans. A.C. Miles and Rush Rhees, *The Human World* 3 (May): 40.

FIVE

Finding the 'Self'

Q: When did you come to Calcutta and why?
A: First to run from myself, then to know myself and then to make a living.

Many of the survey sheets went out by email, and were returned the same way. In all cases, we had no way of knowing the women who responded apart from what they let us know about themselves. There was no space in the sheet for names and addresses, though the introduction did state that the respondent was free to give both and indicate if she wanted to be contacted for the discussions, and whether she was willing to have her name used in the book when it came to be written. As the reader has noticed, after having read thus far, no names have been used, even if they were given; place of origin, profession and age have been used to indicate each of the respondents. This may have seemed unwieldy at times in hampering smooth reading and/or writing, but this seems to be the least we can do to preserve the privacy of all those who shared with us some very intimate pains and pleasures. The citation with which this chapter begins is from one of the women who preserved her anonymity jealously even while answering the questionnaire: all I know about her is from hearsay, heard during the time the survey was in full swing. She did not let us know her name, place of origin or age. She has been quoted in Chapters 3 and 4, telling us how she increased the size of her room with mirrors and how the city of Calcutta can be stretched in every direction to accommodate us, women who come from outside, and our dreams and desires. Her willingness to give her thoughts and experiences alongside the poetry that (male, European) savants had theorized about, guided the conceptual framework of this study in no small measure. The enterprising resource person who was responsible for eliciting her responses is also a horoscope junkie, and so managed to find out that this woman was an Aquarian; all she told us herself was that she worked in advertising and was bored of the job, longing to chuck it up and learn film-making. While this book has been in the making, she has shifted to Delhi. The woman who had initially given us her email id and facilitated our contact has married and gone away. Ironically, since we cannot put an age or a place of origin to this advertising professional wanting to turn filmmaker, we refer to her through her sun sign, so as not to confuse her with the other advertising professionals who have responded, and whose experiences are also recounted here.

Our Aquarian friend, whom we shall have occasion to meet again in this narrative, seems to echo the quest that many women have made their own when they opted to come to Kolkata: to 'find' themselves, if not exactly 'run' away from their already assumed identities, and in this chapter we consider one of the aspects that defines this search for self, especially for women who are working in the city: their jobs. But as we have seen in the previous chapters, it is impossible to concentrate on any one aspect of city life at a time. This chapter begins with jobs held by the women from outside who work in the city, the opportunities, expectations and difficulties that they face in the city, and then explores the ways in which these relate to the notion of 'self'. In that sense, work is taken in its practical as well as affective aspects, meeting financial as well as emotional needs. The self that we have posited at the end of Chapter 4 is also the self that we seek to delineate here: it is a self in relation to others, and this opens the chapter up to an exploration of relationships consequent upon the women's living in the city alone. In this chapter, we approach this issue from three different, but inter-related angles: Firstly, relationships forged in the workplace; secondly, changes in relationships within the extended family, which has sometimes to play host to women coming to live in the city alone for the first time, and finally the attitudes of the city towards the woman who comes from outside: what relationship does the citizen as colleague, relative and as local inhabitant forge with the 'outsider' and what does this mean in practical and affective terms for both parties? Christine Battersby (1998: 38) asked a speculative question: 'What happens to the notion of identity if we treat the embodied female as norm for models of the self?' Some consequences of attempting to do so, unconsciously, are offered in this chapter. Here too, we divide the responses into sections, to delineate the concerns that women coming from outside think are most crucial to the process of 'finding' the self in the context of the city.

WORK OR 'WHAT WILL YOU DO THERE?'

Many women have chosen to come to the city because their home-towns or villages do not offer a diversity of employment opportunities.[1] But we must also note that if you come from a particular place, a particular background, you are able to live more comfortably in certain areas in the city rather than others; you feel at home in certain types of accommodation rather than in others; you either want a single-seater or are content to share; either you have options or do not. The same thing is applicable to your job. With certain kinds of jobs, you have fewer problems finding accommodation; as the journalists and Information Technology employees have already indicated, it is difficult to convince or explain their working hours and habits to either landladies or roommates who do not come from the same profession or background. It is to this gamut of considerations that we turn in our attempt to understand the trials and expectations of the women who come from outside to work in the city.

> The advertising scene is not well developed in Jamshedpur and anyway it is not a place for Humanities-minded people to flourish, so obviously Calcutta has helped me in my occupation (advertising professional from Jamshedpur).

> Durgapur is an industrial town so there are no jobs for humanities people.... I have no idea about the advertising scene in Durgapur, if at all it exists. Right now I am a trainee and I'm doing the rounds of all the depts.—creative, CS, media—everything to understand the work of the agency—so obviously Cal has helped. My training and education are possible due to Cal, otherwise a BA degree is of

no value anywhere. Cal has something for everyone ... engineers will get jobs easily in D'pur, but for me Cal is a good place to start (trainee ad professional, Durgapur).

But here you have some choices, at least, whereas in Bhubaneswar I had limited choices if I wanted to work in a newspaper only. I have sort of settled here and uprooting myself for another job wouldn't be easy for me. Besides I am nearer home working in Kolkata (journalist, Bhubaneswar).

It is easier to get jobs anywhere else other than my place of origin. Well other than govt. jobs and teaching, of course (artist from Agartala).

I was very excited to get a job as a trainee in a reputed multinational bank. My learning curve accelerated very quickly which is not possible in a small town like Ranchi The exposure was very good. I could test my professionalism with the best people in this industry (marketing executive from Ranchi).

Because Calcutta fostered a warm teacher-student relationship so I knew I could count on my college for a job even after years.... Calcutta provides an encouraging ambience to Literature students even as far as careers are concerned which is a rarity elsewhere (media person north Bengal).[2]

Thus even for those who do not come from rural or suburban areas, the city is a place of opportunity and the main reason they come here is to avail of these opportunities. Hence, from a sample size of 250, for the 63 women who come from rural or suburban West Bengal, Calcutta presents an inevitable destination for employment. From this number, 12 out of the 15 working women who responded wanted to stay in the city, while only 3 thought they could take up an offer outside. They are unwilling to go beyond the city for career opportunities, even if they are dissatisfied with their present jobs. They feel they can find better opportunities here itself. But the picture is radically different when it comes to students who are studying in Kolkata, in the age group 18 to 25. Among the 48 students surveyed, 18 felt they would continue to stay in Kolkata and work here, while 30 were open to changing cities for career opportunities. These included responses in both English and Bangla, and so we can say that out of a total sample that includes both students and working women, 52 percent associate Kolkata with job opportunities and, whether they are happy with their living conditions or not, they would like to remain here since they hold jobs that allow them to do so. And out of this 52 percent, the majority are students who have come to Kolkata from rural and suburban West Bengal. Kolkata seems to have given them a taste for the large city, and the confidence to try their fortunes elsewhere.

> Since I do not know how to speak English or Hindi I cannot go outside the state. So I am happy here (22-year-old nurse from Belur).

> Coming to Kolkata has helped me immensely. This opportunity has changed my life. Now my younger sister wants to study BSc in Kolkata if she gets high marks in her Higher Secondary. I can't think of leaving a Bengali ambience, so I don't want to leave Kolkata (nurse from Kontai, Medinipur).

> I came to Kolkata in 1987, after my husband died. I had to seek refuge in my brother's place In Kolkata women have limitless opportunities. I can't go beyond West Bengal (45-year-old ward attendant from Chakdaha).

> I am satisfied with where I am now and I think I'll not get people who are so warm and friendly to outsiders (23-year-old customer care executive, Darjeeling).

> I don't want to leave Kolkata … because it is close to home. The chances of getting a job are much more here. It has given me an education, the Bengali culture and warm heartedness, which I would not have got anywhere else (24-year-old copywriter from Srirampur).

Among the 39 respondents who are from the northeastern part of India, and from north Bengal, whether students or working women at present, 53 percent want to move on to another city if better opportunities come, the breakup being 13 out of 21 students and 10 out of 18 working women. This is explained by the artist from Agartala thus, 'A lot of women from the Northeast have started migrating to the cities for better education and source of income. There are also women who are management trainees or regular job seekers who come to Kolkata for a start.' One of the reasons that lie behind this is the fact that Kolkata is the largest city in the east of the country, and as such, it is seen as being 'near home'. As the artist points out, this is a good place for the first job or as an educational base. But as another current student from Gangtok points out, 'Study-wise I feel Calcutta is best. Its simplicity pulls me and it is cheap also. Once I complete my studies, I look forward to working in another place, like Pune or Bangalore which pays well.' The artist from Agartala has lived in Kolkata since her student days and also started her working life here. As such she has had a long time to analyse the city, and these are her views on why she finally relocated to Delhi:

> Kolkata has this slackness in attitude which sometimes creates unnecessary delays and ultimately reflects poorly on overall deliveries and may eventually lead to diminished career growth prospects. Professionalism and alacrity were certainly qualities that were missing. A mindset of *dekhchi, aajke hobeyna* (I'll see, it won't get done today) were real deterrents for carrying out any task ... the other aspect is that compared to other metros, companies in Kolkata pay less for the same kind of jobs.... Kolkata is a decent city to live in, however, there are less growth prospects if one were to look primarily at a career curve. Cities like Delhi and Mumbai are not only power centres and commercial hubs, corporate houses along with their decision makers are headquartered there. Kolkata has not grown much in terms of new companies setting up base; existing corporate house have only continued to operate with the same tempo.

> Right now there is learning satisfaction, a degree of attachment and working comfort. But I know stagnation is right around the corner. So I must be on the move to arrive somewhere bigtime (media executive, parents currently posted in the Northeast).

Among those who come from the small industrial towns in and around West Bengal, the situation is a little different. Most of these women have been exposed to a cosmopolitan lifestyle in the industrial town culture, where a number of people from all over the country have lived together for years, and due to the size of the town and the distribution into areas by occupational status, the sense of belonging to this or that region of the country grows parallel with the awareness of the diversity of the country itself, because close neighbours in the facing flat or the next door house come from a different part of India. I have first-hand experience of this, coming as I do from a small industrial town myself and I unashamedly still search out women from my own city during college admissions, especially if they happen to be from my own school. As far as women like us are concerned, Kolkata is seen as a stepping stone to higher things, because we are aware of a larger world outside this city, which we often find quite insular. As one of my fellow townswomen put it, 'There was this major culture shock when people asked you on your face what caste are you?' An aspiring filmmaker in BA informed me he was a Barendra brahmin. A leftist activist in MA clarified his *gotra* as Bharadwaj. There was a girl with my surname from the Scheduled Caste, and I had to clarify that I was from the general category. When I was invited to my friends' houses, there were implicit questions about caste and antecedents. In PGs, questions were explicit.[3]

In general, the women from these industrial cosmopolitan areas seem to be looking for growth and feel that after a point Kolkata will cause them to stagnate; used as they are to people moving from their places of origin to search for enhanced job opportunities, they may have initial trouble with convincing their parents about the shift to a larger city, but once the boundaries of educational institutions have been crossed, these are the women who seem the most mobile group. Among the 33 respondents surveyed from industrial towns, there were 13 working women and 11 students in the 20–30 age group. Six students wanted to continue in Kolkata; the rest felt they would go further afield to pursue a career. Of the 13 working women who belonged to the same age group, 6 felt they would stay here, and 7 knew that Kolkata was a temporary stopover as far as jobs were concerned. The total sample size of women from these towns was 28 working women in all age groups surveyed, of whom

11 wanted to leave the city for better opportunities, and 9 felt they could stay here, as it was near home, they were closest to their parents here, and because they were satisfied. However, 54 percent of all women from industrial towns in eastern India, whether students or working women, living in Kolkata, wanted to leave the city for better opportunities in future. Taking into consideration women from all the areas who responded, that is, north Bengal, the Northeast, the industrial towns and other smaller cities in neighbouring states like Odisha, Bihar and Jharkhand, the reasons given for wanting to leave eventually are such:

The reason why I want to leave Cal is coz my growth will stagnate after sometime why coz Cal lags behind the other metros economically ... Cal is facing a brain drain. People go to metros mini-metros all the time. Money is better there, job satisfaction and growth are better there (trainee ad professional, Durgapur).

Kolkata is not as advanced as Bangalore and Mumbai or even Delhi and its suburbs like Gurgaon. Here we lose out on advancement and perks. Kolkata is better than Bhubaneswar. But I am not satisfied entirely. My friends who have gone South or abroad are doing better than me. Kolkata needs to learn a lot. There is a *chalta hai* [everything goes] attitude even among top professionals here, so commitment suffers. There is a vicious circle of poor commitment, and poor wealth and job creation. People are more concerned about their adda (software professional Bhubaneswar).

During 2000 placements I got an offer in Calcutta but I refused as I wanted to stay in Mumbai or at least two years. Then I came to Kolkata on transfer in 2003. Mine is a hardcore finance job, so I feel I am missing out on the action with the Big Boys. I would be completely satisfied but for this. I am considering a relocation (finance executive from Ranchi).

Lots of women in my hometown work. So I can't say that girls/women work less in my hometown. I am not satisfied with my job because the hours are equally long as in Delhi/Mumbai, but the salary is not at par. The compensation package in the cities is better plus the scope to do more challenging work is better (29-year-old content writer, Jamshedpur).

There is more satisfaction in other cities where job is concerned, even a mini metro like Ahmedabad has better options and pay (BPO employee, Dhanbad).

I am satisfied with the nature of my job but perks and pay leave something to be desired again. But Cal is a cheap city so how can I complain? (advertising professional, Dhanbad).

I'm quite happy with my job, it's pretty exciting to practice what you are taught in theory, and I learn something new everyday. Having said that I also know there is no room to grow in Cal, so it's a training ground, after a year or two I will definitely leave Cal for Mumbai (trainee ad professional, Durgapur).

I would not otherwise consider changing cities because I feel very comfortable in Kolkata, but I would definitely consider changing cities if I find a job in another city which is more challenging and would help me grow as a person. Moreover Kolkata by dint of its being more easy going than other cities has the potential of becoming stagnating if one is tied down within a limited field of work (programme coordinator, Ranchi).

I want to go to Mumbai because I feel opportunities would be better there. Also think the South would be good for me (technical writer from Siliguri).

Obviously, Bombay is the place to go. But Bengali channels are doing pretty well for themselves. Our budgets are tight so a production executive must innovate to give the illusion of a big-budgety thing. So I know a lot right now. However, wavelengths differ, there are very few professional cosmopolitan guys around (media executive in a TV channel whose parents are in the Northeast).

I have stayed in two places, Calcutta and Delhi. I think Calcutta has jobs for everyone it's only a question of finding it. Sadly, most Bengalis have a very narrow outlook when it comes to so-called blue collar jobs. Delhi is a much harder place to live. Salaries are better there, but the money doesn't stretch like it does here (36-year-old manager from the hospitality industry who was originally a Calcutta person but left to do an MBA in Delhi after her mother's death and has now come back to work in Kolkata and live alone here).

Though the general trend, even among women form suburban and rural west Bengal is that younger women are more open to mobility, there are some women who do buck the trend, for special reasons that are connected to Kolkata. Among those who chose to stay, was the 29-year-old advertising professional from my own hometown whose reasons are: 'After a while an advertising professional would move on to Bombay/Delhi/Bangalore. But Calcutta is kinder professionally. Because when I fell ill and couldn't do a regular job, my network helped me find freelance work to sustain myself in reasonable comfort'. The 56-year-old university teacher from Burnpur has a different reason for having been in the same job since the 1970s: 'I am in the best place available in the country.' The PhD scholar who returned to her old university from Kanpur and now stays in the university hostel after an experiment of staying in a mess failed, feels, 'I am here from the career point of view, it's not as if the city attracts me. I don't mind it here but it is limited within a small circle, even though it is a metro-politan city.' Another computer engineering student from Mahishadal in Medinipur too has not been able to come to terms with the city. She comes from a place where there is not as much pollution, and her health has suffered as a result of coming here. But 'I am here because I have to study. Later I might possibly continue to remain here when I begin to work.' So the city is a destination, sometimes by choice, at other times by compulsion, and women who live here on their own strive to make the most of it in their own ways. Another 51-year-old teacher, incidentally from the same university, says that only Kolkata could have given her 'my subject and my department' but she is open to moving into another city if 'a more dynamic workplace' is available.

Some of us have actually learnt more about ourselves than we knew when we filled in the questionnaire. This particular respondent did have an opportunity to leave the city and take up a rather prestigious job in Delhi; she returned because she felt her commitment to her discipline and department would not be fulfilled adequately, and also that she would miss the city and the circles she had built up around herself. Thus, what we are engaged in doing, as well as where we come from seems to have some bearing on how we look at the city; almost all of us are here because it is larger than the place we originally lived in. All of us are making the most of this opportunity, even though for many, this is not the end of the road.

THE PEOPLE AT WORK

Who succeeds; whom does the city accept, and does it reject any of the women who come here with hopes and dreams? The advertising professional from Jamshedpur says,

> Most WB suburbans come to study in Calcutta if they are able to groom themselves properly or they are unusually brilliant, they do well for themselves after college. But the majority stay on because they can't go back. It's very poignant but true. They want to work and get married and stay on in Calcutta. Townies mange to get something sooner, but if they are professionally not trained for anything they run the risk of losing jobs or of sexual exploitation.

The suburban women are also aware of the attitude that the city has taken towards them: a 31-year-old journalist from Bally, a suburb of Calcutta has this comment: '[People in Calcutta] look down upon those who come from the districts. On the other hand, those who come from Delhi, Mumbai and Bangalore are privileged.' A student from Durgapur, 24 years old, has been in Kolkata for 5 years. She feels that '[They] treat outsiders with contempt. My friends initially thought that outside Kolkata everything or everyone is rustic and boring and not sociable enough.' Another 21-year-old student form Nabadwip says, 'I remember once being asked with good intentions: 'What do you do when you are at home?' The MPhil student from

Mirik says good humouredly that she is a tribal, namely, someone 'who wears paint and feathers at home.'

This may well be interpreted as lack of sensitivity especially by a young woman who is struggling to find her feet in the city alone. But does this mean that the city, after providing jobs, does not help us to fit into the niche of the city-woman? The experiences of most women on the employment front seem to be pleasant on the whole.

> My most precious memory is that I was then still new to office when my birthday fell on 10 May. It was in the middle of a hectic week of work. I was new to my job in Kolkata, so I was very upset when I could not take leave. What happened was the whole office got a cake and candles in my honour as a surprise, everyone from my department gave me a gift (a huge teddy bear) ... office people are nice and cooperative. My promotion is a boost and it made me believe in fair play. I feel free to express my views. My learning curve is on an upswing after the new responsibilities (MNC executive from Ranchi).

> Q: Has coming to Kolkata helped you in your occupation? How?
> A: Not much industry exposure but some gud ppl, I mean talented ppl her so I can say I learnt a lot from seniors.... I am not happy with my paycheck but other things r gud. Sum ppl r amazing. Like I really get help from seniors (designer from Siliguri).

> Kolkata is a great place to start because people are very patient they will give a novice room to grow which I realize every day at work (MNC marketing executive from Patna).

But of course this depends on the individual places of work and on the people who populate them: intra-office politics are not entirely absent with respect to women who come from outside. The programme coordinator from Ranchi says, 'Employers [are] sceptical but have higher expectations: they often tend to judge you on your small town background and doubt if you will be stable in your job. They also have higher expectation in terms of devoting more time to your job just because you don't have a proper home to go back to.' The technical writer for a pharmaceutical company, from Siliguri has this experience:

When we joined our organization I wanted to know about the structure of the companies so I joined in sales basically also because I wanted to know how well I could compete with the men in our organization which means that I knew that I was doing a tough job. But the amount of non-cooperation I got from my male colleagues was stunning; first they did not like my doing well or getting performance incentives, then they were noisy during my presentations and then they all started spreading stories about me. Actually Calcutta people are helpfully vague if they don't know u; but once they come in close contact with u they will try to pull you down. Actually they succeeded in my case as I had to leave my job and take up a technical writer's job which is a lateral transfer within the same organization but I enjoyed my first job more because the rewards were far more than now.

I know I am gud in my job, but when I got my increment, sum ppl said why I got it and not them as they come from St. Xavier's/La Marts [prestigious private college and schools], but if I am a better designer than them what can I do (designer from Siliguri).

And sometimes, the experience with a colleague at work is not limited to the public or work sphere—by virtue of being a woman who lives away from her family in some sort of accommodation that is most probably not owned by her, she is vulnerable to incidents that originate in the workspace but implicate her status as a woman from 'outside' the city quite directly. A journalist from Bhadreswar tells this story:

A man who lives in the same building as myself and coincidentally works in the same organization had some trouble with my landlady. In a fit of rage he went and informed the police that the lady keeps girls in her home who come in at the dead of night, despite the fact that he is aware f my work and that we work for the same organization. Not only that he had the cheek to come and tell me not to discuss the issue in office.

I will say that for working women it's difficult to make new friends when you've come to a new city; its only colleagues, and if you are in the same dept it's not wise to be too friendly with colleagues because professional blackmail can occur. I think if I had come to study in Kolkata, I would have made far more friends (27-year-old technical writer for pharmaceutical companies, from Siliguri).

Or there is another sort of victimization; a subtle discrimination that will work against her because she is 'from outside', without an established family lineage in the city that often functions on such networks. This then becomes a matter that lurks under the surface of all interactions that happen regularly, from the work-space to leisure activities. Clearly, the woman from outside, living on her own in the city, is a different creature because of her position, and this makes her as well as those who come in contact with her, alive to the subterranean differences between the city woman whose family has roots here, and the city woman who is in the process of putting down her own roots independently, unaided by family history. This immediately sets a woman living on her own in the city apart from others of her age and background. And in fact neither age nor background is enough to equalize women who live in the city and those who come from outside. In the absence of any known markers, one of our respondents said, 'When there is no family-introduction to fall back upon, you are judged on the basis of the college you go to; that is a part of who you are.' Now that may be circumscribed by a number of factors—the oldest and supposedly best college in Kolkata, though co-educational, did not have a separate women's hostel—even if a woman from outside was perfectly capable of gaining entry into it, where would she stay in the absence of a hostel? Generally, university hostels are few and have limited space given the number of women who are admitted in both postgraduate and undergraduate courses. The same goes for certain colleges of commerce that have established reputations. Professional courses like medicine and engineering, luckily, do not fall into this category, but that is not the point. The point at issue here is if colleges are linked to women's future identities in the job market and become standards to judge their worth in the absence of any other markers, then too, women from outside are at a disadvantage: many of these colleges, especially those that are co-educational, do not have accommodation for women coming from outside, and hence many women, despite their capabilities, are deprived of the facilities and resources of a good college which may enhance the student academically and provide her with opportunities for the future.

> On the professional front it's an accepted fact that if you are the progeny of a well-known father/mother, things are easier for you in Calcutta. So outsiders must be more efficient and have more stamina than the Calcuttan. Only then will you be accepted. There is sympathy if you are from outside, but respect and recognition is something you must earn as a professional (media professional, north Bengal).

> When I was in the first year of graduation, I used to teach in the Apex Study Centre which is quite well-known here. The authorities tried to extract the maximum amount of work for the minimum amount of pay. When I refused to do this in no uncertain terms, I became *persona non grata*. I left the job myself. When I stood first class first in the BA exams, they themselves returned with a fresh proposal to teach there again. By then I had learnt not to undervalue myself. I said a firm no. This is something I learnt from life (postgraduate job seeker from Habra, North 24-Parganas).

> During the initial days of my work, my hep colleagues refused to understand why I couldn't go to Someplace Else with them and spend Rs. 1500 which was 1/4th of my salary, on a single night. However in 2003, I was lucky to get one colleague who had lived and worked in Delhi for 4 years before coming home to Calcutta. Both she and her mom understood my problems; sent lunchboxes for me, celebrated my birthday and made me feel very nice (advertising professional from Jamshedpur).

FRIENDS

And that brings us to people: people who start as colleagues or classmates, but become friends and form networks of support; people who do not do so, even if they were meant, by definition to fulfil that role, that is, relatives. The general attitude towards people in the city seems to be hesitant: a 23-year-old student from Medinipur says that Kolkata knows how to make each person feel at home in her own way; yet when it comes to friendship, she seems cautious. Friends can be made, of course, but the extent and the true nature of such friendship always leaves one in doubt. A 19-year-old student from Kharagpur says, 'It is easy to make friends but difficult to know if they really are your friends.' Is this because the outsider is naturally wary or is it because she has had experiences that have made her extra careful? Or can it be explained in the way that the computer professional from Malda looks at it: 'Here I think people are more selfish, so it's not easy to make good friends. But that is my opinion as some other people think that this is a fine city for friendship and love, especially if that person is living alone for privacy.'

But not all women are willing to tread the fine line between outright hostility and the willingness to give each relationship with local people a chance unless conclusively proved otherwise. A number of women, whether they worked or were students, remembered that their colleagues or classmates brought them food from home to compensate for their hostel/PG/mess food or invited them home to a meal. A student, 25, from Asansol said that when the hostel mess staff was on strike, day scholars brought extra tiffin for the hostelites in their class. Yet another 23-year-old student from Asansol remembered 'one day an extremely trendily dressed woman came to the hostel and was asking for me. She had found a purse I had left in the bus a few days ago, and had come to return it: really how little meaning can be attached to modes of dressing! Many strange things have happened to me since then, but I remember this for its totally unexpected nature. I was absolutely new to the city then, and had a fixed idea of what a city entailed, but that was the first time this idea was changed radically.' But still, a larger number of 'outsiders' took the first option and decided that the people they were in contact with here were 'selfish', 'self-centred', 'status conscious', 'only interested in money', 'arrogant' even overtly 'self-conscious'. The reasons were similar but articulated in various ways. For example, people from Kolkata 'suffer from needless self-satisfaction' (21-year-old student from Ranaghat). 'They feel there was no need for us to come to Kolkata to study at all' (18-year-old from Raiganj). Besides, 'I wish people in the city did not have the attitude that they know everything' (19-year-old student, from a village in Medinipur). This might well be explained by the fact that men and women, even adults, who live at home and take its comforts for granted are rarely sensitive enough to discern the myriad daily problems that make up the life of the outsider. They feel that locals are sympathetic only on the surface: their sympathy 'is restricted to Hi and Hello' (21-year-old student from Haldia), but 'when it comes to actual needs, they are nowhere to be found.' Another student from Bokaro Steel City, 21 years old, says that 'people are friendly to you when he/she will feel that your friendship will be beneficial to him/her'. A 24-year-old student from Durgapur who has been here since 1999 and is now adjusted to city life analyses the situation thus 'People outside the city may find the city living style alien. People of Kolkata are not that warm-hearted or involved. Everyone is too busy to fend for others.' In fact the difference between the local people and people who come from outside has been noted and ruminated upon by a number of respondents. Their perception of the difference between themselves and the locals stems from the fact that the former are 'more relaxed, because 'they have someone to fall back upon and I don't'.

> I've also noticed that we are more ambitious and hardworking than Calcuttans coz we had more difficulty and struggle than the Calcutta kid. He or she had all the comforts of home. So we want more than him or her (trainee ad professional, Durgapur).

> 'People are pretty lazy and shallow here; always live for the moment. There's no ambition' (BPO employee from Dhanbad).

> As far as attitude is concerned they are mostly carefree, knowing they have a support system to fall back upon. They are more relaxed, extravagant and less bothered about the consequences of their actions (19-year-old student, Jamshedpur).

> Most of them are a lot more laidback, over-confident, careless and mostly still very dependent on parents (not only financially). They expect more (21-year-old student, Dhanbad).

> People here are accustomed to the fast and diplomatic lifestyle which is not found in other smaller cities. Their mentalities do not match

and they cannot be counted upon during crisis simply because they do not understand (student, Durgapur).

They are much more self-dependent and often loaded with attitude and very aware of their urban status (23-year-old student Ranaghat).

Though they get all the facilities, I think without them too, I can achieve what I ought to. My goal is evident.... I have adjusted and can do whatever a Kolkata person can do (19-year-old student from Shillong).

The process of finding one's feet in the city and one's place among the local people is sensitively described by a 19-year-old economics student from Durgapur:

People of Kolkata have loads of attitude for no good reason. In academic fields, outsiders are equally good as them, some even better. Initially those classmates of mine who belonged to Kolkata maintained a distance in our class that reminds me of an elite circle. But outsiders shared the same thoughts as mine. They have been friendly since the first day and have helped a lot. Then there is a competitive atmosphere, where you have to. There are definitely many things to learn here, like to be broadminded, competitive attitude and general awareness.

Success: How to Get It and What to Do with It

Urban reactions to working women are supposed to be supportive, but the experiences of women from outside reveal that there is an ambiguity there as well, especially when the woman is young, independent and in the new professions that fetch her enough money for a visibly comfortable life. As in the case of all issues connected to women, space is made for them socially, but on condition that they inhabit it with the minimum of self-assertion, such that the structure of social relationships does not change. Even if they do, these changes are inevitably left for the women to handle: they are the ones who face the consequences of their 'freedom', especially the more difficult ones. Pointing to the role of informal norms that regulate social interaction, England (2000) notes their impact upon the behaviour of women. She also argues that such norms form the context for the working of power: women may have gained power through their actions, but they use it or withhold such use in accordance with social norms, whether these norms are internalized by society or internalized by the woman herself. She points out that despite resources the exercise of power becomes difficult when the norms dictate that women do not use power in certain situations. This deters the women who wish to remain without overt visibility within the community whose norms are being followed. For the same reason, women themselves may feel that it is improper to use the power that that they have acquired, and refrain from doing so. However, within patriarchal gender organization, if 'men hold egalitarian norms regarding gender, this normative push towards non-differential treatment of males and females helps redress some of the greater power men typically have in forms other than norms' (ibid.: 53).

In this context, women who live alone in the city often face situations in which the exercise of 'power' brings forth undesirable results, though the power is apparently theirs to use. Is there a sense of irony mixed with a sense of security when the senior university teacher from Asansol says that Kolkata is safe for women like her who live without family support because, 'Neighbours keep constant vigil, are forthcoming with protection. Especially in localities where many people spend their time on the neighbourhood roads'? Perhaps as one grows older, this constant vigil becomes a source of strength, but the younger women who have faced some curiosity describe these experiences differently. Take, for instance, the attitude of older neighbours, male and female, and 'uncles' in housing societies and neighbourhoods:

> Some people are creeps like extra-friendly and all. Like I gave one neighbourhood uncle a blasting; he always used to ask me questions morning and night, so where are you going? Why so late? That's a nice dress? Going to a party? etc., so I got very het up. So I said that

uncle pls stop bothering so much abt where I come and go, bother abt your wife and daughter (BPO employee from Dhanbad).

There are also many people who are interfering; now when I got a good job for three years, sometimes when my father comes to see me, some neighbours tell him that why is he not finding any good alliance for me, and if he wants to live on my money and is that why he is not interested in getting a good alliance for me (computer teacher, Burnpur).

There was a grudging resentment over whatever I have achieved in my residential complex. Senior uncles would stop me and ask me my salary, and they would be sighing and say things like, we worked all our lives for this little money, we ran families, as if I had misappropriated their share! Even the ladies told me that I will have to leave my job when I got married as no mother-in-law will tolerate my long hours. But now whenever I go to my flat with my husband I make it a point to tell them that I am still working (finance executive, Ranchi).

Finding a 'Family'

The woman alone in the city has ample opportunity to get to know uncomfortable truths about people who are supposed to fulfil certain roles and probably do, up to a point. The relation between women who live alone in the city and their blood relatives can well be a micro-study about family formations in the age of changing gender organization fuelled by women's emancipation and entry into the workforce in larger numbers than before. Sociological theory about the family defines it in various ways, including the 'strength of people's feelings and sense of commitment to others' (Newman and Grauerholz 2002: 4). If this definition holds, then 'extended families' could be non-existent as institutions. On the other hand, if blood ties and kinship are the basis for the institution, then extended families are indeed viable entities. However, women who come from outside the city and begin to live within extended families discover that shared blood ties and kinship do not necessarily strengthen feelings and commitment to each other; quite the contrary, in fact, because there are then financial, social and other considerations which inflect the feelings, commitments and kinship.

Carol Stack (1974) defines families as those who assume and recognize responsibility for one another, rather than those who share blood or institutional ties. This assumption of responsibility does not imply that it is always willingly undertaken, or entirely fulfilled, even when undertaken, especially when there are no visible gains for the hosts. Bengali women who come to the city alone inevitably begin by staying in Kolkata with relatives. Those who are in the 40–50 age group even spent a large part of their early days with them. But the experiences that they had, twenty years ago, seem either romantically recalled because the bitter is completely elided and only the sweet remembered, or the affective structures of extended families have changed drastically since then. For example,

> I first stayed with my Mamamoshai's family in Maniktala. I stayed there for nearly 10 years. Then the joint family house was sold. I had made an arrangement with my cousin brother and the promoter to buy one flat for myself. So, it can be said that I still stay where I first came to stay (41-year-old educationist, Chandannagar).

> I arrived in Kolkata to study in 1976. When I came to study, I was protected by my relatives. I stayed in my ancestral home from where I completed my BA (Honours) (45-year-old PSU officer).

Was this possible because families were closer at that time, single women living alone in the city were so few and far between that they were not perceived as threats to city men, young or old, or because the paucity of such women led to a mystique associated with them that rubbed off on the host families? From my early experience of living with relatives, I think all these factors worked in my case. But I had to make an effort in various directions then too. That was the time I learnt the value of appearance in social relationships other than perhaps the closest ones, and also the value of living by certain codes which have fixed interpretations, especially for women. For example, bringing home my male classmates was standard practice, as was maintaining a curfew for myself without being asked to do so. The flip side to this was of course that significant men were never brought anywhere close to the household (now I wonder why). On the other hand, what I did between the time I left and the time I returned, of my own volition, was hardly ever questioned. The interactions with all levels of the family, from younger cousins to grandparents, was not a chore, but perhaps I was lucky that I found some interest in some aspect or other of their lives. This, as I learnt from this survey, may not always be the case. Looking back, I realize that I could describe my experience of living 'at home' with extended family in an alien city using Goffman's theory (1959) of social roles played on the 'front stage', that is, in the public world, and the 'back stage', that is, in the private world. My stay in the house of maternal relatives taught me that the privacy of home was also a construction: that roles were played to varying degrees in the private and the public world, but they were played, nevertheless.

In the general sense, the family, as Kain (1990) points out, is both a living arrangement and a social institution: whether the convenience of the former is allowed to compromise the demands made upon family members by the latter, and to what extent, is tested often in the case of young female relatives coming to stay for indefinite periods with the express purpose of studying or working in the city. Speaking about the location of privacy, Newman and Grauerholz (2002: 41) say that those places are considered 'private' where 'people expect to be left alone or deal with others as they choose'. However, the woman who lives in the extended family in an alien city can hardly take this definition at face value: she cannot deal with others as she chooses in this apparently private family space, because her rights to that space and that privacy are compromised by her dependence on the people who live there, making the space both available and habitable. Again the issue of adjustment arises, and in the extreme instance, it takes the form of 'adjustment' to sexual harassment or assault. At least one of the respondents, still a student, has recounted an experience of being sexually assaulted by a cousin when she came to Kolkata and began to stay at her relatives' house. She is still unable to forget this incident, though she has been here for five years and now lives in the hostel of her own college. Her experience indicates that women who come from the outside are, in fact often at risk even within what is called their 'own homes'. Of course, all women are thus at risk: but those assaulted know, and, we also as witnesses, are beginning to learn, that it is gender construed as a position of powerlessness, that creates a victim in the eyes of the perpetrator.

The woman who is an outsider and lives in the city alone will have no one to shield her 'legitimately' from such a perpetrator especially if the latter happens to be a member of her own extended family within which she is currently staying; at least that is what the perpetrators think. That she is young and an outsider to the city are factors in determining the extent of risk: youth, location and powerlessness are often linked in such cases. The relative poverty of the woman, that she may be a dependent relative, for example, could also be a factor is such assaults. All the factors that indicate powerlessness are inherent in the woman who comes from outside, even when the household she lives in happens to be that of kin. These are supposed to be her own people, but the dynamics of gender hierarchy are in operation here too, and in a most violent fashion. Outsiders are fundamentally dependent upon hospitable relatives for shelter in the city. Poor young women are at risk if they are from outside the immediate family, and more so if they are in a state of dependence of any kind, as outsiders are.

There are, then, several reasons for which living with relatives becomes a burden, for there is the duty of obedience often without the bonus of pleasure and sometimes accompanied by the threat of plain insecurity. Women in the age group 25 to 35, who are now living alone but had started out with relatives, have different experiences to relate. In general, the feeling can be summed up thus:

> Disillusionment with relatives. A turning point in our lives, when we realize that the happy extended family stories that our parents fed us since childhood are all exaggerated. This makes us more individual-istic and daring as we come out of the family institution and learn to judge relatives as mere people (advertising professional, Jamshedpur).

A 21-year-old student from Dhanbad first came to stay with her aunt, but 'after a month all love and hospitality changed.' The programme coordinator from Ranchi, who when asked who she depends on for help, says, 'On friends, colleagues, relatives in that order. This is not the perfect arrangement because it is natural for people to look for help from relatives first. Unfortunately, relatives do not wish to take responsibility especially when you are a woman and I personally do not like to take favours from relatives.' She sums up the attitude of relatives thus

Relatives [are] pitiful or resentful. Pitiful because they have the privilege of being residents of the city and me and the likes of me had to come to the city so they have to take responsibility. One time right after college I was looking for a place to stay I was staying with relatives and many of them were subtly resentful and urged me to return home.

I had a very tough time when I came here. I made the blunder of going to ask for help from my uncle and cousin brothers to help me in buying forms and then for accommodation. But they had no time for me. But when I told my parents there was a communication gap; my parents said that I have misbehaved and they told me to return. But then I said I won't return, and I really had to convince this to my parents. I had full faith in myself and my capabilities and that helped me to make my parents believe me. Moving out was a challenge, but I had to go out without any cooperation from anybody in fact when I was moving out, I got my own taxi and put my luggage in it also (computer professional from Malda).

Even my younger cousins seemed better informed about things in Kolkata. I was constantly teased about this, which left me feeling bitter ... it made me feel insecure, inferior and very, very unsure of myself—worst of all I had to depend on others (23-year-old student, Durgapur).

Relatives apparently are not always comfortable with a single young girl of proven competence living in their midst. They are unable to get rid of her by overt means; she is family after all. Also, their status in the extended family may well be enhanced by their hospitality towards her. But they seem in no mood to be anything more than visibly hospitable and sometimes show their displeasure at her success: 'My relatives are very unhappy that I am doing well in my career' (sales executive from Dhanbad). On the other hand, a number of women also felt that staying with relatives would limit them because, as a 24-year-old student from Durgapur put it, 'I didn't want to be a liability or answerable to anyone.' But there were at least 2 respondents in their twenties who are working women and currently staying with their relatives because they have figured that this will help them to save money on rent and prepare the base for independent living in the city, 'I stay at my relative's place in Ajoynagar.[4] I will stay there till I get a proper job. Then I will take up a PG in an area close to my office. I am also studying for my CA Final and staying with my relatives' cooperation is making it possible to get the care and warmth of home' (CA Internee from Bihar Sharif). A 29-year-old computer teacher from Burnpur stays with her relatives in north Calcutta[5] and finds this convenient because, 'I don't want to spend too much money on rent. So I think staying there is good for that. I also like to stay here with my family members for safety reasons. But I pay for my food because I want to keep my respect high. As my cousin brother stays in Bhilai there are no problems of space or any related problems, so there is peace in the family. I have my own room also so I am happy.'

Sometimes the class backgrounds of the women and the gender stratification and role in the place of origin as well as the destination (K. Santhi 2006) structure the relationship with relatives. Women who do not belong to the urban middle class, but are of the lower income strata from rural agricultural households, are more 'tolerant' of the impositions of the extended family with whom they are staying in the city. Many factors have to be considered in order to understand the woman's position and response to staying within the extended family household in the city. They may have relatively low-paying jobs in the city and hence no option but to live with relatives. The relatives may have left their original homes earlier, and may have moved upwards in society, which puts the newly arrived woman from the suburbs or the rural areas at a disadvantage, and opens her to exploitation. On the other hand, the host relatives may be in the lowest rungs of the urban class hierarchy, yet, by virtue of being urbanites, have or at least feel that they have an advantage over the woman who has come from the rural 'backwaters'. In both cases, the woman who comes from outside and lives within the family home in the city is in a vulnerable position. And the survey reveals that such women, in low paying jobs, from rural backgrounds, living with relatives in the city, do not complain about the attitude of the latter. Is such a woman overawed by the place that she has come to, where she must make a living, a place which is manifestly different from her home? Is she grateful for the mercies shown by her urban relatives in taking her in and providing her with a place to stay? A 22-year-old nurse from Belur says, 'My father's cousin put me up at Dum Dum (north Calcutta). Now I stay with my pishi (paternal aunt) in Baishnabghata (southeastern Calcutta). I have no problems there. I changed my residence to be with my pishi. My pishi, my cousins, my colleagues are all there, so I am not scared.' The fact that a woman in the city may be 'scared' of the very place she has come to make her living is articulated by this respondent. The women who live in arrangements like PG accommodation or rented places or the mess may have felt this fear, not of peculiar circumstances, like walking on a lonely road or staying alone in a room in a strange house, for instance, of the city as city, but they have not articulated it. Once again, we must note that employment and mobility, even when they are linked together, do not mechanically or even necessarily result in an increase in sense of confidence or independence. Whether confidence is related to economic and social circumstances within which the woman has been socialized from her childhood, and to what extent this structures her consequent response to emancipation denoted by increased opportunities for employment and mobility are questions we may well ponder.

It would, however, not do to come to conclusions hastily. The computer teacher from Burnpur, who comes from a small industrial town and has an MA in Philosophy, has the same view: 'I think if there are good relatives, there are no problems. But if there is nobody then there are many problems, for girls there is no 100 percent safe place. By chance if no incident happens then it is your good luck.' But the other women surveyed who said they stayed with relatives and did not mind this arrangement were women from a different background. They held low paying and low-valued jobs in the city as ward assistants, unskilled nurses, and so on, and came from rural agricultural backgrounds with limited language skills. 'I stay at my brother's place in Kasba. I pay Rs. 500 to my brother every month, but otherwise also there is no problem' (45-year-old ward attendant from Chakdaha). A 24-year-old nurse from Contai in Medinipur says, 'I came to stay at my *mamabari* [maternal uncle's house]. I am quite happy there. I have to do domestic chores despite my routine but I do it with a smile on my face in order to keep peace. I also know that staying with my relatives gives me protection and security which staying in a working girls' hostel may lack.' It might be that being thus dominated is something that she has been socialized into taking for granted as women's due, and so it does not seem unnatural to her.

This seems to be the ideal situation for patriarchal gender organization: women are converted into wage-earners, thus apparently entering the labour market, but they still remain docile and bound by the norms put in place when they were unwaged home workers charged with the responsibility of reproducing the conditions in which male labour could become most productive. Why the acceptance of these conditions is tolerable only to the women who are aware of their limitations in terms of education, social skills and earning power is a point that might be ruminated upon. When women enter the workforce, do they not feel empowered because of their economic independence? And if they do, how is this independence performed in social situations? If it is not performed, does society become aware of their empowerment except in a crisis situation or not even then? There is another point that strikes one. In most of the cases described by our respondents, there are clear instances of domestic exchange: labour or money in return for board and lodging. Are some sections of society, that is, the 'lower' classes, able to adopt a more dispassionate attitude to relational ties, using what seem to be quite rational means of exchange in order to keep the so-called ties of blood functional? Do problems arise in middle-class extended families because these families feel it beneath their dignity to go into such direct and clear terms of exchange, using blood ties as a sentimental veneer?

The crucial issue is that the feminist struggle for equal employment opportunity cannot remain limited to employment itself. It should result in a larger social change wrought by the entry of women into the workforce, and the enactment of this arrival on the social stage, such that the effect of changed circumstances extends to both women and the rest of society in general. As a corollary to this, single women who come to the city to earn a living are either to be viewed within the interstices of patriarchal gender organization itself, or through the changes wrought in patriarchal gender organization by their arrival and continued residence in the city. Here are the experiences of two women who came to the city when there were not many like them here:

> When I first came, I did not know how to move about or conduct myself in the city, so if people around me did not help me to adjust myself, I would have made a lot of mistakes. My uncle was a very conservative man and there was no girl of my age in the house. So, I became friendly with the ladies in the neighbourhood. Earlier, neighbours were a source of great help but now its no longer the case (42-year-old educationist, Chandannagar).

> Neighbours keep constant vigil, are forthcoming with protection especially in localities where many people spend their time on the neighbourhood roads (56-year-old university teacher, Burnpur).

Women who have come in the last decade, those now in their late twenties or early thirties, are not so tolerant or even remotely amused by these attitudes. As the advertising professional from Jamshedpur says:

> Men who come from outside and do well, soon become insiders while women who come from outside, more so if they stay unmarried, remain outsiders. People who are permanent residents are benign as long as the girl assigns them the role of a benevolent moral guardian/protector. Once you assert yourself or simply do your own thing, it becomes everyone's business to know all about you, judge you and condemn you.

A 41-year-old woman from Durgapur, who lived in Kolkata through her college and university days and worked here too (she is now married and living here with her husband) recalls an incident that illustrates this comment:

> I believe people are friendly and helpful. But if they are friendly and helpful, they expect a young girl to obey them and be grateful to them. But that is not possible always. What happens is that when someone who is single asserts her independence a lot of eyebrows are raised. For example, I was very friendly with my classmate in LBC (Lady Brabourne College), whose parents lived in Calcutta. After I got a job, I requested them to find a PG for me, and they asked me to stay with them as a PG, paying a nominal amount, which was a wonderful arrangement. My friend was already married, and they were very nice towards me. But when they learnt that I was dating my colleague, they were extremely angry. They had a conservative mind-set, and they didn't believe in love marriages and all that. My friend intervened on my behalf, but things had gone all haywire already, and I had to leave their house. Only after I married did they come and bless me at our reception.

The people whose house the woman lived in were not related to her; they could well have left her to her own devices, as she was an adult and presumably, able to take care of herself. On the other hand, though they were not her relatives, they were concerned about her welfare simply because she was a woman alone in the city and they felt that their intrusion was justified. They took it upon themselves to play the role of what sociologists would term 'fictive kin', a bond that women living in patriarchal social organization can interpret either as interference or as concern. Many women who participated in the survey themselves said that people in the city, whoever they are, relatives, friends, neighbours or complete strangers, display 'needless curiosity' towards single women who have come to the city from outside and live here on their own. The opposite view will obviously be that of a society in which patriarchal gender organization prevails so that a woman by virtue of her gender, needs protection and intrusion into her life. Some of the respondents also had this view. Accepting that the norms of society are as they are, they take the functional approach: if people left women completely alone, would they come to their aid when these very women needed help? The artist from Agartala, for example, feels, 'most people are generally friendly. Most others feel it to be 'intrusive' but I feel that if you don't know your next-door neighbour or your landlord, it's sad'. I have myself the experience of putting up with many queries that, if one were to preserve one's privacy jealously, would constitute gross violation, but in many cases, I have learnt to answer these with as much good humour and equanimity as I could muster in the circumstances, thinking that these people did come to my aid when necessary, and that their support was crucial. This is a learnt reaction; in the initial stages, and at a younger age, one would be surprised if the woman is diplomatic enough to react thus. But as the Agartala artist explains, 'Community and neighbourhood [para] concept is very strong and people belong.'

DOES THE CITY LEAVE YOU ALONE?

A unique concept across Kolkata is that a *parar chele* (neighbourhood boys) are their own neighbourhood watchmen. 'No woman would feel unsafe if she belongs to that para.' This is akin to what Lefebvre describes as a rural community. At one time, everyone knew everyone else in the neighbourhood, and each individual felt himself supported, under close supervision but assisted, much like in a village (Lefebvre 2003: 151). Is this an inversion of urban alienation? Is curiosity the price one pays for a continuation of local networks of help and support, especially when there are no institutions like the family or a set of kin who will 'protect' the single woman who lives on her own? If a woman needs help from someone, does she have to open her life to public scrutiny and live by public standards in return for that help? Does the neighbourhood community act as watchdog for security as well as like the moral police for 'unprotected' women from outside the city who inhabit the neighbourhood? These are the questions that the experiences of these women throw up to contemporary urban society.

Specifically, these questions divide Calcutta into 'safe' but conservative neighbourhoods where women from outside have the benefit of protection from the local people, but have to submit to their sometimes unwelcome scrutiny and questions. Then there are 'progressive' neighbourhoods where no one bothers about who lives where and how: but safety is often not compromised because local people come forward in a crisis. The reverse of both these situations are also common: the conservative neighbourhood may merely point fingers and say that the woman deserved what she got when an untoward situation occurs, and the progressive neighbourhood may shrug its shoulders and adopt a policy of non-interference. In both cases, the woman has two clear choices: she may continue to live in the area and bear the brunt of public censure or cope with indifference, or she may, if she can afford it, leave. An apparent progressiveness as well as curiosity disguised as bonhomie characterizes different strata of the Bengali middle class and upper middle class. Their residence in the older north Calcutta areas or the newer better planned and maintained, more modern south Calcutta areas do make a difference, which is why we have seen many women choose the latter over the former as places of residence.

> I am not sure whether permanent residents of the city are sympathetic or not, but often people say, aha, you're staying so far off from all your relatives and friends, alone in the city ... now whether this is called sympathy I shall not be able to say, but when you need their help actually, there's no one around. In a busy city like Kolkata, no has the time to stand by anyone else. Even though they stand beside a single woman and act as if they are sympathetic, their sympathy is for their own gains, motivated by their own needs (student, 21, Jalpaiguri).

Shall we look at these responses as age-driven? Are women who are in their mid-thirties and beyond, socialized into accepting community participation in their lives because they have, at some deeper level, accepted that the social organization of patriarchy has to be gradually articulated to fit their changed lifestyles, rather than radically opposed? Is it because we were part of the vanguard of women who dared to do what had hitherto not been done that we were open to certain compromises just to make our presence and activities more acceptable, more innocuous, not excite continuous comment while we got on with our lives? Are the women who have followed us impatient with our compromises because they did not have to face the initial struggle to leave homes and families behind? What for us was a challenge, an 'adventure' had, in the next twenty years, become a 'normal' socially accepted path for women. So they seem to have taken on the next phase of socialization, the next stage in creating social consensus about their lives and lifestyles in the areas where they live and work. Instead of 'adjustment' with patriarchal society's unchanged norms about the proper conduct of women, working or not, outsider or not, staying alone or not, younger women want these 'norms' to be exposed for what they are: what these women themselves call 'needless curiosity' or 'interference'. The usual patriarchal explanation of this is that women now are more 'intolerant', flaunt their independence to a greater degree and pose larger threats to the structures deemed normal by hegemonic gender organization. It is possible that at least the women who have come to the city in the last decade have done so carrying with them the gradual benefits of some change in the general perception of women's 'natural' status, and are no longer amenable to fitting into the earlier role requirements of being naturally submissive and seen-but-not-heard? When they enter the sphere outside their immediate homes (and sometimes even within their own homes), they are perceived as being impatient with things that earlier generations 'adjusted' to. This decrease in the perceived levels of adjustment stands out starkly for women who are outsiders, because by virtue of their status as female outsiders with no visible protectors they stand out anyway.

And that this perception may be right, but is not necessarily harmful or even detrimental, that they may even make the institution change into something which offers the woman more space in the public sphere than was traditionally granted to her within it, emerges from what this finance executive from Ranchi had to say:

Many times people cautioned my in-laws because they thought that I won't be able to adjust to family life and girls from hostels do not have the same commitment to family as girls who have stayed at home. Actually we are thought of as selfish women who will immediately divorce if anything does not meet with our approval. This feeling was there in Bombay also (finance executive from Ranchi, now married and living with her in-laws in Tollygunge).

But is it not a gain of feminist struggles that this should be so? What was earlier a rare occasion, that is, that a single woman should leave the 'safety' of her home to work or study in another city, has now been accepted as more or less normal within a particular class, and is slowly gaining acceptance in rural and semi-urban areas as well. Should not women who have crossed this stage without a sense of struggle, now engage with deeper layers of patriarchal socialization that dictate that even when they have left home to work and live alone, they must still conform to norms that were meant to be followed by women who were neither seen nor heard? But this also raises a related albeit uncomfortable question. If there were no interference or curiosity on the part of the groups or individuals who, in this case, can be said to represent 'society', if women were to be 'left alone' to pursue their own lives with complete freedom, would they be safe? We shall raise the specific question of women's safety at a later stage. But here, we must face this issue squarely: does this interference and/ or curiosity always work to women's detriment, especially in the case of women from outside the city who live alone without 'protection'? This only underlines the fact that the woman who can now do several things which the earlier generations could not, has reached a certain stage: yet that stage is itself situated within a larger socio-historical context which has not exactly changed to accommodate her without many contradictions coming to the surface.

Any woman who has gone to the police station to register a case of what is lightly known as 'eve teasing' without the support of some organization or a man, will know that those who are empowered to 'protect' women are not exactly eager to fulfil their roles. Neither do they have the resources, means or mentalities to effectively do so. Is 'social protection' then a viable alternative, and should women suffer the unwanted interest of such self-appointed social protectors? Has the women's movement been able to address the issue of women living alone in a society that is still manifestly patriarchal, despite the increased visibility and mobility of women in the public sphere? The experiences of the women who have come to the city from outside to participate in the public sphere reiterate this question. They also alert us to the fact that the concrete consequences of actions that foreground resistance to some norm (and perhaps hope to become norms themselves) are also situated within a context, of which the time and the social space are but broad markers. The internal differentiation within the area demarcated by these boundaries also impacts upon the consequences.

The women themselves have forged certain networks, communities and support systems that will help them to deal with these realities. These are predicated on the fact that these women, once they have arrived in the city and have learnt to work their way around, can function as support for other women and for each other. Thus, they have fashioned relationships and bonds that did not exist in traditional structures of family and friendship. We turn in the next chapter to an account of the degree to which these new forms of sociability have become part of urban life, inflecting established patriarchal gender ideology and its quotidian working towards visible transformation.

NOTES

[1] Details of women's migration to the city for different regions of the country and covering the different 'types' of migration enumerated in Fawcett et al (1984) are to be found in K. Shanthi (2006).

[2] This does not refer to a particular city but an area in the state of West Bengal. Since this is the way the respondent described her home, it has been retained in the narrative.

[3] Gotra is a very small subsect within a caste group, named after a mythical male ancestor. Those who share the same gotra cannot marry within the group. The Scheduled Castes and Scheduled Tribes as well as people belonging to Other Backward Castes (OBCs) are distinguished from the 'General Category' for admission to educational institutions and

employment in mainly the public sector. The noun 'scheduled' comes from the schedule of the Indian Constitution that lists the historically disadvantaged communities for whom 'reservations' or affirmative action is mandated.

4   See Figure A2.5, and also Figure A2.2 for location of the area relative to the Central office district.

5   See Figure A2.6.

WORKS CITED

Battersby, C. 1998. *The Phenomenal Woman: Feminist Metaphysics and the Patterns of Identity*, New York: Routledge.

England, Paula. 2000. 'Conceptualizing Women's Empowerment in Countries of the North', in Harriet B. Presser and Gita Sen, eds, *Women's Empowerment and Demographic Processes: Moving Beyond Cairo*, Oxford: Oxford University Press.

Fawcett, J.T., S. Khoo, and P.C. Smith. 1984. *Women in the Cities of Asia: Migration and Urban Adaptation*, Boulder, Co: Westview Press.

Goffman, E. 1959. *The Presentation of Self in Everyday Life*, New York: Anchor.

Kain, E. 1990. *The Myth of Family Decline*, Lexington, Ma: Lexington Books.

Newman, D.M., and L. Grauerholz. 2002. *Sociology of Families*, Southern Oaks, Ca: SAGE Publications.

Lefebvre, Henri. [1974] 2003. 'The Other Parises', in Elden, E. Lebas and E. Kofman, eds, *Key Writings*, Athlone Contemporary European Thinkers Series, London: Continuum: 151–59.

Shanthi, K. 2006. 'Female Labour Migration in India: Insights From NSSO Data', Madras School of Economics, Working Paper 4.

Stack, Carol B. 1974. *All Our Kin: Strategies for Survival in a Black Community*, New York: Harper.

Friendships: Creating a Community

Writing in 1938, Louis Wirth describes city life as involving a much greater degree of interdependence, a volatile form which people can hardly control.[1] We consider the measures taken by women themselves to build up relationships that will help them to negotiate the difficulties and share the triumphs of the city that they inhabit as outsiders. As Wirth points out, these new relationships and communities are a function of urbanity, and form a substitute for traditional family ties. But we shall also see that these relationships and ties are forged in the context of the city: they generate corresponding relationships that emerge between the outsider, singly or collectively, and the people of the city as well. In the previous chapter, our respondents identified friendships as crucial to the process of dwelling in the alien city. In this chapter we consider this theme in detail as it applies to a woman coming from elsewhere, for whom networks of friends are sources of sustenance, both emotional and practical. After first considering the nature of friendships in general and then female friendships, the issues that emerge from the respondents' own views regarding factors influencing making and keeping friendships, are considered in separate subsections in the latter part of the chapter.

In Simmel's view (1903), sociability is a playful form of socialization where the 'concrete motives bound up with life's goals fall away', making sociability an end in itself. If this is taken literally, then the friendships that women who come to the city from outside forge with one another and sometimes with citizens cannot be classified as sociability. For these relationships are not exactly devoid of concrete motives as Simmel demands. On the other hand, neither are they what relationship theory designates as 'instrumental' relationships which have a particular goal in view, and are limited by that goal. Stack

(1974) studied the relationships between networks of poor African American women who tended to think of each other as 'family' and depended more upon each other for support and solutions rather than on their kin by marriage or by blood. This provided a different concept of family even while it extended the idea of friendship. Later work in the contextual theorization of friendships, as advocated by Adams and Allan (1998: 1–2), shifts the focus from the dominant 'attributes' perspective within psychology, onto the properties of individuals within relationships rather than on the relationships themselves. Thus a fuller and more sophisticated understanding of the internal dynamics of the relationships became possible. Here too, interaction rather than mere action was emphasized, and as part of the concern with relational properties, the dynamic, processual aspects of relationships and how they develop and change over time has been highlighted far more than in earlier attributional approaches. Adams and Allan themselves add the 'contextual' approach, which they explain as 'the conditions external to the development, maintenance and dissolution of specific friendships, those elements which surround friendships, but are not directly inherent in them, the extrinsic rather than the intrinsic' (ibid.).

What counts as 'extrinsic' to relationships? Adams and Allan maintain that 'researchers can contextualize a given phenomenon in quite different ways, each carrying its own assumptions, strengths and limitations'. For our purposes, this context is already defined: women who come from outside the city form relationships with each other more easily than they do with citizens. And the contexts within which these friendships flourished began usually with colleagues, classmates from outside the city, and with those with whom one shared accommodation.

> Friendships with Calcutta residents happened with time. With outsiders, friendships were instantaneous. But I have made a few good friends over the years ... the most difficult and the simplest thing [in city life for an outsider] is getting a reliable support system. Friendships made during hostel-life must be nurtured by every young girl (media executive, north Bengal).

For older women who have been working for long and have been living in the city for awhile, the people who benefit from their work become close to them. The 53-year-old surgeon from Silchar says, 'I did not have friends [earlier] because in our times, brothers and sisters were more important than friends. But as I am growing old, I can see that I have made many good and respectable friends, even a long-term patient can become friendly, not just the patient but his or her entire family'. A 39-year-old interior decorator, self-employed originally from Bokaro, says, 'I rely on my two employees. I have employed a very reliable husband-wife team and they respect me very much. We are very close like family. I have learnt good Bengali from them.... If a client is happy with my work, the whole family becomes close, I get birthday presents and bouquets from my clients every year. I feel self-satisfaction in this'. The senior PSU officer Murshidabad has pleasant experiences from the time she bought her plot of land in Salt Lake, where she now owns a double storey house: 'I was the only lady in the cooperative. But the men were very helpful, they arranged for the lawyer, contractor, everyone was nice.' Now, her tenants provide her support. She also feels that she is safe because her neighbours are interested in her welfare. 'In the cooperative, there are families who are now like my own family. I think values are very strong and clear. In Delhi and Bombay, the next door neighbour has not even seen you, but here everyone is concerned about me so I am also.' But, as usual, there is a different view, and it comes from the software engineer from Bhubaneswar. She has been in the city since 1990, and is now 32 years old, financially secure and owns her own flat. Initially, she was disgusted at the discrimination shown by city residents because she spoke Oriya more fluently than Bangla. Can this be connected to her experience in buying her own place? Did the fact that she was a woman alone, and also one who was culturally different from the Kolkata milieu, lead to a negative experience about getting her own place in Kolkata? She says:

I don't think people [in Kolkata] are very sympathetic. Even when I was buying my flat, my promoter tried to swindle me, my property agent also did. When I was a student we faced routine harassment from local boys. Only my colleagues are sympathetic. But that is because we work in a professional environment.

The 'complicated, volatile, fragile form of mutual dependence' that Wirth points to is slowly becoming stronger and more cemented in the lives of women who live alone in the city without the cushion of immediate family. A student from Durgapur says, 'Kolkata has gifted me with really good friends: some who are my mother's age to a child. I think it is easier to make friends here as friendship has not got any fixed definition or age-bar in Kolkata. Back home it was only classmates I thought could be friends'. The basis of friendship, in societies that are structured, may well be age and similarity of experience, but in a situation where a woman has come from outside and cannot only depend upon people of her own age, she has to extend her circle of acquaintances further. In her home milieu, the familial relations that she would have drawn upon are not available, but the relations that she herself creates are often named in familial terms. Yet these are not similar to familial relations, they are friendships, built upon the shared elements of city life and on mutual dependence, and not embedded in any history. The relationship is constructed purely on the value of the individuals involved and the situation that brings them together, rather than any prior reference to family ties or other antecedents, though they are built within the context of work and habitation.

Generally, friendships are seen as relationships of equals, and some theorists of female friendship like O'Connor (1998) have even designated them as reinforcing the class, religion, ethnic and gender differences that structure the society within which the friendships are located. Similarity thus becomes an important condition for friendship, while the friendship based on similarity is itself a means of substantiating social differences. Women who come to the city from outside, however, often experience a different reality because of their peculiar circumstances. This is articulated by our respondent, whose earlier conception of friendship as age-specific has changed in a milieu that is more diverse than the one she was exposed to at home. This may be because her needs are more varied and her responsibilities in fulfilling them are different in the city than they were in her place of origin. She is in contact with many more people, and open to a variety of relationships with many more of them. One could extend this by saying that as women venture out of the confines of home into the public sphere this is more likely to happen whether they are citizens or women who come to the city from outside. In that case, the experiences of the women who come to the city from outside alert us to this variety and extension that mark the traditional view of friendship as women's mobility and visibility in the public sphere increases.

There is also the consideration that 'no city can be the perfect place to make friends because of the competition' (content writer from Jamshedpur, who has been here since her college days). This comment is interesting if viewed against the difference between male and female intimacy in the patriarchal capitalist context. Stacey Oliker (1998) has argued that the growth of individualism as an ideology that facilitated modernism, democracy and capitalism was associated with autonomy, self-interest and competition in the public sphere, which was then occupied by men. Intimacy was typically contained within the private familial sphere which was seen as dominated, managed an operated by women. The different structural locations of men and women thus shaped the relationships that they formed. Thus, the identification of the city with the public sphere, where friendships, that is, intimacy, cannot be fully realized because of competition seems to echo this classical structuring of relationships along gendered lines: except that with the entry of women into the so-called public sphere, one would expect that such demarcation would begin to be compromised, if not completely changed. One of the issues that we must keep in mind as we proceed to explore women's entry into the public sphere as well as their need to form relationships outside the patriarchal family for their own support and emotional sustenance is precisely whether what were earlier perceived as gendered demarcations continue to characterize intimacy and what are the implications of both change and continuity in this context.

A possible direction for this change is indicated by the programme coordinator from Ranchi when she says, 'It is easy to make friends in Kolkata because people in general are more amicable and social than in other cities where life is faster.... However, ... there will only be a few real and dependable friends because congeniality can never be the sole basis of friendship.' As this respondent is aware, 'there is nothing more concrete on which to base the friendship'. We have already noted that the contexts of friendship cannot be strictly demarcated as external to the relationship. Rather, the circumstances in which the relationship is constructed would seem to be a crucial factor in determining its nature. That some form of similarity beyond class, gender, ethnicity and race can function as the basis of friendship is clear. We must note that such a response is possible when the basis of a constructed community, however nebulous, is discerned by individuals who seem to share this sense of difference and collect around this shared feeling to actually construct the community. In structuring this fragile support system for themselves, and striving to maintain the balance between privacy and community, women find support among other women like themselves. Circles or networks are thus crafted from the resources that you can call up.

Sayer (2000) describes community as being based on shared beliefs and common identities, and upon the decision of those who share to be identified as a community. He identifies two essentials that define community: there must be real pragmatic bonds between people which can stand up to external pressure. This does not signal a mere exclusionary wish but something universally proposed and viable within their situated particularities. Communities are embedded in wider social systems, and their members participate in wider divisions of labour, sharing infrastructure, language, economic and cultural resources and phenomena (ibid.: 179). Thus the communities set up among women who come from outside and live alone in the city are founded on their shared sense of externality to the city in varying degrees, and their shared necessity to cope with the various aspects of the city, also to varying degrees. These variations structure the relationships that are formed. As the sales executive from Dhanbad says when she needs help with anything, 'I first contact my friends. They are mostly outsiders like me, both men and women and all working today. Even if someone is hitched up, we include the boyfriend/girlfriend in the group; they do all the running around.' This is an instance of what Marks (1998) calls 'inclusive intimacy' which increases and strengthens the support system, embedding the primary relationship within ever-widening circles. The 41-year-old from Durgapur remembers, 'In my hostel we girls bonded instantly and those friendships have stayed. I also played cupid for two friends, who are now very happily married.... We all relied on each other to an extent that even today, my friends are more important than many of these so-called relatives, and I make no bones about that.'

The nurse from Belur says, 'I know many women who are like me, who have come from outside. The main worry is how to get a good job. Secure accommodation is also a worry; whenever we get a chance, I talk to these girls. We discuss problems and the way out. I can tell these girls everything that is in my heart. I am not so friendly with Kolkata girls.... Kolkata people will always be a little different from others. There will always be a communication gap'. A home tutor from Kanthi, Medinipur, says, 'Compared to my hometown, people here are much more mechanical. Life has made people here more self-centred.' The same is echoed by a school-teacher from Murshidabad, 'It was difficult to adjust with the city at first, people seemed indifferent and unhelpful, selfish, and their double-faced natures slowly began to be exposed. I think you should behave with a person in the exactly same way as he deserves.' So one gravitates towards women from outside like oneself.

> I depend on my roommate and her family for emotional and practical support. I also rely on a few ex-colleagues for effective support.... I found accommodation in Gol Park for my friend from Ranchi, cared for her physically and financially during her illness until her parents came and even then I had to navigate them. That same friend taught me how to email in 1999 and write CVs and covering letters via email for jobs. My friends from outside have helped me during illnesses; my roommate has been a pillar of strength. And she is corroborated by the programme coordinator from Ranchi, 'Peers and their families are mostly sympathetic, even empathetic. I have had friends [whose] mothers ... have cooked for me so that I could have a feel of home. My colleagues ... have got lunch for me almost every day. In case of illness my colleagues and friends who are residents of Kolkata have ... have tried to help every possible way (29-year-old advertising professional).

Another set of relationships develop with local friends' families, who turn out to be more supportive than blood relatives. The journalist from Bhubaneswar says, 'At first I stayed with my friend's uncle and aunt. I stayed with them for a month and they were the *most* hospitable people I've ever met.... Even after I moved out, they are still family to me'. The ad trainee from Durgapur says, 'Rishika, this friend of mine and I became like sisters, her family is the sweetest, although I am a Bengali and she is a Marwari, there was no probs. Even reg food, aunty told me to cook and eat non-veg if I liked, which was very progressive of her.' Later, when it was decided that her friend would get married and leave for Mumbai, 'her parents are saying not to shift till I get married coz I can take her place'. She has become so much like family, she says that whenever any of her friends from outside are in trouble or need of places to stay, 'I tell Rishika's parents all the time to help out with their connections.' A marketing executive from Ranchi says, 'Kolkattans are famous for their helpfulness. For example, when I came from Ranchi, my father's friend whom he has not seen since college offered to let me stay in his home without taking any money. He only found the Sinthee PG for me.' An MNC executive from Patna explains why she is happy in the city, '1stly Bengalis are very friendly people easy-going also. My best friends are Bengalis and their moms are always calling me over.' A technical writer from Siliguri, when she first came, 'stayed at my friend's house, interestingly, she was my penfriend, but then she became my friend as she came down to visit after the 10th exams. So we had grown pretty close. [Later] I shifted to a PG in Karunamoyee in Salt Lake, but till date I have a close relationship with her parents.'

Friendships with other women who come from outside the city often spring up from the very beginning itself; for example, from hostels, when women from different places are thrown together as soon as they come to the city. Hostel mates understand each other mainly because they form part of a similar crowd; women from the hostel of a single institution have a similar perspective, some of them feel that this kind of similarity does not occur in the messes where people from all walks of life live together. The project assistant from Kanpur remembers her first experience which identified her with another hostelmate who was naturally, an outsider, like her: 'I joined

Jadavpur University in 1998. There were two of us, my friend from Shillong, and I from Kanpur, both from the Delhi Board. Local people in our class took it for granted that we were not very bright, Delhi Board people were not academically oriented. The first tutorial, she came first, I got the second highest. Even now I am in touch with my hostel friends ... all the friends I think of as my extended family in Kolkata are from outside.'

Thus, the basis for friendship was the similarity born of exclusion, which could be perhaps a variety of what O'Connor (1998) has provocatively called the friendship based upon victimization. Women from outside seem more angry than despairing about the attitudes of the city people towards them, and hence can only be called victims by some stretch of the imagination. People in the host city are seen by some women as difficult to get on with for several reasons. 'By and large I have found it easier to be friends with people who are Calcuttans by choice rather than Calcuttans by birth' (media professional, north Bengal). The reasons cited for this were generally of a pattern. 'It is easy to make friends in Kolkata with people like myself or non-Bengali residents of Kolkata, or colleagues. Even as a student I found Bengali day scholars pompous and selfish' (software professional Bhubaneswar). 'We rely on friends from our own place. They are there for us anytime anywhere though we might not have talked with each other back home' (student from Gangtok). For women from outside, there seems to be a specific problem: women from the city who it seems are often anathema to the outsiders:

> Mostly Bengali women above 45 are difficult to handle.... I have many horrible stories. A divorced lady is given so much attention that is negative, and my life was getting worse. It was then that my real friends told me to get rid of these bad elements and get out of self-pity ... men of my community know that I am the bahu of [the family I was married into], also I am so tall that Bengali men are mostly shorter than me (39-year-old interior designer, self-employed, from Bokaro Steel City).

> Don't get me wrong, but Calcutta women are such whining, clinging babes, and the pseuds are the worst, all big talk and then they'll get

married according to caste and whatnot, so you never know where they stand. Calcutta men, if they have never gone out of Cal and worked their asses out in another city are insufferable. But a Bengali guy who's gone outside Cal and come back—he's gorgeous, and you know why? He's every bit as sensitive and sensible (media executive in TV channel, 30 plus).

This does not mean that women from outside generally gang up together; many, as we have seen, are comfortable with local people too. As one respondent pointed out, not all Kolkata people ware unfriendly, as not all outsiders vibe well with other outsiders. The ad trainee from Durgapur says, 'I have very few friends, though most people are like me, work in Kolkata with family elsewhere. But this isn't a conscious decision. I stay with wonderful people [my best friend's parents]. And I have never faced anything. In fact my landlady gets more tensed up if anything is wrong with me than my mum'. An executive with the channel Aajtak from Siliguri says, 'Kolkata is a city of variety. I have seen real warm hearted people who have offered me [a place] to stay with them without any rent. But there are people who can be manipulative and opportunist and even suspicious.' A media trainee from Bolpur, 23 years old, also agrees, 'The reactions are mixed. Sometimes they are sympathetic. I remember one of my classmates taking me to her house and making me feel at home, knowing I was far away from my own home.' The Programme coordinator from Ranchi explains, 'Let me put it this way—my closest friends have always been outsiders like me [maybe owing to the empathy factor] who settled down with jobs mostly in Kolkata. But I have a number of friends from Calcutta, few close, mostly from my workplaces and some from college—they too are close.'

SELF AS 'OTHER'

Just as a community must be able to withstand threats to the pragmatic bonds between its members, it is also liable to define itself as different from those whom it constructs as the 'other'. Local people, who see the women who come from outside as 'different' often have certain reservations about them, and these stem from the nature of the society in which the outsiders as well as the citizens live together. With regard to single 'unprotected' women who live alone, the chief fear is of course their relations with men in general, and men related to them in particular. As the 34-year-old executive from Jamshedpur said, women were wary of these unattached, unchaperoned girls from whom they thought they should protect their vulnerable sons. According to the programme coordinator from Ranchi, 'Most people are apprehensive [they fear that these women would get involved in sexual relationships which would affect them] and avoid letting out houses to single women or even two women. People in the city should be sensitized towards being more open to women who come from outside and want to reside in Kolkata; very few single women even if they have jobs if they don't have parents moving over to Kolkata can set up homes in Kolkata on their own. This is because of the sceptical attitude people have towards single women which can create tremendous pressure on them mentally.' But she also points out that 'the guys at the local phone booth, cyber cafes, grocery, etc., are appreciative and sympathetic because we are women from another town living on our own terms in an alien place and doing relatively well for ourselves'. But perhaps we must remember that she was living in Gol Park in a relatively upper middle-class area, while the advertising professional from Jamshedpur, living in a lower middle-class south of Jadavpur PG, had a different experience, 'Girls from outside generally come to study and stay on with jobs. Free from restrictions of family and with money in their pockets a few do stray but most of the girls are disciplined and hardworking and well-groomed go-getters. Now stay-at-home women see them as a threat. We are all vamps for them. And men will be men. So there is absolutely no help from residents especially if they have to take sides in a confrontation. The only safety net is the network of your own making.'

The student from Gangtok agrees: 'They have a very narrow and sad view of women who stay on their own. They feel that we are immoral.' She is echoed by the sales executive from Dhanbad, 'The prob is that city guys see them as easy lay and city women are so insecure, it's like if u are alone u would want to go round with every

guy u see, that's not the case so people here need to grow up a bit.'
The issue of 'protection' and 'ownership' is rather crudely marked out
in these instances: and the women who come from outside, rather
than being seen as in need of protection in an alien city, are seen as
predators because they are unattached to a male or a family. Hence the
status of a single woman especially from 'outside' is ambiguous, and
her identity is constructed in a way that patriarchal society imagines
and teaches its members to imagine as 'insulting'.

For women ostensibly 'past' the age of marriage and still living
alone and independently, the problem takes on different a dimension.
In reply to the question 'Do you think Kolkata is safe for women like
you who have no family support to fall back upon?' The hospitality
industry manager, 36, says,

> I don't think it is safe if you are personable, attractive and well
> groomed after a certain age. In our society people do wonder what
> is wrong with her why is she living alone, is she promiscuous or a
> lesbian or frigid or what? ... I can't explain to all and sundry that I
> have a taxing job or that I haven't met a man who has excited me
> enough for me to give up my freedom. And why should I? But these
> questions or speculations do happen, and after a certain age, men do
> pass questionable judgements on character.

The Locals

This is a variation on the same theme: that women living away from
an identifiable family set-up are to be viewed with suspicion, and
capable of upsetting the balance of 'normal' social life, whatever
their age and professional pursuits. Forced to be imagined thus
by virtue of being female and 'outsiders', the women from outside
too have formed some views about the locals: Most of them fail
to understand the sort of mental and physical stress that outsiders
undergo. Even the financial pressure is incomprehensible to them,
according to a 23-year-old student from Bardhaman. As the designer
from Siliguri says,

Women who r Cal types r such a bore. Here lots of women work, but their attitudes r so backward it's unbelievable. I mean they give the monies to hubby or daddy … my colleague is saving her sal to buy gold for hr wedding. If there r plans 4 an office outing/eating out she always says baritey permission pabona [I won't be permitted to go by my family] or else ppl will try to b intellectuals. I think I am expected to be overawed by Calcutta also coz I cum from a small town. I was speaking of a lounge bar I'd bn to in my last vacation in Bom which is better than Cal ones and these guys were all like do you know everything, so there's this kind of disrespect dat's hard to pin down but dat's there.

In different ways, different women from various backgrounds and different cities have felt this superior attitude that they claim is flaunted by Calcutta people, especially the women. 'Those who are local to Calcutta, for example, my classmates, they view outsiders as lower than them' (21-year-old student from Balurghat). The superiority complex is not of recent vintage; it has been there for decades, as the 53-year-old doctor from Silchar has also had to face it: 'I came from a very small town. I was a very simple girl. So I also overcame great hurdles and hindrances. We were simple people so we were criticized for our simple dress and attire. We were also criticized for our Bengali which is different from the spoken Bengali of Calcutta. Owing to all these difficulties my studies were suffering.' The finance executive from Ranchi said, 'I was very anxious not to look out of place. I felt I was always inferior to the Calcutta crowd…. Sure, it was childish but I went through a phase of trying on different outfits and hairstyles and hanging out with cool folks and being bindaas.'

Firstly, I almost fainted at the sight of people wearing tube and spaghetti tops to college/university … having the urge to dress bold, wearing make-up during daytime and trying to mould myself like a city girl was initially very difficult. I would term it as my days of identity crisis … one does it to be one among the crowd…. I also had to hear from a haughty girl that she improved my dress-sense after spending a year at JU…. But once I realized that all this serves no end and I had to reshape and work at my goal with which I had to originally come to the city, the rest seemed blurred. I chalked out my essentials and today feel a little good about getting a decent-type job before all these city-girls could. When they were busy buying clothes and accessories, I learnt things that would help me fulfil my dreams (student from Durgapur).

'City' Culture

The freedom of the city and the campus could come as quite a shock to many of the girls from small conservative or closed places, where everyone knew everyone else and certain types of behaviour in public was absolutely taboo. In reply to the question 'What do you still recall from your first days in the city and why do you think this is memorable?' a 20-year-old student from Kharagpur replied, 'To watch couples walking hand in hand, which is unusual in my place.' The advertising professional from Jamshedpur also felt shaken: 'I went to Jadavpur University and saw girls of my own age (18–19 year olds) smoking for the first time in my life which thoroughly unsettled me. I had never seen real women smoking in my milieu. I had just seen them in movies and serials like Tara.' Jamshedpur is a cosmopolitan city and quite different from a West Bengal village, but a 22-year-old student who came to Kolkata from such a village seven years after the advertising professional from Jamshedpur, to the same university, had exactly the same experience: 'I saw that there was no communication between people who lived in the same neighbourhood, and also I saw women smoking, something that I could never imagine in the village.' A 23-year-old student from Durgapur, 'thinking of quitting studies for a well-deserved job' relived her initial experiences with Kolkata people: 'At the university, classmates went to my place to see if I could be taken in inside their group. I was unaware of their intention. Only after judging me by my wardrobe contents, convent background and a family with well-settled people, did they go ahead to talk to me. This was later disclosed by one of them during her cold war with the others.' The two women from Jamshedpur and Durgapur are from similar backgrounds, from industrial cities where people from all over the country lived around the industrial plant, educated in English-medium convent schools, the former older and now working in advertising, the latter who 'came here as a student, but just after my graduation I got a job with a very reputed company. Being an arts graduate and a fresher on top of that, this came to me as a most welcome break. So Kolkata has definitely been helpful (in terms of occupation)'.

Her success in securing a good job is based on her merits, merits which do not stand her in good stead when it comes to the nitty-gritties of daily living and fighting tooth and nail to preserve one's dignity and composure. Describing a quarrel with her Kolkata friends, she was horrified to note that even parents were dragged into the fray. Later, 'My friends had told me that I not being a city-girl couldn't 'break' the mouth of the girl who had abused my parents, and that had it been this friend (a Kolkata born and bred) in my place, she would have made that girl regret that she was ever born. I was told that being a small-city girl, I lacked the quick wit and the courage to fight. About this I am still thinking!' This entire syndrome is succinctly analysed by a 21-year-old student from Kharagpur, who says, 'Often, women who come from the village or the mofussil towns find it difficult to adjust to the city culture. Hence two groups are formed, one of city students and one of those who have come from outside, which creates an additional pressure. Often simple rural girls are traumatized by being trapped in the complexities of city life.' Their experiences with Kolkata people indicate perhaps the fact that Kolkata is hospitable on the surface but ambiguous beneath. And the general idea that a good job or a good academic career will force city people to respect you, needs re-thinking. This was a view that I myself had held as a result of my own experiences until this survey threw up such incidents as those described above. All the more does it make one reflect upon what the media person from north Bengal, who has experienced Kolkata's attitude to the single female students as well as to the divorced woman from outside the city, living on her own, has to say: 'People born and brought up in Calcutta ... have strange superiority complexes; this is true even of the seemingly liberated Calcuttans, you scratch the surface and all those prejudices tumble out. And especially if a woman from outside does well, the unspoken feeling is that she is taking away the rights of a Calcutta born man [and woman].'

Competing with the 'Locals'

Of a different order, but stemming from the same root is this experience of the postgraduate job seeker from Habra:

> A regularly published poet from the literary journal *Desh* took a poem
> of mine to read. He promised that he would get in published. He
> kept his promise—he did get it published, but in his own name. So
> how does it matter—this is the nature of our tawdry fame! Later I
> met him at the book fair and said to him, 'That was a good poem—
> unfortunately it was not written by you.'

Anyone who has the slightest acquaintance with the literary
circles of this city will understand the volatility of this encounter.
This may well be peculiar to Kolkata—the desire to become part
of the much vaunted cultural scene, the fierce competition that this
involves and the self-seekers who indulge in this rat-race are all butts
of satire—from those who have no interest in going the same route
themselves. For a female aspirant who is not from the city and has
no influential lineage, the fear of exploitation always looms large,
and this exploitation can vary from the emotional to the sexual. A
graphic account of a young woman from outside the city who aspires
to make a mark in the literary world is contained in Aparajita's 1996
novel *Debolina,* which we have cited in Chapter 2 as one of the few
instances in Bangla literature where the experiences of a woman
coming to the city from outside forms the content. The experience
of our respondent seems to be an echo of this story about a certain
section of the city's intellectual circle, their lust for quick fame, their
veneer of liberalism and their insecurity camouflaged by superiority
complexes.

'Alone' in the City

All the same, women from outside do find both love and friendship in Kolkata, and these are not always offered by men or women

like themselves who have come from outside. Sometimes, when a relationship goes wrong: 'I received tremendous mental emotional and financial support from my hostel mates during my divorce, more so when it was a so-called love marriage. If my friends didn't stand by me I would have collapsed' (media executive from North Bengal). At other times, one has to face such problems all alone, and often it is quite early in one's stay in the city: 'When I was totally alone, I had the experience of being cheated which taught me to be alert (20-year-old student, Bardhaman). Among the students who responded, a 19-year-old from Assam expressed her critique of the survey questionnaire thus: 'I think you have missed out on a very important aspect of our lives, that is, acquaintances and relationship that we come across in order to fight our loneliness. Some of which turn into bitter experiences and some that remain stable forever.' The loneliness of the large city especially for a woman from a smaller place where support and intrusiveness go hand in hand, is perhaps the fuel for all the relationships, failed and successful, that these women enter into, and each one, as they admit themselves, is a learning experience, which teaches the woman more about herself as well as about the world outside.

There were a number of women who said that Kolkata had given them their husbands, but there is still sometimes the ambiguity of being an outsider, as we will hear from finance executive from Ranchi: 'When I came back [from Bombay] and started dating, I used to also hang out with my husband's college group so it was difficult to catch the little inside jokes. I used to mind very much, but then I adjusted.' The computer teacher from Burnpur realizes that 'Kolkata is not like Burnpur or Santiniketan (where she was in college), so at first I did not have friends. Now my colleagues are my friends. It's easy to make friends because of language. I can speak Bengali and English everywhere. What I like here is that a boy and girl can be sincere friends.' But the sincere friendship is also not always as sincere as it looks and women who come from outside may well become victims because, as the BPO employee from Dhanbad recounts: 'My very good friend, she is also an UPite like me, she had a love affair with a Bong guy for 6 yrs, now this guy dumped her after he returned from his honeymoon, telling her he married a Bong girl and he wanted to be fair to his wife so he tested their compatibility in the honeymoon but now he is satisfied so he has to tell his gf the truth. He can't have an extramarital, his family and blah blah. Now if we had families living here, this jerk would be screwed, but he got away.'

> I knew a girl.... She was my roommate ... she was jilted by her boyfriend and treated very badly because he was not scared of the consequences as she lived alone. I used to help my roommate but her problem was so serious that I couldn't have done anything much (relationship manager from Chandannagar).

A 22-year-old working woman from Debagram, Nadia, feels that Kolkata has given her one thing she could not have got else-where—her boyfriend—yet she says that it was Kolkata that had snatched him away from her and will perhaps do so again in the future. She is reluctant to go back to her village for a period longer than a week, because her boyfriend will not be there. The insecurity that she has experienced in the relationship seems to have made her wary of trusting people. As she says, 'Kolkata teaches you to think thousand times before you trust anyone. Or else you will be betrayed again and again. I was cheated in my first year. [My friend] Banasree in her final year [of college].' A 22-year-old student who gave her origin as a village in West Bengal, said that she knew many women like herself, who had come from outside the city. The main problem they faced was: 'Some opportunistic Calcutta boys take advantage of their loneliness.' This is borne out by at least one experience that was recounted to us in the first person. An MPhil student in Women's Studies at Calcutta University said that her boyfriend wanted to go abroad to study and asked her to lend him a substantial sum of money, which he promised to repay as soon as he started getting his stipend as a graduate student. She gave it to him. Three years have passed—he has sent some money, but the bulk of the sum remains unpaid. She has developed a way of looking at this incident: 'I don't think of this as my stupidity—I did what I thought was correct because I trusted him. It is his failure that he was unable to honour that trust.'

MEN: SUITABLE AND OTHERWISE

The structure of relationships has changed, and so have women's ways of understanding these changes and coping with them. The woman in this case may have initially broken down at being cheated, emotionally and financially, by the man in question, but now her feeling is that the man has not been able to live up to an ethical imperative, thereby proving himself deficient as a human being. However, if this incident is looked at in general functional terms rather than in ethical abstracts, one would want to ask if such incidents can occur because single women living alone in the city are too trusting, do not choose their friends carefully and are also prone to dependence. Many of the respondents have thought about this question and analysed the subtleties; a media executive in a TV channel says: 'The romantic problems. Girls who live alone develop this need for leaning onto guys who may be just using them sexually. A lot get dumped and they really become a mess. There's no one at home to answer to, there's a lot more liberty for those who come from a conservative home. And those who come from these very dad-centric home become arrogant when they earn themselves. It's like I can do anything now. But there's deep insecurity about themselves, talent, everything.' A sales executive from Dhanbad adds: 'I have been staying here on my own for 10 years, generally people are okay, but in tight situation it would be nice to have a dad/bro/boyfriend around.' A manager in the hospitality industry adds: 'I would like to make one thing clear, that although after a certain age, especially when one has been living on one's own for some years, most women feel sentimental about wanting to lean on a strong man during a crisis, I can say from my own experience that I am most comfortable doing things on my own.'

One can look at this situation as ironic; after all, aren't women who have struggled with making themselves independent in all senses expected to cherish their independence to the extent that they will not enter into relationships? Some women, like a 42-year-old educationist from Chandannagar, do report the struggle to retain their independence in the face of merciless campaigns by near and dear ones to fit them back into the frames: 'When my relations pass marriage proposals to me I feel very uncomfortable, especially in front of younger relations. In my view if the right time for something has passed, doing it at the wrong time is a mistake so the question of marriage does not arise for me. So I would like this unnecessary interference to stop.' A journalist from Bhadreswar adds: "'Women like me" are considered problems for parents. Neighbours are always ready to extend full sympathy to our parents; if only they would agree. They are also ready to hunt for grooms. And any social occasion can be a big bother especially if u have to look out for prospective in-laws who have been fixed by relatives. U have no option but to be arrogant and then that triggers another chain of events. U are not only single but have been spotted as arrogant, a result of staying single for so long.' But then, are not typical relationships what society has trained women to desire? And just because women are living independently in a city and providing for themselves, is it to be automatically assumed that they are not interested in heterosexual relationships? The advertising professional from Jamshedpur explains it thus; 'No one wants to stay in the provinces or districts anymore—in the 1960s and 1970s, it was men who came here in search of jobs, futures, whatever—in the 1990s, it is girls, parents who aspire for better things tell them, go and do something, a course, a degree, and in one case I know, at least, a girl who used to stay in my PG, they were four sisters, no brother, her father said he wanted each of his daughters to be a son, but her mother said something even more interesting, she said, we don't have enough money to get boys for all of you, so if you go to Calcutta, get jobs, look for your own husbands as well. Three of the sisters are here, they live in the same PG, their greatest lament is that we have lived here for so long, worked in offices, we still haven't found a suitable boy.'

Does this mean that the journey to the city is a quest for the suitable boy, ultimately? That the appearances of emancipation and self-reliance are ultimately subsumed by that which patriarchal society designates as the most primitive of all feminine desires? It is perhaps also lonely; couples prefer couples, as the 51-year-old university teacher says. To add to this, if you do succeed in finding a man who you are convinced is able to understand your true worth, the era of adjustments has just begun.

Perhaps one can conclude that the quest for stability in a city is now defined as part of the 'normal' process of 'growing up' in the lives of women from smaller places, a necessary stage in their quest for self; just as the women's movement has made women's working a 'normal' part of this same process, women from smaller towns, who feel stifled in their environs of origin are now amenable to the idea of moving to an unknown, and often apparently inhospitable environment of the city to fulfil this necessity. Why should this be contradictory to their desire to settle down to marriage, why should the latter desire be seen as exclusive of the former, is a debate that must figure, eventually, on the agenda of feminist theory and practice in India. Looked at from another perspective, why should not the single woman in the city want to enter into a stable long-term relationship whose terms may be differently defined from those prevalent in what we know as 'typical' relationships? Would not the single woman living alone in the city require companionship and intimacy along with friendship with those who she may define as part of her 'community'? For is not the burden of single female existence in the city extremely wearying? What are the rewards of an independence that is the result of daily battles hard-fought, and territory that keeps slipping away if you do not continue the fight every waking and subconscious minute? 'If you want to enjoy or freak out on your off-day, eyebrows are raised automatically. A single woman is expected to spend time with her parents or visit ailing aunts on her off day', says a 29-year-old journalist, Bhadreswar. But does not this constant struggle equip you for a differently structured relationship, because, as the finance executive from Ranchi says, 'There is a lot of change for us. In fact more than the girls who get married from home as they leave one home for another. But I have had to change my entire lifestyle, be answerable to not just my husband but the entire family. So I think if someone like me gets married, there is a higher level of commitment. What I feel is that in fact a working woman who has stayed alone will probably make a better life partner because she will be more efficient, panic less and be a real support to others.'

Does this not in very basic ways indicate a change in the role a woman is assigned in patriarchal gender organization? The role of wife is being rearticulated by these women who have chosen to marry, and it remains to be seen to what extent the single woman living in the city, who brings to the marriage her own skills and emotions produced by her independent existence, impacts upon the reorganization of marital equations. Another consideration is that if marriage, the accepted institutionalization of sexual union, is under stress from the 'encroachment' of such women who have ventured to live life without the protection of males in the urban space that has traditionally been seen as threatening to their 'modesty', then their breaking of the norms of sexual choice must surely create problems of earth shattering proportions?

LOVE: BIDDEN AND FORBIDDEN

The city is a large receptacle, and probably that is why fissures in heteronormativity are available on looking for them; perhaps, then, heteronormativity need not be oppressive here. Among some of the responses were hints at same-sex relationships, fraught with ambiguity, but the source of the ambiguity lay in the very questionnaire itself, for what we asked was

> Q: Are there any problems in women sharing homes with other women in terms of landlord's suspicious of relations between girls?
> Answer 1: My landlady is not suspicious, we are all from good families, she has full faith in us; I also am friendly with my roommates.
> Answer 2: We are all very alert about unnatural relations between two girls because we don't want to stay with such elements ourselves. In fact, we all should be so I don't blame landlords if they are suspicious.... I have not met any girl of that kind so far and even if they were of that kind, I would prefer not to know their identity as I would be totally scared.
> Answer 3: Like lesbianism? Must be. Kol is quite conservative I believe, not like B'lore where gays live together openly.

From the ways in which those who took the cue answered, the range of attitudes exhibited towards lesbianism by women who live alone in the city seems large. For instance, 'It's highly unfortunate for lesbians and other women if they have to share space because everyone will be uncomfortable in that scenario. So I think its best if that is not the case'. But some respondents felt differently; a media executive said, 'thr r sum girls who give friendship between girl-girl a bad name, I don't want to spk abt them bcos I dnt kno them.' Do we find echoes of what Oliker (1998) would explain as caused by the spread of modern sexology which caused the fading of intimate, romantic same-sex friendship prevalent in the nineteenth and early twentieth centuries in the West? O'Connor's view of this situation is:

> There is no cultural ideal of friendship between women and the cultural and social space for women's friendship is limited. The boundaries between such relationships and lesbianism are much more permeable than heretofore—a phenomenon which Faderman has suggested was not unrelated to women's increasing economic independence and the economic viability of a life style not involving men. In this context, depicting women's close ties with each other as sexual and stigmatizing them acts as a further cultural inhibitor of these relationships (118).

It is clear from this that heterosexuality is taken as a norm, and any difference, individual or collective, is seen as a deviation. And this is evident in the way many women who come from outside think about other women who seem to them, in the private space of the mess or the PG or the hostel room, to be in a sexual relationship.

> I think I have shared my PG with a lesbian couple. I don't want to go into details, but I think my landlord also suspected something was wrong. But we didn't ever discuss this with anybody or even amongst ourselves. I think the most we spoke about was that one girl was dressed up in a very macho way and she was very reserved also. They stayed for 7–8 months and then they both went to Delhi with new jobs. But there was no problem. In fact we would also chat. I felt slightly uncomfortable but didn't think too much about it and my landlord-landlady wouldn't have said anything directly because they would not have wanted any scandal (technical writer, Siliguri).

Clearly, this ranges from a refusal to accept that same-sex relation-ships can be within the scope of 'normalcy', to an ambiguity about them; it extends to a refusal to think that friendships between girls can cross the boundary of the purely platonic. As is clear from her response, the technical writer has lived with women she thinks were in a sexual relationship with each other, but there appeared nothing 'abnormal' about them; so, does her generally held view that this was somehow wrong or bad, now remain as strongly held as before? But we might mark another aspect of her response; she says that no one talked about it though everyone, apparently, suspected. This makes lesbianism sound like a crime that has been committed; it is as if women who are sexually involved with each other are running from the scene of some crime, hiding their identities from the world. One reason cited for this is homophobia, and as we have seen, since every-thing, from clothes to professions to religion are taken into account when accommodation is offered to women from outside, keeping one's sexual orientation a close secret seems to be the wisest thing to do. Otherwise something like this might occur: 'When I was staying in the Bagha Jatin PG, a lower middle-class lesbian couple had come to stay. They very foolishly and indecently decided to sleep together under one mosquito net. Something made the other girls suspicious, and our landlady and her mother-in-law packed them off at 5 am in the morning. This incident became a legend, to be recounted with much gusto and horror.'

This happened in one of the PGs located south of Jadavpur, whereas the incident recounted by the technical writer occurred in a more centralized 'advanced' part of the city. That may have been the reason why in the latter case, it was an open secret, which no one talked about, while elsewhere the people involved, like the landlady in the former case, did not know what to do and treated it as a reprehensible and evil thing, getting rid of it immediately. Also, in the latter case, the women in question may have flaunted their relationship in ways that were more emphatic than seemed acceptable. This was apparently not the case in the former instance. This may be why lesbian couples who come from outside the city and live together are extremely sensitive upon this issue. Yet, since both the partners come from outside the city, it is perfectly normal for them, as it is for many heterosexual women, to stay together on a room-sharing or flat-sharing basis. They are wary, even many years into the relationship, that the actual dynamics between them might be a cause for comment. The programme coordinator from Ranchi, who knows of a friend being driven out of her PG room on suspicion that she was a lesbian, which she was not, said in reply to this question: 'This is not yet a common phenomenon amongst landlords in Kolkata. Unfortunately (or fortunately for lesbians) they still like to believe things as homosexuality does not exist within 'normal' girls. But this attitude of non-acceptance can be dangerous and needs to be addressed for if this suspicion finds roots in the conservative middle-class society of Calcutta it would become totally impossible for women to live freely let alone find accommodation. I would suggest that this could also be a strong argument for legalizing homosexuality in India'.

Even the student from Nabadwip says that what landlords (and perhaps women themselves) fear about women living together is the possibility of group formation, not the threat of homosexuality, which, she says is 'beyond the horizon of expectation of people in the city'. Either there is this head-in-the-sand attitude or there is total aversion for same sex relationships. Hence the women actually involved in such relationships seem to go to great lengths to keep the truth as close to their chests as practicable. What the company executive from Jamshedpur says explains this reticence as particularly related to Kolkata. 'I have seen women who are lesbians face tremendous trauma in the city, the city is very backward in these cases. Such things are pretty okay in Bombay'. This is echoed by a student who comes from Bolpur, and has recounted this incident: 'One of the women I know has a relationship with another woman. And once this was known to the people in her office, there were many kinds of obscene comments, she became the butt of many jokes and mockery. When the woman I knew became really traumatized after all this happened, I tried to counsel her as far as I was able, trying to help her regain her equilibrium, advising her to ignore these comments made by her office colleagues. Because is not the matter of who lives with whom a matter that is solely confined to the private sphere?' However, as another respondent put it, 'I have not heard of same-sex couples living openly anywhere in Kolkata, so obviously there is a problem'. But apparently the city does not think so, for the advertising professional from Jamshedpur who was witness to the incident in the Bagha Jatin PG described above, says, 'By and large lesbianism hasn't yet become part of the social fabric simply because it's taboo, and in fact very few homosexuals can afford to jeopardize their financial and social independence by declaring their sexuality. So despite media attention even in the vernacular media, few landlords would really suspect two girls to be sexually involved with each other form the very beginning. But if they do, God help the girls.'

The city may be seen as offering space for a woman's sexuality to blossom following its own proclivities because she is here alone and does not have to bear very close scrutiny from her immediate family. On being asked: 'Are you satisfied with your life as a city woman? Indicate if there are things you want changed about your conditions or about the city/people which will make it easier for women like you to live and work here?' the Aquarian answered: 'Yes I want to live in Cal. I am very happy here. I think we should just stretch Calcutta instead of complaining about the city. Stretch it whichever way we want it to. Calcutta is very flexible'. But there is a flip side to this, as always. Should she find herself in a situation of rejection for her orientation that she expresses in closed circles for her own safety, should her sexual preference be exposed to a larger, unsympathetic world, then, she does not have close family to protect her or shelter her. On the other hand, would the close family want to protect and shelter a woman who has broken norms? Until the woman is in a socially justifiable sphere, that is, her rebellion is limited to living outside her home town for higher purposes like a better education or a paying job perhaps families would stand by her and support her. But what happens when it comes to an assertion of self that shatters the myth of heterosexuality as normal, and offers the woman a chance to express her self in ways that are labelled deviant by society? The city can well be held responsible for the increased opportunities to explore and act according to sexual orientation. Does the city then rally to her support?

Relationships conducted with people of the same sex or with those of the opposite sex, whether friendships or romantic love, take on a different complexion for women who live in the city alone, for a variety of reasons. We live in a time when romance is a consumer good, much like friendship, loyalty and dependence/dependability. But there is also a parallel emphasis on independence, individuality and success. Apparently, there are no contradictions between these two sets of imperatives that constantly assault our senses through the media. But you only need to live in the here and now to understand, if not articulate, that the contradictions are stubbornly present, if not totally irresoluble. This throws up a number of questions about interactions between men and women in a heteronormative patriarchal society. It is a little disturbing to characterize one's immediate milieu thus: another more popular way of saying it would be 'normal' society. Here we have considered only a miniscule group of very specific women: those who have come to the city from the outside.

We proceeded on the assumption that since most of those we have spoken to either did not bring an intimate romantic and sexual relationship with them to the city, and that some of them actually used the city as a place of refuge and rehabilitation after such a relationship ended, their involvement with aspects of what we commonly understand as 'love' would be inflected by their lives as outsiders in the city. Those who agreed that they 'found' love in the form of a husband or a boyfriend in the city appeared to be moving towards some form of acknowledged permanence within the context of the city itself, their status as 'outsiders', by their own admission, becoming a factor in such change. Does the city, practically, psychologically, symbolically, play a role in the formation, maintenance and dissolution of sexual love and intimacy? Does it sow the seeds of what appears as transgression because it is anonymous and large, accommodating and progressive? I would like to end this chapter with one of the most sobering accounts that I encountered in the course of this survey that I now share with the reader. It does not pretend to answer any of the questions that I have asked above. It seems, rather, to be built out of these questions and indeed leads to several more questions which follow the narrative.

This story is about two women, one of whom was contacted by our resource person and the other, her friend, contacted through her. I quote here the description of the incident emailed to me by the resource person who met her contact out shopping one day a few months after the survey was over:

> I met her, apparently happily married, with her husband, wrists full of bangles.... But when her husband moved away a little, she told me she and her friend were involved with each other, then the friend went away to Delhi, and she herself got married—she was almost in tears when she told me this, but quickly managed to hide her feelings and was all smiles and tinkling bangles by the time her husband returned.

For the woman who comes to the city from outside, this is the contradiction that she carries within herself. This too is a part of the education a city imparts to the woman from outside. It is the city that offers her the possibility of shaping a self whose sexual orientation is different from what is perceived as 'normal', and yet it is the city that shrugs its shoulders and turns in another direction when that self is under attack. Should we expect (and why should we expect?) that the city will offer us a shoulder to cry upon or a space to house our pain? A 21-year-old student from Nabadwip says about people from the city, 'Though they are sympathetic, they actually lack sympathy. So the sympathy becomes a millstone around their necks.' For the city is ultimately, for all that we imagine it to be, another institution regulated by hegemonic gender ideology, except that the mechanism of regulation may be better concealed by other ruses of freedom.

Perhaps the wariness about romantic and sexual relationships that women who come here from outside confess to feeling arises from this palpable unease. What pride can one take in the city which, as naturally as any other small, obscure place, excludes the possibilities of variety in relationships from the most obvious to the most subtle? Should we accept that the opportunity for transgression and sense of freedom that many women have identified as a gain of city life actually reflects the indifference and alienation that is also said to characterize urbanity?

For it is the city that also teaches the ability to 'adjust', to suppress one's inclinations and one's city-generated self, when one comes up against a taboo. Was the 'friend' described above, who left for Delhi in between her relationship with another woman from outside, referring to an acknowledgement of her experience of intimacy when she said: '[Calcutta's] made me very free very myself, very clued in.... I have outgrown who I was. I feel free to take any shape.'

It seems trivial to record here that the survey was conducted before the incident described above occurred, so the exhilaration of knowing one's own self had not yet been dampened by the harsh reality of suppression. After all, the pain that the transformation of this relationship eventually brings is emblematic of the double-edged gifts from the city; one wonders, whether after this incident occurred, the friend still thought, 'I was spiritually born in Calcutta. I will die in its dust and glory. I am following my dreams.' Did it remain the flexible space that stretched to accommodate her? Because afterwards, was it not the same city that closed its jaws upon her fledgling self that it had helped her to realize, and then, lulling it into a fragile sense of being 'clued in' and in control, swiftly devoured her?

If these words are too violent, I would like to remind the reader that this act of sawing off a part of your self for the convenience of being able to live according to social norms, the act that we innocuously call 'adjustment' is doubtless a violent act, as mentioned earlier (see Chapter 5). For the woman from outside, the discovery of self is often expressed through the relationships that she forges in the city, relationships which bind her both to her self as it emerges and the city as it provides a habitus and a subjective focus. Apparently the city offers the woman living alone a chance to live with herself. She is not answerable to anyone unless she chooses to be so. How does she then constitute her independence in relation to love and physical intimacy as bound up culturally with the moral issues of fidelity, loyalty and betrayal? Both the protagonists in this story were women from outside the city, making their way in an alien setting, battling with all kinds of obstructions, real and imagined: obstructions and difficulties that we have come to gain some knowledge of in the previous pages. The expression, if not the very realization, of their sexual orientation was catalysed by the city itself. It seems, from all that we have heard and experienced, that the city encourages such desires and preferences, hitherto unrealized, literally and metaphorically, in shaping the contours of one's self. But it is the same city that teaches the limits of transgression through the exacting of adjustment.

The home may be where one can act according to one's own will without having to put on an act. But the city teaches us, in its imposition of a certain form and content upon the very ideas of emancipation and freedom, that compromises may kill one but they have to be made. What they are made for may vary, but the taste of freedom and the undertow of compromise to maintain a certain degree of that freedom is invariably learnt in the city. The self that the city constructs is always amenable to being destroyed without a tremor by the city itself. Women who come from outside the city are drawn by its vastness, its ability to contain differences and hold opportunities. They are lulled into thinking that they will be able to preserve the sense of self in the habitation provided by the city. And then, the indifference or the callousness or just the expertise for adjustment that these women have developed in order to survive in the city congeals into a ravishment (and I use this word with all its sexist baggage) of self in the context of the city. When they step beyond the lines that circumscribe its limited core, they encounter a harsh reality: the city pretends to be a space of freedom but conceals its dangerous limitations underneath a glittering, indifferent sprawl.

Note

1   'While traditional ties of human association are weakened, urban existence involves a much greater degree of interdependence between man and man and a more complicated fragile, volatile form of mutual interrelations over many phases of which the individual as such can scarcely exert any control' (Louis Wirth 1938). See Appendix 1 for the age range, occupation and language of response for survey respondents.

WORKS CITED

Adams, R.G., and G. Allan. eds. 1998. *Placing Friendship in Context*, Cambridge: Cambridge University Press.

Marks, S.R. 1998. 'The Gendered Contexts of Inclusive Intimacy: The Hawthorne Women at Work and Home', in R.G. Adams and G. Allan, eds, *Placing Friendship in Context*, Cambridge: Cambridge University Press: 43–70.

O'Connor, P. 1998. 'Women's Friendships in a Postmodern World', in R.G. Adams and G. Allan, eds, *Placing Friendship in Context*, Cambridge: Cambridge University Press: 117–35.

Oliker, S.J. 1998. 'The Modernisation of Friendship', in R.G. Adams and G. Allan, eds, *Placing Friendship in Context*, Cambridge: Cambridge University Press: 17–42.

Sayer, Andrew. 2000. *Realism and Social Science*, London: SAGE Publications.

Simmel, G. [1903] 1971. 'The Metropolis and Mental Life', in D.N. Levine, ed., *On Individuality and Social Forms: Selected Writings*, Chicago: Chicago University Press: 314–29.

Stack, Carol B. 1974. *All Our Kin: Strategies for Survival in a Black Community*, New York: Harper and Row.

Wirth, Louis. [1938] 2000. 'Urbanism as a Way of Life', in R.T. LeGates and F. Stout, eds, *The City Reader*, 2nd ed., New York: Routledge: 97–105.

SEVEN

The 'Safe' City and Outsider Women

Without the social drama that comes into existence through the focusing and intensification of group activity, there is not a single function performed in the city that cannot be performed ... in the open country ... in its various and many sided life, in its very opportunities for social disharmony and conflict, the city creates drama; the suburbs lack it. (Mumford 1937)

There is so much drama in Calcutta, in the streets, in the pavements. I love to watch people, there is so much fluidness (advertising professional referred to in text as 'Aquarian').

Is Kolkata safe for women like you who have no family support to fall back upon? Why/why not?

I don't like to be safe and yes it is too safe (Aquarian, working in advertising).

Yes, of course, because it depends upon the woman concerned. Her bearing, her profession and her conduct will determine her safety. Nowadays so many young girls come to Calcutta. They must be very careful to be away from temptations (41-year-old educationist, Chandannagar).

Let us begin with the Aquarian's response that clearly and directly interrogates the premise on which the question: 'Is Kolkata safe for women like you who have no family support to fall back upon? Why/why not?' is based. Why should safety and security of women be an issue that must be included in a study such as this? Is it to be taken for granted that like the basic necessities of life—a home in the city, a means to remain there, that is, a job, a support system comprising friends—the safety of women in the city too is a basic necessity? 'Safety' is a very basic concern with women in cities or elsewhere; it seems to be a characteristic of patriarchal society that this should be so. Safety is, or at least has been seen until now, as a gendered question whose nature is still under consideration. After all, the safety of men has not been an issue, and when there are some indications made that this should also be so, it appears to be quite a novelty. And that takes us to the second response to the same question. Safety is not an abstract concern, and concerns the state of society external to the person whose safety is at issue and is related to the person herself. Women who have come to the city from outside have broken a few norms by simply being there, in a space that is not the home they were born into, and without protection from sundry males. This places the focus more squarely on safety and makes this an even more live issue. The norms of patriarchy, apparently challenged by these women, must assert their functionality in two different ways: on the one hand by creating this sense of insecurity and on the other by offering 'protection' in some form or other. Women are socialized by patriarchal gender ideology to expect this kind of protection, and must nurture the desire to benefit from it. But some of the women who have lived alone in the city and done a number of things that they were socialized to think of as 'man's work', may well chaff at this 'protection'. We will explore the gamut of these themes related to safety, taking a cue, as before, from the concerns voiced by the respondents.

SAFETY AND SATISFACTION

Are you satisfied with your life (in the city)? If not, why?

I am not satisfied, this question is bugging. I was taught at home to want a regular life, but what is regular? I don't want a job; want more and more risk. I want adventure (Aquarian, Advertising professional, age not revealed).

Not many women who responded to the survey actually said this; but in their replies to the question 'What has Calcutta given you that you could not have got anywhere else?' this feeling of exploring the hitherto unexplored, of charting untrodden territories ripples just below the surface. As the journalist from Bally says, Kolkata 'has brought me up'. The answers to this same question begin from the practical:

> I thought I will be a doctor, but when I couldn't clear entrance exams and had to go in for general stream, I think bcos of the fact that I was in Cal, I could prepare for my mgmnt entrances properly and efficiently otherwise my life would have taken a different turn (26-year-old MNC executive from Dhanbad).

> I have got industry exposure. I get good study materials (CA internee from Bihar Sharif).

It included the range of opportunities and confidence resulting from those opportunities that can be discerned clearly:

> I got the confidence to do Mass Comm and work only after [I began to live in] Calcutta. I was a mediocre student, so my parents were not very hopeful about my prospects. But after my graduation they felt I have changed, as I also became very ambitious (content writer from Jamshedpur).

> Everything that I am today, I am due to the opportunities given by Kolkata. Being a single lady, Kolkata has given me respect and dignity that I don't think I would have got anywhere (educationist from Chandannagar, 41).

> Had it not been for Kolkata I would not have been able to transcend the expectations of my parents/relatives/neighbours back home to go into something conventional (programme coordinator, Ranchi).

The answers extend to intangibles that include a sense of self-respect and fulfilment from doing what one desires in the way that one desires to do it, which for men and women, is a cause for satisfaction; for women who have struggled to reach that state without the support and 'safety' that both men and women take for granted until they leave their homes in family-based societies such as ours, the sense of achievement is perhaps greater:

> Calcutta has given me a lot of intangible satisfaction. When I came here in '94, for a year I earned just enough to keep myself in a PG and pay for my conveyance. But I had to interact with a lot of people for my freelance work and got tremendous confidence from the whole exercise. It was a learning experience more valuable than any degree. Also Calcutta professionally is seeing a wonderful upsurge and it feels good that I am also a part of this rejuvenation (36-year-old hospitality manager).

> The freedom to live life my way to a greater extent than Jamshedpur, and any other place in India I have visited so far (advertising professional, Jamshedpur, 29).

> I was a tomboy with 3 brothers. I did not fit into the goody-goody atmosphere of Lady Brabourne College hostel. Initially I was a rebel and a misfit. Then I started enjoying myself thoroughly. My exposure to the styles and ways of Calcutta girls made me realize I was different. So I was learning to discover the feminine side of me. I could live on my own terms and take tremendous risks in my personal life because Calcutta gave me a support system (media professional from North Bengal).

> In my generation in Calcutta there are still some women who are unmarried, but in Bardhaman this is not so. So here at least you can stay as you wish, and people will give you respect (44-year-old doctor).

> I think the role of educationists has not lost its relevance in Calcutta as it has in other parts of the country. Even today, I get a lot of enthusiasm for History. I am also fortunate to be associated with social institutions. So I am working in a larger sphere (42-year-old educationist, Chandannagar).

> I feel like a Calcutta person definitely because of its music, literature and the arts (hospitality manager).

Ironically, in these statements one can find the causes of the city's discomfort with such women. They are indebted to the city for providing the very places and situations that were taboo for them as women before they came here. Now, the city itself seems to have reared up in protest at their defiance because they are regulars in places where women are not supposed to be; even the places that are normally inhabited by them without comment, or ought to be, are made threatening to them. 'When I first came to Cal I was living with parents and went everywhere in our car, so I thought Cal was actually pretty decent for women, I mean after Delhi where you are constantly on the edge, here you are pretty safe. But when I started to live here alone, I realized I am pretty unsafe, there are plenty of wolves, people think you are an easy lay, or else you are pretty wild and all that. So people's attitude change in your face' (27-year-old media executive, parents currently in the Northeast). An office administrator, 25, from Bokaro, recounted a bad incident on the road and added 'a girl feels safer if her family is staying in the locality for say 50 years.' The latent feeling of insecurity may be explained thus: 'Permanent residents seem to know each other on sibling terms and close ranks when outsiders don't know those familiar endearing terms (46-year-old university teacher from Burnpur). But some women feel differently:

> I go to Chandni every day, which is not very safe, and return by Metro quite late, but even then, I feel confident (29-year-old systems administration executive originally from Bokaro).

> It is much safer than other cities because people don't try to take undue advantage now and then (23-year-old customer care executive from Darjeeling).

This is in stark contrast to the places these women come from, as they themselves have pointed out:

> [Calcutta] is a step forward from Bokaro. Bokaro is so unsafe and backward.

> Girls don't move about alone in Dhanbad, how can they work?

I felt very safe in Kolkata after Patna and Delhi (B school) (26-year-old MNC executive from Patna).

Kolkata is very different from Patna. So I was very scared in the first month.

When I started to go to Brabourne Road alone I was very scared. [But] on the whole people are good though some elements are bad. Eve-teasing is very low even in the Burrabazar area, which is lucky for us (26-year-old CA student doing Internship, from Bihar Sharif).

Kolkata is very safe compared to Ranchi where no girl goes out after 7 pm. In Ranchi very few ladies work. In Kolkata the culture of the place is different. So women are free to study and work in newer areas (marketing executive, Ranchi).

It is easier for ladies to work in Kolkata than in Bokaro. In Bokaro women can work only as teachers. Law and order situation makes life very difficult for women (39-year-old interior decorator, self-employed).

WHAT IS 'SAFETY'?

In general, Kolkata is known as a 'safe' city, but what is the actual nature of this safety? Women who have lived alone here can explain the meaning of safety in different ways:

I think it is safe, again if you keep your decency. At my age, dangers are minimized. But I was also young. So as I have said, it depends on the girl. Being unmarried and young if a girl lives alone, everyone is curious. They observe her minutely. Then if they think she is easy and a fast type of girl, they will not hesitate. Even in Calcutta where Bengali men are more homely or cowardly, there is great need for modesty. Women staying with families will blame the girl from outside, not the family men (44-year-old gynaecologist from Bardhaman).

It's safe as long as it's in safe hours. Then everything matters. Unemployed youths go out of their way to bother you if you are smartly dressed and unescorted. I think it's their insecurity but if they molest me or anyone like me, the police and public will blame me for my dress (sales executive Dhanbad).

Many women feel that Kolkata is certainly safer than any other city in the country especially for women living away from home. The artist from Agartala has an explanation for this:

Kolkata is a cosmopolitan city and the outlook is pretty much tolerant. People treat each other in a civilized manner in the sense that even when one would speak with a stranger, it is with politeness first. A woman in general would not feel intimidated at the outset. The city has culture. People here respect women. They are great worshippers of powerful female gods like Durga, Kali and that spills over into the very approach to womankind in general. Literacy/knowledge/ education also liberates the people of Kolkata. Gender-discrimination concept is not all-embracing in the city and therefore a woman does not have to constantly face prejudices and feel threatened in some way or other. Average Kolkattans are not snobbish (unless they have studied at La Marts). The culture of para, adda and goppo bring out warmth and a sense of humour rarely found in other cities.

THE MANY FACES OF 'SAFETY'

These contrasting views are about the same city; they reflect the difference in experiences, inflected by the different places and arrangements the women have lived in, not to mention their professional backgrounds and their expectations from the city itself. By now it must be clear to the reader that all these factors are related to one another in complex ways. People's fears (expressed insecurities) are largely a function of whether or not they are part of uniplex or multiplex social networks when the nature of their relations and lifestyles are taken into account (Walklate 2001: 81). The Left realist view is that we need to understand the importance of local knowl-edges and local context in fuelling people's expressed fears (ibid.). What Stanko (1990) calls the 'climate of unsafety' proves to be an adequate expression of the perception of fear and explains the threat of insecurity as well as the need for safety. As Walklate (2001: 90) explains, 'the concept of safety, then, placed a gendered understand-ing of fear (and by implication, risk) at the centre of the exploration of the fear of crime by asking the question about whose standards are used as marker of what might count as rational or irrational fear.' By concentrating on fear in a given situation, we shift the terms from 'safety' to 'fear'.

For one thing, the degree to which you perceive yourself to be safe varies over time. As the PSU officer from Murshidabad explains, 'Bengal has a tradition of respect and enlightened view of women.... So women are not only safe, they are respected also.' But a woman of a similar age, engaged in a different profession, remarks that travelling has become more difficult these days, and perhaps it is because she must travel to work that she has noticed a change in the city that she records thus: 'Society has also become very disorderly. Earlier there was a public decorum maintained but now the respect for women has declined and even women of mature age are sub-jected to disrespect' (42-year-old educationist from Chandannagar). The doctor from Silchar, 53 years old, says, 'Calcutta was safer in the past days. Nowadays there are criminal elements in the society of decent people, so girls re not safe even when they live with their parents.' The National Crime Records Bureau statistics show that West Bengal in 2013, has recorded the highest incidence of crimes against women in the country, a total of 30,942 cases being reported. Kolkata is ranked as the third in the list of unsafe cities for women. Whether this must be interpreted as a sign of awareness and alertness reflected in more crimes being reported and recorded or as more women being in situations of risk, or more actual crimes against women occurring, or varying combinations of all three possibilities is an open question. The fact remains that the earlier idea of Calcutta as a 'safe' city can now be seen as a limited if not completely changed description: a reality that women like the ones quoted above, who have seen this change occur, are witness to.

Women have very precise problems about the visible security or lack of it: 'There is a sense of insecurity in all areas.' 'There is sexual harassment daily on roads and transport.' 'Because I am a woman, where I stay, there are innumerable rebukes and threats, especially from the older people, which I find laughable.' These restraints often veer close to oppression, and women perceive it as such.

I am not allowed to act independently according to my own tastes (21-year-old student from Gangarampur, South Dinajpur district).

However much we say that times have changed and women are now more emancipated, we shall be wrong. And it is easy to realize this in Kolkata. In many places, in crowded trains and buses, in dark streets, women are far from secure (19-year-old student from Beharampur).

The experiences that I have had in travelling in and to the city are perhaps those without which no woman's life is apparently 'fulfilled' in the true sense of the term (22 year old from Ashoknagar).

Q: Is Kolkata safe for women like you who have no family support to fall back upon? Why/why not?

Yes, by and large. But I believe things have changed for the worse now (41-year-old from Durgapur, currently a housewife, earlier studying and working in Kolkata).

My friends who live and work in north Calcutta face eve-teasing a lot, and in the south also there is harassment in the autos or stuffed buses (24-year-old student, Durgapur).

Calcutta is changing and people are not so helpful as before. In 1999 I went to college by bus, having forgotten to take my purse, and I told the conductor he said that I don't have to bother. The same thing happened while coming back because I forgot to borrow money from my friends ... I am sure that it is not very safe. Because today people have become very rude and they are not very considerate about anyone. Recently I was pushed out of the metro in rush hour and no one even looked at me (content writer from Jamshedpur).

'As Safe as Houses'?

As some of the responses recorded above show, whether you feel 'safe' is also related to the area in which you live. 'I feel Kolkata is relatively safe. Or maybe the area I stay in has been safe for me until now. No matter what time of night it is I have returned home safe and sound. Even though I have no family support, the people around are eager to help and do whatever they can to make us feel at home' (journalist from Bhubaneswar). This is the reason why finding a house to live in is such an important task: the locality in which you live, as we have seen, must suit your profession and self-image; if there is a mismatch between these two, the support of neighbours cannot be availed of, and consequently, security at home and especially in the neighbourhood is threatened. As a woman living alone in the city, without the support of immediate family, you cannot reject all overtures from those who make them with good intentions, simply because they also carry the baggage of intrusive curiosity. And this is why the matter of curious or intrusive neighbours also assumes paramount importance. An incident that was recounted to me in the early stages of this project has remained in my mind as an epitome of this inevitability. What do you do when in the dead of night your visiting brother is shoved around by local toughs who have set up an alcohol adda next to your rented room? This incident triggered off the discussion that I record below. There are two possible courses of action, both suggested by women who live alone in the city:

First: File an FIR talk to the local MP [whom one knows by virtue of the fact that she is a teacher at the university where the girl and this advisor, have studied].

Second: Talk to your landlady. Make her feel responsible for your well-being. When we lived in this area, we used to get eve-teased like crazy. Then I spoke to the landlady, why should this happen to us, it is not as if we are dressing provocatively or anything, we don't hang around with men in the neighbourhood, or come and go at all odd hours, so why should this happen? Then she spoke to the local club boys. They identified the fellows who were doing it, they took whatever action, but it stopped. I didn't wear jeans as long as I stayed there. And I've seen [the girl whose brother was roughed up] coming back home with her boyfriend at eleven in the night, and of course she wears jeans too.

There are, of course, many pertinent questions that arise from both these strategies, and the women themselves went on to reflect on the ramifications of each position.

First: But does this mean you can't do whatever you want just because you are a woman staying alone? The local toughs are your guardians?

Second: You advised her to file an FIR—what happened then?

First: Well, they did file an FIR but the next morning the local people from the neighbourhood came and began to ask why the police had to be dragged into a local affair.... I don't know what happened then because the girl [to whom it happened] did not get back to me, I had told her to file the FIR, but when the next morning's incident took place, she thought I had done it to mess up her happiness

Second: There you are then. She can't afford to live anywhere else, she'll have to stay there, the police might come once, it's not sure that they will do even that and the local boys will stay there even after the police are gone. You have to deal with these things.

LEARNING SAFETY

The experience of freedom that women who come from outside the city enjoy, the development of an ability to cope with everything, the confidence in one's abilities in the situational space of the city are also seriously compromised and often brought to a crisis by the city itself. Did we know how and when to file an FIR in our home towns? Did an FIR even exist within the range of our possible actions? Many women who have been city-bred and aware of the women's movement and its activities, either in the immediate locality or country-wide, will think that this is a redundant question: especially if they are younger women, coming into adulthood in the last twenty years, during which events like the Uniform Civil Code debate foregrounded by the Shah Bano case, the Vishakha judgement resulting in Supreme Court directives for prevention of sexual harassment in the workplace, the laws against sexual harassment of women in the workplace, against domestic violence, and to facilitate reservation for women in Parliament have been the focus of media attention. These issues have gone some distance in making people aware of the rights that may be asserted and demanded, and the basic structures of redressal in the case of sexual assault, harassment, violence, and so on. However, there is a general wariness about enforcers of the law, despite the opening of women's cells in many police stations across Calcutta. Women are actually afraid to go to the police station to lodge a complaint if they are unsupported, and even more so if they come from outside the city. How can they be sure of the consequences of their filing an FIR or even making a General Diary in the place where they stay? The simplest of things have sometimes unthinkable consequences, as the incident recounted above shows. On the other hand, the mechanism of filing an FIR, the need for doing so, and the support that is required by all women, but by women outsiders in the city particularly, seem to be lessons that the city has taught the women who come here from the outside.

And there are many other new things to learn from/in the city, too: for example, dealing with being cheated. Some women remember this as their first experience of the city. A 22-year-old student from Durgapur says that 'an early morning quarrel with an auto driver 'was her first memorable experience in the city, and that this was memorable because 'it immediately created a one-sided view of the city.' Other women also recall instances of being duped by people because it was obvious that they were not locals

Everyone waits for an opportunity to fool and dupe us. During Puja time a group of 8–9 boys enter our house and demand huge amount of money and the neighbours quietly enjoy the fun (student from Sikkim).

From rickshawallahs to shopkeepers, everyone charges the hostel-girls extra. Once I came from 8B to the hostel for 10 rupees (this would cost at the most 6 rupees) (23-year-old job-seeker from Coochbehar).

The auto driver knew we were from outside and charged two rupees extra (21-year-old student from Dhanbad).

Some women, like a 24-year-old student from Asansol, have analysed the issue impartially. The 24 year old's experience is that it is not possible to reply directly to the question whether Calcutta is secure for single women who come from outside. She says, 'Kolkata is itself not an individual person, many kinds of people live here, there are people of both kinds here, those who help and those who do not, and both kinds exist in large numbers. On the other hand, a particular person may be very helpful for one woman, but may well remain silent when it comes to another woman.' Therefore, since security itself is relative and contextual and individual specific, women who come from outside have to learn to manufacture their own security when they do not have the solidity of an established home in the area to fall back upon.

How to Behave with 'Outsiders'

Self-consciousness seems to be the first strategy: 'Safety is no problem. Although Salt Lake is not called that safe, but I have faced no incident. But I am very alert of any problem so maybe my alertness is the reason' (computer professional from Malda). That the notion of safety for women is a social construct is thus brought harshly home to women living alone and away from their families. Since they have occasion to test the attitude of society towards women as individuals, and must of necessity tackle the consequences of being a discrete unit in the city unsupported, ostensibly, by various networks of kinship, on a daily basis, these women actually experience the level of acceptance that women as a group enjoy after their right to work outside the home has become socialized to a degree that it is now considered 'normal'. Given this apparent social acceptance, has society itself changed in any way such that women can, in lived experience, enjoy this freedom? The 51-year-old teacher from Giridih points out, 'It is safe if you do not break social norms'. And the 26-year-old computer teacher from Burnpur, who lives with her relatives says that there are certain conditions for safety. 'It is safe if those conditions are fulfilled.' For example, the sales executive from Dhanbad felt, 'When I get out of the Metro at Rabindra Sarovar station and walk to my PG it doesn't make sense to take a cab for 7 minutes' walk but I feel it's very unsafe after 9:30 pm, especially with so many hookers around. Once someone was following me so when I screamed a few people said I shouldn't be out so late, but the problem is, will these people do my work?' The hours of work, the area, the clothes the woman wears, her attitudes, all these are as important factors determining the woman's safety in the city as are the attitudes of different people in different areas of the city to different 'kinds' of women of various age groups.

This is certainly true for all women, whether they come from outside or not: but as the media professional who lived with her parents earlier in the same city pointed out, the existence of family support, or as the university teacher from Burnpur said 'living here for generations so that people know you on first name terms in the neighbourhood' does make a difference. For the women who come from outside the city the neighbourhood knows who they are and what they do and look carefully at every move before deciding whether they are 'worthy' of protection, as the incident of the FIR recounted above would indicate.

As we have seen, older women who have lived here alone for a long time seem more amenable to 'interference' from different groups of people—relatives, neighbours—and thus feel that they are 'safe'. As an MNC executive from Dhanbad, recounting an incident of harassment that she faced put it, 'This can happen to any girl—but you do feel safer if you have been living in the locality for say fifty years!' But what of those who refuse to put up with such 'concern'? What about younger women who have different views on how life is to be lived? They are guardian-less because everyone in the city, man or woman, stranger or intimate, is their guardian. As the media professional from north Bengal says, 'The chief problems are those in overcoming attitudes of traditional Calcutta orthodoxy and patriarchy.' Men who come to the city from outside have been doing so for years, they are part of a culture that is well entrenched, and in patriarchal social systems, they are the party with whom power resides. They may be comparatively at a disadvantage because of their status as outsiders a well as because of their religion or ethnicity, but still their position is different from that of women. Women who live in the city have been in the neighbourhood from birth; they have imbibed the fine balance of their localities, and in the event of a controversy, will be judged by their families' reputations first and foremost, not to mention the fact that their families' support will also be forthcoming.

Women learn to cope with these situations in several ways. One, of course, is the jeans syndrome: the dress code that suits the locality and the accommodation may not suit the woman herself, but for the sake of her own well-being, having grown up in a milieu that blames violence against women upon the woman's clothes, it is imperative that she conform. 'Even when I wear jeans, I wear a salwar kurta the next day, or a sari, so that people can see I wear everything and I am not an ultra mod girl. When my parents come, I introduce them to the mudi shop; I take my mother to the parlour so that my locality people know that I have a family like them' (27-year-old marketing executive from Ranchi). Apart from this, women who live alone develop several survival skills, to emphasize upon the world that they are not alone even if they are living in the city away from their families. As the hospitality industry manager says:

> For women living alone, commuting is a problem, accommodation is a problem, men are a problem. So you learn to drive, get proper accommodation and you learn to fend off unwelcome attention; or you sit back and enjoy and go with the flow. But problems are there in a megacity with a swelling population and it needs an organized attitude. One has to really firm. I have seen a sense of humour helps more than taking offence in such situations.

Most difficult is adjusting to the water and climate here ... then I had to learn about the city about roads and shops, shortcuts also the language. After that Kolkata is easy to live in. The turning point is when I learnt driving in 1999. Now I know streets better than many born in Kolkata so that gives me great self-satisfaction. I think bank account and driving are very important for anyone (39-year-old interior designer from Bokaro).

SEXUAL HARASSMENT

Most younger women coming from the suburbs or the small towns of West Bengal are vocal about the sexual harassment they have to face in public transport and on the roads—perhaps those who come from small towns and industrial settlements in other states, like Ranchi or Dhanbad or Patna or Gaya, think of these as relatively less obtrusive compared to what they have to face in their home cities—they have in general compared Kolkata favourably to their cities of origin. For instance, a 21-year-old student from Dhanbad says, 'Kolkata preferably is the safest for women. A lot less eve-teasing in public transport and public places. Men are more sympathetic than my hometown.' But those who come from different parts of the state complain that this is one of the chief difficulties of city life, despite the fact that there are so many advantages of living in the city. Safety issues range from the classic to the unthought of. Suppose we also go down the scale thus, beginning with incidents of blatant harassment in public spaces. The 25-year-old office administrator from Bokaro says, 'I had a bad incident once in 2002, I am in an auto at 10 pm from Jodhpur Park to Gariahat (I was returning from a wedding to stay over at my relatives) when a man sitting next to me behaved very badly with me. So I told the auto driver to stop and asked him to get out and then slapped him. This was in Gol Park petrol pump. The man started abusing me with choicest gaalis and the sad part was every man over there watched the scene but no one said anything to the man. One man kept saying *uni ki korechen apnake* (what did he do to you). Finally I called up my cousins to come and get me.... I should have gone to the police. But I totally lost confidence after the crowd's reaction.' However, the programme coordinator from Ranchi has been more fortunate. She argues that

> Kolkata on a relative scale is safer for women than most cities in India. Apparently people, especially men, are more sensitive and respectful [this could however be a chauvinist trait] towards women and are generally helpful and led by emotions and ideologies. The police and the administration is also better in terms of safety of women than other cities. An experience proving both: One time when I complained of eve-teasing to the police, I had to go to the police station alone to give a statement against the accused. Police station was not a friendly place to be in and it was late in the evening and I was not comfortable. So I called two of my male colleagues and my landlord and they were in the PS within half an hour of my call and I felt very safe. The police though unrefined were very cooperative. The incident had happened on the road right at Gariahat and the man had turned abusive, and while I stood alone fighting him, none of the passersby had stopped to help.

Women are aware of this hit-or-miss status of safety in public places; if you are lucky, you might be supported, but it is purely a matter of luck. 'Kolkata is safe or unsafe as any big city with a village mentality. Whenever I have protested against eve-teasing in public transport no one has sided with me, not even the women. Friends working in sectors like media/marketing say that women are treated as ornaments (software professional from Bhubaneswar). Hence, it is best to be alert, even when you are in supposedly safe circumstances: the instances of company drivers turning predatory has not happened in Kolkata yet, but the instance in Bangalore in 2007 is enough to make women wary: 'I also have to travel over eastern India, so that way it's becoming a problem when the flight lands at 2 am and outside the airport its quite scary even with a company driver, Howrah is safer than airport' (sales executive, Dhanbad).

SAFETY DEVICES AND STRATEGIES

Some women who have lived in other cities as well reason that Kolkata is safer because of its 'family' nature. 'I think it is not as safe as Mumbai, but much safer than other cities because Calcutta is dominated by family people, so they think twice about doing anything dirty' (finance executive from Ranchi, who has lived for a while in Bombay). 'Family fabrication is built on concrete grounds. Women are either *didi, boudi, mashi ma* or *dida*.[1] Each occupies a place of pride in the household and around. People do not look upon single women as prey as they do in Delhi; one does not need to judge and measure before making friends like they do here in Delhi. In general the outlook of people in Kolkata is uncomplicated and laissez faire' (designer and artist, from Agartala, who lived in Kolkata for 8 years before shifting to Delhi on work). But of course, family values do not ensure a foolproof system for the single woman living alone in the city. Rather, the absence of family itself becomes the loss of a safety net for some of the girls who have had bad experiences with relationships in the city. As the BPO employee from Dhanbad said, after recounting the experience of a friend who lived alone in the city and got dumped after 7 years of a relationship, 'Family is very important. It's true we get more freedom but we also pay the price.'

Is a family, for the victim as well as the predator, an adequate safety net to keep women safe from what patriarchal society has constructed as the 'natural' inclination of men towards women? The journalist from Bhadreshwar points out that some people feel 'that outsiders ought to be warned against metro monsters and told about the dangers of the city'. Though this can be irritating at times, the fact remains that for her, Kolkata is replete with 'certain hypocrisies'. In reply to the question: 'Indicate if there are things you would like changed about the city/your own living conditions that would make it easier for women like you to live and work here', the designer from Siliguri says: 'Calcutta [needs] to reduce double standards+hypocrisy in attitude to working women+working women from outside.' And perhaps this subtle indication of hypocrisy despite the apparent family veneer that some take as guarantors of safety is gestured towards by the hospitality industry manager who says:

In posh social situations, I have had to handle some unruly behaviour like pick-up lines from men who are obviously married and whose wives are in the same room. I have had model friends who face the same problem even now when they are married and with children. I have also got persistent offers for modelling even when I have told them I am not interested.

I've been propositioned and it had nothing to do with me. I mean I have quite a snooty façade, which is probably because of my family. My parents wanted me to study for the IAS, I came into the media; it was my choice and I have to own responsibility for it. But Cal is pretty low in certain ways, even highbrow cultured people are really leches in disguise. Anyway I have frozen them myself (27-year-old media executive in a TV channel).

One way is carefully limiting the circle you mix in. The 44-year-old doctor from Burdwan indicates this when she says, 'As a lady living alone I have to be choosy whom I meet or invite when I have time. So my friends are my cousins, their wives and my close friend and her husband who are also from outside Kolkata.' Many years of having to stay as a single woman in Kolkata, as well as her profession, have exposed her to certain harsh realities. So in response to the question, 'Are people who are permanent residents of the city sympathetic to outsiders?' she retorts, 'I don't know what is meant by sympathy. There is danger in excessive sympathy from unknown people, through interaction with my patients I hear many social evils, but I have no personal experience.'

The nature of your profession is important, as the doctor from Burdwan says, 'Some women from outside come to Kolkata for modelling/acting. These women if they are desperate face many problems. However if they come to me I will tell them first to be responsible to your bodily health and not have any unwanted pregnancy.' Also, it is crucial that landlords or landladies should understand what the professional demands of the women staying in their houses as paying guests or as tenants are. This is why the journalist from Bhubaneswar made sure that she found the right place to stay before she and her flatmate in the same profession moved in: 'We did come across people who were not too comfortable with my hours of work. So we kept looking and searching for a place where the landlord knows how and when we work. Only when we were absolutely convinced that they wouldn't complain did we take the house.' As the advertising professional from Jamshedpur says, 'How do you explain to your 54-year-old landlady who has never worked all her life and whose husband is a retired govt. babu that you had to work till 11:30 at night for a presentation tomorrow at 9 am? And that the man who came to drop you was your senior colleague as tired as you working for 15 hours and pissed because he couldn't return home to his wife and son early? It happened to me.'

And even in corners that one would least expect them to turn up, safety concerns lurk—what one would never have thought of as a 'safety issue' becomes so inflected when it involves a woman staying alone and a group of people—men, women together or separately, who perceive her as the other. Automatically, her status as single, literally and metaphorically puts her in a position of powerlessness: 'I am totally and absolutely powerless in many basic ways, subject to humiliations by my landlord, shows of insolence/superiority which are very demeaning to my self-esteem,' says the advertising professional from Jamshedpur. She is echoed by a 21-year-old student from Ranaghat whose first impressions of the city include a feeling of helplessness in the unfamiliar surroundings of her paying guest accommodation. The 'unwanted advice of a number of people' seems to make the 25-year-old student insecure. A number of students living in messes south of Jadavpur complain about the behaviour of the landladies, a complaint that becomes even more strident if it is a Paying Guest arrangement, that is, if the woman has to depend to a larger extent on the householder. A 19-year-old from Debagram, Nadia, recounts a strange experience: 'I had come [to the PG accommodation] just a few days earlier. One day I was sleeping in my room in the afternoon, when the [landlady] woke me up with a great deal of urgency, as if bandits had attacked the place. She pulled me up and shoved me into another room and locked me up. After a while I was let out; then I learnt she was taking precautions because a male electrician had come to the house. I have not yet been able to digest this experience.' The innate ambiguity which local people feel towards girls who come from outside, especially if the former have to live in close proximity with the latter, begins with such bizarre incidents, and sometimes reaches an extreme:

> These three girls whom I know personally decided to take up a house. They followed all the rules and regulations sincerely. No late nights, no boys allowed. They're very simple and decent girls. One day the rickshawallah charged them really high so an argument broke out. The para people kept watching, and finally when they refused to pay him extra, he accused them of smelling of alcohol and a neighbour accused them of being girls with bad character. The argument got heated and one of the girls broke down seeing a woman of her mother's age accusing her and treating them so badly for no reason. Things got so bad that they had to leave the house at three in the morning. One of them wanted to return home forever. Now they too have a mindblock for people from this place whom they will never be able to accept [student from Gangtok].

> Once I was standing with some friends in Esplanade. There were no buses to Jadavpur. Suddenly a gentleman came up to [a senior girl] standing right beside me and said, 'How much do I have to pay for you to come with me?'

This kind of propositioning, which one encounters once in a while and can straightaway identify as violent, is of a different sort from the slow attrition practiced by some men. 'There are some young boys who frequent the addas of 8B bus-stand: the way they keep running after girls from the [Jadavpur] Ladies Hostel, saying, 'Excuse me! Excuse me!' is really irritating.' A 24-year-old student from Asansol first came to the city and began to stay in a hostel at Lansdown Rd. She says she changed her accommodation because 'the boys of the neighbourhood club used to make continuous demands. Because I am a polite person, I used to honour their requests, I could not say no.' Perhaps the 24-year-old library science student from Raiganj makes the most valid point when she says that Kolkata taught her 'how a single woman should conduct herself.' This would not have been possible if she had not come here alone, away from her family;

as another student noted, her local counterparts who live in Kolkata with their families are more laid back and 'do not care about the consequences of their actions'. This is obviously because the women from outside are always on their guard about the kind of image they present to the world at large: what they are perceived to be, rather than what they actually are, seems to have an important bearing on their safety and can be one of their most effective strategies for protecting themselves. 'People tend to become very persistent when they learn that you live alone. They become very curious about your personal life as well. Since I am in the hospitality industry, grooming and a pleasant demeanour are a must. Since I am single by choice, I have to be extra careful that I am not sending out mixed signals, and sometimes it is very tiring. Sometimes you do feel like snapping,' says the manager from the hospitality industry.

It is difficult, then, for women not to be wary all the time. Sexual harassment is certainly an issue, but it is one of many, perhaps an important one, even the most important one, but still one among a number, when women have to protect themselves on multiple fronts. As the working woman from Debagram, Nadia, says, 'Many people used us. They made us waste our money and our time. You have to be careful always. Sexual harassment is nothing new in our country: 99 percent of women grow up being sexually harassed. There is nothing to be gained in saying this with great fanfare. There is nothing to be gained in shouting about it either. It is not so easy to change society. We have ourselves created barricades in our own path. So staying alone is truly frightening.' Women staying alone in the city are reluctant to believe that the city has become safe for them because they have equal job opportunities and perform certain tasks for themselves that male relatives would have performed, had they been at home. Even their enhanced financial situation which ought to have fostered a sense of independence, (and does, to some extent) does not cancel out the fact that their gender is ultimately the primary concern. Rather, they are more circumspect and careful about describing their status as 'independent' women living alone in the city: 'It is almost impossible for a single woman to travel alone at night in the city. If you work in a private firm, you might have to stay in office until late at night on many occasions; in such circumstances, the roads are not at all safe, and it is desirable that the government takes steps to remedy this' (25-year-old student from Bolpur). A 19-year-old student from Darjeeling sums it up when she says that the city is safe, 'If you are at the right place at the right time with the right person.' In other words, your safety cannot be anyone's concern other than your own, and you are responsible for setting up the conditions which will ensure that you are not at risk.

A 20-year-old student from Durgapur said that the city was safe 'provided you don't jump into danger like crossing the Calcutta Maidan in the dark'. There is no hard and fast rule that says that women who come from outside are less prone to taking risks like walking in the dark alone on the Maidan[2] which is a huge stretch of open space housing many sports clubs and bordered on one side by the boundaries of Fort William. To all intents and purposes, after dark, when the clubs close, the players go home and the Fort, tucked away far behind the road, protected by walls, disappears into the night, the vast open space becomes the haunt of lovers or those using love as an excuse to seek other pleasures and those who are out to make a fast buck from such seekers. It is a breezy beautiful place that one may sit in to talk or ruminate, as are the leafy dark expanses of the Dhakuria Lakes[3] in south Calcutta. But one would do this at one's own risk, despite the fact that these places are patrolled by law-keepers, who also think of these locations as sources of income. Their duty, as they perceive it, is to keep the city free of whatever they, in their wisdom, construe as obscenity: whether that is a woman unaccompanied or a couple necking depends completely on their mood and desire for ready cash. Hence, these places in the city are best avoided not only by women but by anyone not wanting to get into needless trouble. Evidently, there is a fine line between safety and the consequences of foolhardiness; tempting fate is not the wise option to take, and women who are responsible for their own security and aware that they have to handle it themselves are evidently more sensitive to this line of demarcation.

To me the mechanisms women put in place for their own safety do not seem an aspect of the much discussed 'adjustment', simply because it appears that certain givens have to be taken into account by women in patriarchal society without exception. Whatever be the woman's position vis-à-vis the city, it is not only women who come from outside and live alone in the city who have to be careful not to do anything foolhardy, but also all women in general. The former will probably be more acutely aware of this limit rather than the latter for whom this may not appear to be an issue until it is actually staring her in the face because she does not bear the burden of her own security, living as she does, with family and within certain entrenched networks as a permanent resident of the city. We may thus challenge, as Goodey (1997) has done, the assumption based on a certain reading of the empirical evidence that presumed that women were fearful (and therefore risk avoiders) while men were fearless (and so risk-seekers). This would substantiate Lupton's view (1999) that people are put in perceived 'risk positions' arising out of a metaphorical capacity for concerns produced by locally constructed and locally understood structures of feeling, generated by myth, folklore, received wisdom, perceptions, and so on. So the 'myth' of Calcutta as a safe city may be tested by the experiences of women coming from outside at a level different from the perceptions of those who have been here from birth or have the support of families.

'SAFETY' AND THE WOMAN 'OUTSIDER'

We must note that these are indications of possibilities merely. One might at the most say that since the women who responded to this survey have already taken the risk of staying alone in an alien environment and are in various stages of learning how to cope with it, they are likely to be acutely sensitive to dangers that can compromise just this activity that they have chosen to undertake. As the 25-year-old student from Beharampur put it, 'Where I am insecure, it is not because I am a single woman but because I am single and a woman.' There is much food for thought in this. Both the conditions that describe the position of the respondents are contentious in the context of patriarchal society within which struggles for women's emancipation are waged. Consequently, the single woman who has come to the city from outside, has to cope with three factors simultaneously: the conditions of being single, a woman, and from outside. In such a situation, there are people who act according to patriarchal norms, proclaiming that they will protect her—not in any gallantly romantic fashion, but out of sheer duty. How fragile and complex this sense of duty must be is evident when it conflicts with the profit motive. This is clear from the incident described below, where despite the fact that the owner of the mess continuously asserts that you are 'his' responsibility, he cannot—or does not—do anything to protect you when you perceive a need for it, for fear that too much investigation into the affair will give his mess a bad name and consequently be bad for business.

Let us consider two versions of an incident that occurred in a mess south of Jadavpur, in the late evening. Firstly, the narrative of one of the women who was present throughout the incident:

> Three of us were chatting on the terrace, and one of us said, look there's a man behind the tank. I thought she was joking. The other girl with us felt scared and went off downstairs. We were also scared, we started yelling, Who is it, and hearing this the boy jumped off the tank and began to come towards us ... we were screaming, and one of the boarders and Jethima (the landlord's mother) also started shouting from downstairs. The man started coming towards us. We were stunned. Then there were thuds and thumps, we thought maybe there were more people, two or three more. Sometimes when we don't get the connection on our mobiles, or when we have to put out our clothes to dry, we do go up to the terrace ... later there were sacks found there on the terrace, we said to dada [the landlord] these sacks were left on your terrace, why didn't you say anything? Dada said, those are our sacks. But Boudi (his wife) said they were not ... next day, when I came back from the office, I got off the auto, there was a man sitting on the truck, as soon as he saw me he started yelling who is it, who is it, just like we had done the previous day ... they were joking with us.

The landlord recounts the same incident:

> At around nine o' clock one evening, three of the girls were on the terrace, two boys had climbed upon the tank to steal. The girls saw

them and started screaming, the boy jumped onto the next door
terrace. At first there was some tension, but later it settled down.
My house is on the main road, there are shops surrounding the
house, taxis plying all night, no one from outside dares to pass any
comments.

These are the two versions of the same incident: from the point
of view of the of the women boarders, and from the point of view
mess-owner. Several questions arise: why does the wife of the
mess-owner (here referred to as Boudi) stop her husband from
going upstairs when there are girls screaming for help? After all the
girls are his 'responsibility' (see Chapter 4 for his views on this).
When there is someone inside the house inhabited by eleven girls,
in the middle of the evening (he himself says that it was around
9–9:30 pm, his house is on the main road, adjoining the bus-stop)
what prevented him from going to enquire what the matter was when
they called for help? What could have happened to him in these
circumstances? One assumes that as he says this to our resource
person, he too believes this. So, since he is so sure that nothing
could have happened, why did he not go up and check to see what
was going on? This gives the entire incident an even more ominous
undertone; right in the middle of the area, bordering an arterial
road, close to a very busy junction in the southern parts of Calcutta
in the late evening when people are out and about, three women
from outside the city are accosted on the terrace of the place they
temporarily call home, and nothing happens, no enquiries are set in
train, no discussion follows, one of the women even gets taunted,
but 'things settle down'.

This is not an isolated incident; there have been similar cases
in the same place. The same respondent told us, 'My friend used
to live in the room facing the road. At night while she studied, the
curtain was not drawn, she was being watched from the house across
the street. They whistle at us ... throw pebbles at the window.'
Also, 'the house next door is under construction, a number of
people routinely sit there in the evenings, get drunk, we do have
to go upstairs sometimes, put our clothes out to dry, especially on

Sundays when many clothes have to be washed.' Now this seems to be a potentially dangerous situation, waiting to happen. What, for instance would have happened if the girls had not gone upstairs together that evening? What if only one of them had gone up? They were witness to the fact that two men were there; the landlord also agrees that there were two men. Yet, this does not seem to have been taken seriously, no one tries to find out who the men were, no extra care is taken for their security. The women felt themselves in what Lupton (1999) would call a perceived 'risk position' because they were in an environment that they understood on their own terms as both the location of their 'home' in the city and a possible place of risk: was it because they were staying alone in the city as outsiders with no immediate family support to fall back upon? On the other hand, the landlord's view is that thinking of his house as the location of a possible risk is absolutely laughable. Or does he take pains to present it as laughable because there are several attendant concerns, not the least of them being a 'good name' for the mess which is crucial to business?

A set of norms flowing from patriarchal social organization, regulate all varieties of 'life' involved in this incident: there is also hard economics which keeps this organization in operation in this fashion. The women appear to understand the dynamics:

> We all decided that we would take the matter to the local committee ... I myself went; they did nothing, these are local boys after all ... we stopped going to the terrace ... the terrace is locked and we have the keys. At night Dada goes up to check before he goes to bed. We knew he would not do anything else; we are here for a few days anyway, we'll shift in a few days. These are boys from the locality, the house owner, the local committee all know who they are, there are many considerations, party (the ruling CPI-M) is there, and many other things, they must have also felt that if they pursued the matter the mess would get a bad name (implying that it would be bad for business, later) ... the people in Kolkata are rather selfish. People from small towns or villages are different.

The plea here is for some sort of regulation that will balance the space within which these interactions occur: what would be the expectations of the women from the landlord, which they could demand be fulfilled as their rights as tenants? How would these be articulated in a strictly formal, contractual sense? Is it possible to demand the implementation of such formalization? The landlords on their part have begun to move in this direction, with their own set of rules and practices tangibly and intangibly aligned to the gender organization in which the situation of women living away from their families in an alien city, independently, did not arise. Hence the idea of protection, social when more personalized protection is not available, is imposed upon the women, and certainly there is a price that must be exacted in return. The women have to abide by a number of rules, to maintain what is often referred to as 'decorum'. Mess owners ask, by their own admission, for 'forms (to be filled up), identification photo, what are you studying, what proof is there? Submit Xeroxes of your identity card and admit card. Don't make too much noise. You must return by 10 o'clock, no drinks allowed.' But when it comes to their security, there seem to be no rules or efforts on the part of the 'authorities'. The advertising professional from Jamshedpur tells us, 'In conservative neighbourhoods like Bagha Jatin[4] where you have the *parar dada* (the local toughs who call the shots) culture it's so unsafe that girls have had to leave at a night's notice. There is no safety net. You are paying a lump sum every month with no security whatever.'

The landlord has a story of his own of course. This is not a related incident; the only reason why we recount the incident here is to draw attention to the fact that the matter of security and the woman's continued residence in a mess or PG, is dependent purely on the landlord's own perception, and there may be nothing the boarder can do to dispel his views. This proves to be of excruciating importance, for she can find herself without a roof over her head if the landlord decides that she does not maintain the decorum whose (unwritten) rules only he is privy to. As one landlord told us,

One of the girls told me, I need to open an account in a bank, they will send someone to enquire, don't tell them this is a mess, say that I am a tenant, not a boarder. The person came—it turned out that she was applying for a loan. I told the person from the bank the truth. Then I made her leave—gave her notice to clear the seat within ten days. I did not like her attitude. She suddenly left for home without informing me, how do I know whether she has gone elsewhere or not? She will leave without information, that I cannot accept.

This is not restricted to these messes that have mushroomed south of Jadavpur (see Figure A2.3), an area where most households that harbour such mess arrangements are lower middle class aspiring to make some money and consequently looking for upward mobility through running a mess. The functional argument may well be that the girls are completely unknown and live within the family, as do paying guests. Hence certain 'rules and regulations' are necessary. One might, however, point out that the girls face the same problem; they too are alone in an alien city, within an alien family and have to be prepared for any eventuality. So are the 'precautions' taken by the mess owners and hosts of paying guests more justified than those which the women could demand? Are these owners more at risk than the women themselves? In the circumstances, are the regulations imposed ways of preventing the untoward from occurring, or a mate-rialization of the patriarchal idea of protecting women, even (perhaps mostly) from themselves, so as to absolve men of any responsibility for their actions including harassing, teasing, voyeurism or violence? Otherwise, how can we explain the abdication of the much vaunted 'responsibility' for protection in a potentially threatening situation, even while insisting on being provided with information and reserving the right to make snap judgements in controlling something as crucial as accommodation? And is there any explanation of this other than that protecting women from themselves is the only way of absolving men, both protectors and predators? Is this form of 'protection' and 'responsibility' for women the only way to elicit acceptable social behaviour from men?

HEALTH AND THE 'SAFETY'

Apart from the social scene, the roads at night, the neighbourhood toughs who will turn from protector into predator at the slightest hint of a step perceived as put in the wrong place, there is also, curiously enough, the woman herself, by which I mean that the most disturbing reality is the possibility of illness, a possibility that has been pointed to by a number of women. The university teacher, 51 year old, from Giridih says, 'One cannot afford to be ill in the city if one is single and not very rich. The extended family is always on the outside'. Health, therefore, is an added dimension of what may be perceived as safety and security for the woman from outside, living alone in the city, and all of them are aware that this is not a problem they would have to solve alone were they living at home. Another student from Nadia makes this point even clearer, 'At home, sometimes, I used to enjoy being ill; I would be everyone's centre of attention. But here, being depressed also has an effect on bodily health. And at home, I was someone' (21-year-old from Nabadwip).

Initially we did not include a specific question about health in the survey; but the gynaecologist from Bardhaman said, 'Your questions are comprehensive. But some health-related questions can be added. Some girls come to Kolkata during teenage years from their homes. They face lack of nutrition, increased stress, indisciplined lifestyle can occur. This is an important point. This has adverse effects on skin, hair, female functions, childbearing, and so on.' This prompted us to make health a separate question in the second version of the questionnaire. This elicited several insights: for example, 'During illness I really get scared. Even if you carry a good reference, the doctor will not take you seriously when you are alone. I have noticed that. So I get insecure when I'm ill. I always bring my landlady and tell her to pretend she is my blood relative' (sales executive from Dhanbad). The 56-year-old university teacher who has been here since the 1970s sums it up thus: 'The city causes many health hazards. One must take extra care to remain healthy. Excessive humidity leads to a variety of problems; it would help if the city were cleaner and the air fresher and [there was] less sound.' The women from the Northeast and north Bengal, even those from smaller cities, have all said that the pollution and the garbage are matters of concern for them; these translate into health problems. A couple of women mentioned the quantity of iron in the water that led to hair loss; some mentioned getting malaria (as many as five times, in one case). As the programme coordinator from Ranchi says:

> I have fallen seriously ill ... more than once in the city and each time it has been an experience. Initially I would even have trouble finding a doctor. Primarily because Calcutta does not have a good directory of doctors or health care centres and in a new city and given the dubious records of doctors it is difficult to decide which doctor to go to. As I started knowing people who were residents of the city (more so after I started working) I got to know of reliable doctors.... Another problem I faced was when I got ill with jaundice, malaria and appendicitis (at different times) at the PG and the college/university hostel I was staying in. The hostel rules mention that in case anyone is ill one has to vacate the hostel immediately and that calls for a lot of stress for the person who gets ill. When I had jaundice my PG landlady refused to take any responsibility and mistreated (pun intended) me to the extent that the doctor said that I could have died of dehydration. However, I would like to mention that I have always received a lot of help from friends from the city and outside, like me.... Apart from this it is important to mention that 95 percent (that would be roughly 20) of the girls I know who moved to Calcutta from outside and have been living alone have had either jaundice or malaria or typhoid or acute dysentery. If I were living at home none of these problems would have occurred, just because I would have had people to take care of me when I got ill and I would not have to lift a finger.

Others also have similar experiences. 'During student days my friend had appendicitis and then we were all very scared. Luckily her parents came almost immediately' (finance executive Ranchi). Even doctors have this worry about who will provide the much needed 'backup'. As the doctor from Bardhaman says, 'If I am ill or if there is an emergency, who will help me? These things you have to decide with a clear head. Fortunately my relatives are good but everyone might not have this great help.' Others are, in fact, not so privileged—'I don't rely on anyone. I hope I don't fall sick, dats all' (designer, Siliguri). Or take the relationship manager from Chandannagar, who may be putting herself at severe risk because 'I have a medical problem currently which I have to show a doctor but I am not getting time to make an appointment. If I lived at home then my parents would have fixed an appointment based on my availability.' This again boils down to how much one is able to care for one's own self. In normal circumstances, the idea of living within a family translates into the fact that members care for one another; in patriarchal gender ideology, the woman of the house is given the responsibility of caring for everyone, a trait she socializes her daughters into, such that when they have what is popularly known as their 'own' families, they can continue the tradition. From my own experience I can say that looking after one's own needs is the most difficult part of staying alone; it is easy enough to take care of others' concerns, but one's own somehow become submerged in the daily trivia. The training of self-effacement, even when imbibed from one's milieu and not directly imparted still remains a powerful regulator of one's actions and learning to take equal interest in one's own well-being is a kind of reverse training that the city might well give. Those who have lived here long enough would realize after a point that the excuse of being too busy or too preoccupied with other things to look after oneself, would inevitably lead to some sort of crisis that will be even more difficult to tackle; hence, the city should get the credit not only for making us self-reliant but for actually forcing us to notice ourselves, as well:

At 20 I was still a child and at the mercy of the PG people. At 28 when I fell seriously ill (an accident, a gynae operation, a cardiac ailment) me and my friends (3 outsiders and one girl from Calcutta though I depend upon her mainly for emotional support as she couldn't stay away from home or do a lot of running around owing to home constraints) were prepared. We managed MRI tests, ECG, and blood tests, USG and biopsy tests; virtually all kinds, hospital admissions, keeping all the bills in order, everything. In fact due to our energy and initiative, we did better than what my aging parents would have done had I stayed at home. So I think those of us who stay on and grow up and build a strong support system manage to be pretty strong and efficient in dealing with our illnesses (advertising professional from Jamshedpur).

THE PRACTICE OF 'SELFING'

The city has taught us what constitutes emancipation, of self-sufficiency and of solidarity as well; yet, are these practices always compatible? The ideology of emancipation, for example is severely compromised by the city itself; if you decide like many women, to depend upon yourself alone, to curl up within and make sure you are not accessible to most people, as a defence mechanism, then this mode of emancipation remains inflected by patriarchy and its privileging of the single self-sufficient hero type. Any alternatives of being part of communities and networks which are willing to share pain and pleasure are seen in effect to be 'feminine', and since the order of values in patriarchal societies privileges the masculine, these so-called feminine emotions seem fit to be either shunned or concealed. Women who use this shield as a strategy for security and survival in the city seem to be compromising to a violent extent with their selves in the name of freeing themselves from the norms imposed upon them by patriarchy. This seems another manifestation of the syndrome we have discussed earlier; making oneself completely unobtrusive by assuming various postures of adjustment, succumbing to interventions that range from the most innocuous to the most intrusive.

A total aversion to the natural friction that occurs between people may be a part of this attitude. Of course, women who live together will not necessarily bond just because they are women, even if they do have a common problem. A 22-year-old working woman from Debagram, Nadia, says that she 'prefer(s) to depend upon myself when I have any problems.' This may be because the city has caused her to 'lose my natural inclination to trust everyone and behave well with everyone ... because some people take advantage. Because I stayed in a hostel, many people sought shelter. Some were very good though.' But at the same time, she says, 'when I am in dire need of help, I have always found good people who can help me, and I'm sure that will be so in the future as well.'

Landlords, hostel superintendents and those who keep paying guests are all aware that sharing space is itself a very intrusive activity, one that has the potential to be fraught with violence. We cannot assume that this will be any different with respect to women; besides we are all women who have been socialized from childhood to live in a society that is hierarchized according to gender, class, age and in our interactions with each other, too, this process of socialization cannot be discounted, consciously or sub-consciously. Only the nature of violence will be different for different configurations of these social categories, one inflecting the other according to the dimensions of the specific circumstance in which they come into play. Landlords say, 'The girls are not all close to one another: two are friends, but they are against a third. But if they have to attack the landlord, then there is complete unity.' In the incident of the intruders on the terrace, recounted above, the resource person who spoke to the girls in the mess asked them why they could not go together to the local committee to complain when there were men found on the terrace in the evening. One of them replied, 'We don't have that kind of relationship amongst ourselves. When I was in a private hostel in Bardhaman, one day we had a snake that entered our downstairs rooms. It was dark, load shedding, we got a torch and all of us together killed the snake. The Superintendent shut herself up in the upstairs quarters where she lived, she locked the collapsible gate. Then we all complained together: there was a guard who lived there with his family, at least he could have come to help. But here we don't have that kind of unity.' On the contrary, some of the women involved in this incident spoke of another of their messmates who, through the entire duration of this incident with the men on the terrace, did not get involved at all in the commotion. Yet the men who came may well have attacked her because she often went upstairs alone to speak privately to her boyfriend on her mobile. But when the incident happened, she said to people who asked, that she often went upstairs, nothing untoward ever happened, implying that those who had been there that day had done something to invite such attention and intrusion from the local boys.

Is it because of such reasons and incidents that women decide that they cannot depend upon anyone other than themselves in case of an emergency? Let us consider the response to our question 'Whom do you depend upon if you need help? Are you happy with this arrangement?' Let us first consider the answers of those who replied that they depended upon friends, but were very specific; these friends were their roommates or hostel mates who understood what the problem could be, and came to help. As for local friends, there were a number of comments upon the friends made from the city, one continuous refrain being that they could not be depended upon. Younger women, especially students who had been staying in the city for a shorter period than the older working women, said that their impression of their batchmates who stayed at home, that is, city women, was that they were 'much more relaxed'. This is a telling comment, especially coming from younger women who have been in the city for a short while, but long enough, apparently, to understand the attitudinal differences between themselves and the city women. It is because of this attitude that many women specified that they preferred to depend upon friends who came from outside.

We have earlier discussed the attitude of relatives towards women who came from outside and were successful in making a niche for themselves; when these women were in trouble, they felt that relatives were the last people they could go to, though this, they were aware, was an unnatural thing. A 22-year-old student from Haldia also felt that she had to rely on her friends, but 'you cannot depend upon them like you can on family'. She feels that she is '33 percent secure in the city, and 50 percent satisfied with the friends that she has to rely on in times of trouble.' Another 21-year-old student from Gangarampur in South Dinajpur district says that she depends on herself almost all the time, and sometimes on friends. But 'sometimes I feel really helpless, especially when I fall ill, and friends cannot be with me all the time.'

The differentiation is increasingly clear: not all friends can be helpful in all kinds of situations, but, more importantly, not all of them can be counted upon to understand the gravity of the problem itself.

Hence a 22-year-old student from Durgapur says that she depends on people 'who have had similar experiences before' to help her through. Another set of women depend upon the men whom they have themselves chosen for romantic relationships after coming to the city. These are curiously fragile dependences, as many of the women who have done so realize quite clearly. A 20-year-old student who describes her place of origin as 'the narrow-minded mentality of the suburbs' is one of these women, in a relationship since she came to the city, but hesitant to give it the finality or the solidity that is expected (by middle-aged romantics like me, perhaps) of women of her age who fall in love. She says that she depends on her boyfriend when in need, 'and I am satisfied with this dependence, though I am not sure how satisfied, but because there is someone to fall back upon, my anxieties have decreased a great deal.'

It is true that staying alone, and taking care of one's day-to-day needs by oneself creates what a senior university teacher from Asansol calls 'multiple networks' which one can fall back upon in times of trouble. But it also creates a sense of 'self-reliance, confidence and maturity' according to a 34-year-old company executive from Jamshedpur. A 28-year-old teacher from Nagaland says that she relies on her 'instincts and guts and of course friends and well wishers.' But is there a contradiction between depending on oneself and asking for the help of friends when required? Are these two ways of dealing with problems incompatible with each other? We had no inkling of the possible contradiction that apparently may be perceived in these two strategies when we asked the question about whom the respondent depended upon in times of trouble. A number of those who answered this question, however, construed this as an enquiry into their level of independence, and answered accordingly: 'I'm independent, I would rather not depend on anyone else (18-year-old student from Gangtok, Sikkim)'; 'I've always fought my own battles myself' (22-year-old student from Sikkim). 'I depend on myself, and my own power of thinking with reason' (22-year-old student from Murshidabad); and a 27-year-old student from Balurghat added, 'I don't like relying on anyone for help.'

Echoing such sentiments is a 31-year-old journalist from Bally; 'I prefer to solve my problems by straight means without asking anyone for help.' Another 20-year-old student from Shibpur, Howrah, says that she cannot depend completely on anyone, while a 21 year old from Durgapur says that she depends upon 'advice from friends and confidence in oneself. If you believe in yourself, you will not have to depend on anyone else.' Perhaps this attitude culminates in a kind of self-sufficiency—a 22-year-old student from Kajora village near Durgapur, says that she is 'unable to depend upon anyone for help. I try to solve the problem myself. If there is absolutely no way out, then I ask friends for help. The locals here always come forward because I am an outsider and help me.' A 27-year-old MNC executive puts it bluntly, 'I don't rely on anyone; I hope I don't fall sick, that's all.' As a 26-year-old computer professional from Malda says, 'I rely on no one but myself. This makes me confident because I do not think that anyone will do what I can do for me.' A 51-year-old woman who has been in the city since she was sixteen says, 'I rely on myself and I have gotten to like it that way.'

A 22-year-old student from Lucknow whose coming to Kolkata was, she says, 'not a choice, somehow things unfolded in such a way that I came here. I will call it destiny' feels that her local friends 'have someone to fall back upon, but I don't.' Having been here for two years now, she has begun to wonder, 'I feel that this living away from home has made me too independent and privacy conscious. I sometimes feel scared that one day I will lose this feeling of being free; I think I have become very, very individualistic.' Thus she interrogates the very idea of individualism that we have learnt to accept as a positive value; what she points to is the alienating nature of such individualism that rejects friendship or dependence on people as weaknesses or as intrusion upon one's privacy and isolation of the self. Ironically there are so many intrusions and violations that we accept unquestioningly too, in order to bear the burden of independence.

The definition of this independence, as long as it is restricted to a single atomized and de-gendered self which craves, struggles and wins the right to have its sovereignty undisturbed and its supremacy unquestioned, remains a masculine, or even a patriarchal ideal because it has been construed as such by patriarchal society in which our relationships occur, our fears and securities are located. These are seen as attributes of maleness that women have been deprived of by patriarchy and now aspire for in their bid towards freedom. If we proceed to gender this 'self', it will lead us to simplified reductions of the feminine as indicative of community and the masculine as indicative of individualism.

Does this mean that one must succumb to individualism and independence that are structured as male if one wants emancipation that remains a feminist goal? Visweswaran (1994: 57) explains it thus: 'Women falling outside sign chains of possible subject positions could be compelled to construct themselves as lone individuals, even in relation to their friends'. She arrives at this conclusion through an analysis of class differences among women involved in the freedom movement in Tamil Nadu, arguing that women in the nationalist movement were acting differently from the way society expected women to act. In our study, women who come to the city from outside to work and study, and live alone have acted in ways that are becoming accepted in society. This acceptance is understood by the women themselves and by society as the breaking of certain norms of female behaviour only to attempt to acquire certain norms of behaviour and thinking that have thus far been identified as male. The very rationale out of which they have acted and continue to do so, as well as the actions themselves, have been construed as gender-neutral. But if the issue is posited as dependence *vs.* autonomy or individuality *vs.* community within the current hegemonic social structure, this neutrality is revealed as only apparent. Women are here identified as the Other of men, and hence their mentalities and actions understood as being at the opposite pole from those of men. Now when women attempt to act and think in ways that were traditionally not seen as normal for them, their actions and thoughts can hardly be seen as gender-neutral. Rather, as they themselves sometimes point out, they are perceived as, and perceive themselves as, acting like men. The burden of demystification of value neutral, de-gendered positions is to be borne by both men and women. As long as the male-female binary and hierarchy persists in social organization, a contradiction will remain between emancipation and gender, because the question 'freedom from what' and 'freedom to do what' may be answered by goals that patriarchy may claim are value-neutral but which feminist critique has shown to be male.

The respondents of this survey have brought this question into sharper focus. Women who populate this study often find themselves unable to occupy the subject positions offered by capitalist patriarchy, and the result is in some cases, as we have seen, their inclination to think of themselves as lone individuals. They are also tempted to think of themselves as independent because they have managed to take advantage of the capitalist de-gendering of labour and achieve an equality of opportunity that functions notionally in the workplace. This indicates a contradiction between what is perceived as emancipation from traditional boundaries of work and movement open to women and the role descriptions offered to women as gendered beings within patriarchal class-divided society. So we are faced with a double dilemma: should they demand equality of opportunity and take the consequences of visibility and mobility in the public sphere and simultaneously demand 'safety' and 'security' from society at large? Does patriarchy have any method for providing them with both of these: apparently equal employment opportunity, and gendered spaces to live and work in, which need at a conservative estimate, some kind of attitudinal change on the part of men who are cast as protectors and predators by patriarchal gender organization itself?

This again is not a problem faced exclusively by women who live alone in the city: but their articulation of these contradictions will, one hopes, serve to bring the issue into view, and invite direct engagement. But this is only one part of the question. The other part is what women who, to all intents and purposes, have the requisite means of emancipation—financial and social independence and autonomy—think of their position. It appears that some of them think of themselves as loners because they are in positions that the society around them does not yet routinely allot to women. They sometimes find solidarity with each other because of their status as outsiders: what O'Connor (1998) would call the friendship born of victimhood. Whether victimhood can be the basis of friendship at all is a separate question. What we want to address here is the perceived contradiction between 'independence' and 'friendship'. Is there really a contradiction between being independent and being part of multiple networks? Does forming networks in the spaces that we inhabit detract from our sense of independent self and make us somehow weaker? How can dependence on friends whom we trust detract from our self-confidence and/or our self-reliance? Does our staying alone in the city mean that we shun relationships of trust and friendship? Is our sense of community only limited to giving, and are we scared to ask for help and do not know what to do to receive it? Can this not culminate in a martyr-complex resulting from the 'sacrifice' that woman in patriarchal society is supposed to take as her duty?

On the other hand, the figure of the lone woman in patriarchal society excites curiosity of all kinds, as well as pity, compassion and even romance and mystery. Are the women who emphasize their separation and independence succumbing to an amalgam of these even while trying to resist what they see as the typically feminine? And finally, the theme that we have been returning to again and again: does the incidence of emancipation for women mean that they duplicate the structure of emancipation as defined by patriarchy and subscribe to the definition of freedom that is taken as 'natural' by this structure? Does freedom necessarily mean the rejection of the values of community and values derived from human relationships in favour of values that privilege reticence and individualism? And from the ethical point of view, can such freedom be termed feminist in any sense?

This study has placed our experiences as women involved in a social milieu at a particular conjuncture under the focus of what we have thus far learnt to define as value-neutral. But we have attempted to demonstrate, in previous chapters, that such aspirations as we have imbibed as value-neutral from the prevailing social semiotic system are in truth far from being so. In fact, they are all valued in particular forms and in specific manifestations that uphold a standard in the real circumstances which we inhabit. It will not be difficult to recognize these standards as masculine. The contradiction is not, therefore, between the feeling of self-confidence on the one hand and reliance on people whom we trust on the other; rather it lies in thinking, as women and as human beings, that such a contradiction actually exists. The reason for this is the fact that we have been socialized into believing that emotional self-centredness and self-reliance exclude attachments and dependence. And as women we have deemed it natural to assume that emancipation means to transcend the latter which has traditionally been identified as feminine and seen as negative and binding upon us. Our aspiration when we are in search of emancipation naturally is in the opposite direction from dependence and emotional attachment. But the experiences that we have recorded here directly interrogate this assumption and cause us to ponder upon the method by which we as feminists have demarcated our goals. Have we made the error of assuming that certain key states and conditions of being are value-neutral only because it is claimed (and by whom is this claim made?) that they are naturally so? Have we not thus been untrue to our own perceptions, practices and understanding that should have alerted us that patriarchy nestles in the very language of unexpressed thought? The experience of this project has enabled me to raise these questions to myself and bring them up for discussion.

NOTES

1 Sister, sister-in-law, maternal aunt, maternal grandmother.
2 See Figures A2.4 and A2.5.
3 See Figure A2.3.
4 See Figures A2.2 and A2.4.

WORKS CITED

Goodey, J. 1997. 'Boys Don't Cry: Masculinities, Fear of Crime and Fearlessness', *British Journal of Criminology* 37, 3: 401–18.

Lupton, Deborah. 1999. *Risk, Key Ideas Series*, London: Routledge.

Mumford, Lewis. [1937] 2000. 'What Is a City?', in R.T. LeGates and F. Stout, eds, *The City Reader*, New York: Routledge: 92–96.

O'Connor, P. 1998. 'Women's Friendships in a Postmodern World', in R.G. Adams and G. Allan, eds, *Placing Friendship in Context*, Cambridge: Cambridge University Press: 117–35.

Stanko, E.A. 1990. *Everyday Violence*, London: Virago.

Visweswaran, Kamala. 1994. 'Betrayal: An Analysis in Three Acts', in *Fictions of Feminist Ethnography*, Minneapolis: University of Minnesota Press: 40–59.

Walklate, Sandra. 2001. *Imagining the Victim of Crime*, London: Open University Press.

EIGHT

The 'Self' and the City: New Roles

The city in its complete sense ... is a geographical plexus, an economic organisation, an institutional process, a theatre of action and an aesthetic symbol of collective unity. (Mumford 1937: 94)

The main difference between my life here and my life at home is that now I'm independent, taking my own decisions about the good and the bad.... I manage everything on my own. At home my parents had always guided me. I was dependent on them (19-year-old student from Shillong).

People I meet for work treat me with respect when they know that I am staying here on my own for 10 years. Cal gives good returns on investment—in terms of people at least so I have made some great relationships here and I am a city woman if city woman is someone who takes her own decisions and moves about freely and feeds and clothes herself. This is thanks to Cal. I feel like a city woman but not specifically like a Calcuttan. I can adjust to any metro but not to any small town.

The 27-year-old sales executive who said this summed up the entire exercise of the survey and what it has sought to explore: the experience of staying alone in an urban society that dresses its underpinnings in the patriarchal gender ideology with a veneer of progress, but is reluctant to articulate itself to the needs and demands of women who take this progress as an opportunity to scale heights, great and small, that were not available to them earlier. Thus when Mumford talks, in 1937, of the city as an aesthetic symbol of collective unity, the disparities of neither class nor gender infringe upon his vision. But when women come to an Indian city in the twenty-first century looking for just this equality in a vision of collectivity, they discover that the symbol is purely aesthetic, not beautiful—including the realities of class and gender oppression—occur only in their systemic elision, which erases their presence from this collective unity. In order to make the city a functional 'collective unity', Mumford's aesthetic collectivity has to be refigured to accommodate class and gender. Our respondents have shared with us their attempts to do this. In reflecting upon their efforts we realize that when a woman does take up the opportunity to come to the city, her discoveries as well as her struggles to make patriarchal society accept those achievements work to engineer changes in the varied range of roles women are interpellated by in contemporary society. These roles may often interrogate patriarchal gender ideology and the consequent gender organization of contemporary society. They change the woman concerned irrevocably, often, but not always, through the conflictual situations that then become inevitable between the woman and the society she lives in. They make minute, but in the long run, significant, contributions to the change in basic social structures themselves. The experience of a single woman from a small town or the rural areas or suburbs, living in the city on her own, is one such order of experience that so-called progressive urban society is now faced with. K. Shanthi (2006) points out that women's decisions to move from their place of origin are influenced by several factors, amongst which she counts the social role of the woman who is moving and the role of woman in the space which she is moving into. The existing gender stratification in the origin and destination areas influences her decision to move. Besides, her capacity for making and carrying out autonomous decisions also is crucial. The important question is whether she has the resources, mental and material, to exert this autonomy.

As Shanthi (2006) has explained, the main issue in which these ruminations are grounded is whether the potential and processes of migration are affected by the expectations, relations and hierarchies associated with being female or male, and belonging to different classes, castes and so on. How do women benefit/lose by virtue of being women, and are the opportunities and outcomes for women equal to those gained by men who have taken similar steps? Though these questions may easily be answered from the common sense point of view, we may invoke some theoretical systematization of the issues at stake. Paula England (2000: 46) identifies the 'disparate impact' as distinguished from the 'disparate treatment' of sex in the implementation and working of norm and rules by which society is sustained. Men and women are said to receive disparate treatment when different rights and responsibilities are earmarked for them due to the difference of gender. The disparate impact of gender is felt when norms and rules do not explicitly demand that different treatment is to be meted out to women and men; rather rights and responsibilities are assigned on the basis of criteria according to which women and men are on an average differently situated, such that the results are unfavourable to one group. As we have seen, this differentiation operates everywhere, from accommodation to risk in a society organized according to the norms of patriarchal gender ideology. The experiences of women who come from outside to the city illustrate the disparate impact of gender that women have to face even as they begin to take advantage of laws and rules that seek to mitigate the consequences of disparate treatment due to gender. And all the attendant trauma of quotidian tension, adjustment and compromise as well as the micro-level gains of self-confidence, functional efficiency and capability and satisfaction that we have explored through the women's own narratives thus far are encapsulated in the quotation with which this chapter begins.

Women who responded to the survey provided us with a range of insights in reply to the questions 'What is the most difficult part about city life for an outsider? Can this difficulty be easily solved? If so, how? If not what do you think should be done?'

> It's a feeling of powerlessness; as a single woman, without a man's protection/identity. It cannot be easily solved. City life is very tough when you're part of the fabric of patriarchal society yet outside it in a very basic way. You have no husband or father here (29-year-old advertising professional).

> I may not show it but within myself I remain an outsider—that hesitation (*sankoch*) is still there (21-year-old student from Jalpaiguri).

Firstly, adjusting to the fact that you are really an outsider, and know-ing your boundaries. Some girls go too far. I feel everyone needs to realize their limitations and make those your strengths. You don't have a dad or a brother or a husband here, so what? I learnt driving … I learnt to operate my bank account, I learnt not to exceed my credit card limit … (27-year-old media executive).

I think the most difficult part is knowing what you want from life and the city and how you are going to get there. This determines everything else. It also scary, as Calcutta gives you the freedom to drift.… This difficulty can be solved though not easily. It took me a whole year to understand what I wanted to do (36-year-old hos-pitality manager).

Most difficult part is how to establish yourself properly. Without that I think there is no chance of staying in Kolkata with self-respect. So career should be top priority, thereafter the world is open with opportunities. Since I did not have much exposure I did not choose a new career but a tried and tested profession. But now so many avenues are open to women and they should take full advantage of it (45-year-old educationist).

This variety in responses shows that myriad aspects of city-life are most crucial to different women: whether it is an overcoming of powerlessness, an acceptance of self-dependence or turning the feeling of being an outsider into a strength or a hurdle to be brushed aside through one's own efforts, each woman who comes to the city emerges as a different person through the experience. Sometimes, the city takes over the roots; it tempts the woman with her achieve-ments to aspire for larger fields of action. The programme coordi-nator from Ranchi has been through this experience: 'I had begun to feel stuck in Kolkata and hence wanted to move out. This is the problem with Kolkata—it offers an easy life which tempts people to stick on till they find out they could have done much more. This includes not exploiting the resources and facilities that are existent in Kolkata.' The finance executive, also from Ranchi, agrees. She wants to move out because, as mentioned earlier, 'mine is a hard-core finance job so I feel that I am missing out on the action with the big boys'. So the first step out of home has expanded even the horizon of possibilities for many women. From the time that they were unable to cross a busy road to the time that Kolkata has become too small to contain their abilities and aspirations form a journey that they have undertaken, for good or ill, with the city as goal. As the finance executive says, 'I think surviving on one's own really develops one's overall personality.' But this does not automatically mean that such development can be acted upon. For example, the 24-year-old computer professional from Malda is caught on the horns of a dilemma, because her aspirations, after coming to the city, have far outstripped her parents' conception of what a woman can be 'allowed' to do on her own: 'I want to go out, but this is not possible for me as my family is very conservative. I have refused placement in Hyderabad where starting salary level is more than what my boss is getting here. But this sacrifice/compromise I have made keeping family peace in mind.'

This is not a rare situation; women who have come to the city alone have, necessarily felt the lack of fit between the way they come to see the world and the way the world still insists on seeing them. One of the ways of overcoming this dilemma stemming from contradictory visions suggested by a respondent living in a south Kolkata mess doing an MPhil in women's studies at Calcutta University is economic independence. She points out that women like her classmates who earn salaries ranging from 20,000 to 30,000 rupees a month (this was at the time of the survey in 2007), are able to send money home as well as stay in a flat with Rs. 5,000 rent. Then there are no questions: 'she can go and come as she likes no one bothers whether she should stay here or go elsewhere, and how she is staying, because she is earning so much. Only if you are dependent on someone else financially does the question arise of whether this is a necessary expense, whether you should stay in the city: all those problems. If you are financially independent, there are no problems.' This is echoed by a 20-year-old student of chemistry from Khalatpur village in Howrah district, who answers the question whom do you depend upon when you need help with this statement: 'I depend upon my parents, whom I call whenever I need help. I am not satisfied with this arrangement because until I can earn myself, I shall not be satisfied.' Another 23-year-old student from Medinipur says that though she depends on some people to help her in times of need, 'what is most helpful at such times is money.'

There are a number of problems with which the city presents the single woman from outside. As the media executive from Shillong says, they include 'accommodation, transport, working hours, office environment; an outsider can only feel secured if he/she earns a hand-some amount.' But is the availability of ready cash the only possible solution to the trials of being a single female outsider in the city? If that were so, only women above a certain income range would think of their encounter with the city as productive, as a contribution to their formation of self. Yet almost all the women who responded to this survey agreed that their sojourn in the city has given them far more than can be calculated in concrete or monetary terms, even when these terms were high on the list of acquisitions. For instance, there is the opportunity for experience. Inevitably, when the city has thrown up a problem, it has either provided or compelled the woman to search within herself for the resources that will help in solving the problem. This is in fact the most formative experience of the crafting of a self to which women who come to the city from the outside will testify:

> Most difficult part of the city life is taking the right decisions and dif-
> ferentiating between good and bad. It can be solved with our maturity,
> determination and strong will (19-year-old student from Assam).

> It took me a whole year to understand what I wanted to do, when I
> came here in '94. For a year I earned just enough to keep myself in
> PG and pay for my conveyance. But I had to interact with a lot of
> people for my freelance articles and got tremendous confidence from
> the whole experience. It was a learning experience, more valuable
> than my degree (hospitality manager).

> Getting confidence from inside is the most important. I think every
> girl should have a clear planning in her mind what she wants to do
> in Calcutta. I was confused when I came, so I was not confident. But
> when she does something [studies/job] well, then she automatically
> gets confident and everyone respects her, then it does not matter if

she is a boy or girl, when she will get married, why she stays outside her home, etc. (computer institute faculty, Burnpur).

Getting firm footing—acco job r 2 most imp things. I think mental strength is very imp. u can't crack when u r alone, no one else will solve my probs (designer, Siliguri).

Finding the right guidance for career is very important, as what you do means what your place in society is (office administrator, Bokaro).

The best empowerment is perhaps financial and intellectual achievements. Once you attain a certain social status no one will have the guts to mess with you (29-year-old ad professional, Jamshedpur).

To get a good job. Yes, it is easy if you are well qualified and have an aptitude for hard and smart work. Every outsider must enter a metro with a fixed ambition and work towards that goal (finance executive, Ranchi).

It is salutary to note that the emphasis is inevitably on work, which defines the woman, rather than traditional categories of feminine self-definition that are more related to emotional and familial matters. And this is quite natural, because for the woman from outside, her key to continued residence in the city is what she does there. As many of the respondents pointed out, the initial challenge of getting herself an occupation and then excelling at it must be met head on, because unlike her city sisters, the woman from outside must justify her staying here with every step she takes. It is not a natural course of action for her; each moment she spends here, in the initial stages, must be accounted for to herself and to those she has left behind as well as those among whom she lives. This is a continuous struggle, exhilarating when you win, acutely depressing when you see that there is no way of overcoming the odds against you. There is also the ambiguity: you may be successful, but you cannot bear the loneliness or the alienation; you may not have the wherewithal to stay on, but you cannot bear to leave, whether it is because it will be an admission of defeat, or whether your home town is simply boring. Thus once the stage of financial insecurity has been crossed and the woman has proved herself good at what she does, the lessons, practical and psychic, learnt from the struggle, crystallize to form her sense of self. Hence, women from smaller places prize their experiences in the city because it gives them more exposure. As a woman from Manipur who has only recently joined her first job after studying in Calcutta since 2001 says, 'The people of Calcutta are really very educated and this really helped us to improve ourselves and in extending our knowledge knowing that we are competing with them. In the city everyone is independent. Everybody, men and women, are working in the same office according to his/her abilities/capabilities which encourages us to be self-dependent.' A 24-year-old student from Asansol takes all of these bits of realization together and wraps it up in a ruminative statement, providing an insight into the actual resources that living in the city alone demands from a single woman:

> I think calling it 'social' security makes it a little complicated; rather one might say it is the form and structure of Kolkata's unique life-practices. In the beginning, it is this that creates the most difficulties. The easiest solution is that you must be much braver than normal, and unless some really serious thing occurs, there is no need to suffer from a sense of helplessness. On a personal level I at least have not faced any larger or more serious problem than this.

Older women, however, are not always so hopeful. Perhaps there is a strain that single life in the city imposes which ultimately has a dampening effect upon the enthusiasm and the wonder that characterizes the earlier years. The 51-year-old university teacher finds that the most difficult things are 'adjusting to the city-bred temperament, acquiring a certain language, learning to wear social masks. One can choose not to change and be less successful'. However, for an 18-year-old from Siliguri, the city has taught her what she graphically describes as 'stickability, tenacity, fighting spirit'. Clearly, she does not yet consider that she can be less successful or is not yet wearied by the constant juggling of social masks. One might look at these two opinions as two extremes on a scale, graded according to age. The continuous negotiations may well wear one down; but the fact that this is not a permanent, general or even inevitable consequence of staying alone in the city as a woman from outside must never be lost to view. If that becomes the case for many of us who have been living in the city for a number of years, then we might begin to question the validity, the necessity and even the successes of our own struggles. For surely, in this vast conglomerate of people and places and situations, you must, especially after you have stayed here for awhile, find space for yourself, where the continuous negotiations which are tedious beyond a point cannot be submerged in being what you are: what, in fact, the city has contributed to making you. Rather, I would like to subscribe to a more balanced view that comes from the advertising professional from Jamshedpur, who has acquired the ability to look back upon her struggles in the city and assess their worth in the context of her current stability.

> But still I must say that despite everything, it's a tough life and everyone's trying hard to succeed in snagging a degree and a job and a man and a flat (in no particular order). Everyone works hard, harder and smarter than the homebodies who live with parents ever did. One way to combat this is to make friends ... among those of your own kind—women who come from outside.

It is evident from these observations that the entire experience of coming away from an established but restricted environment into an open and fluid situation that you can structure for yourself, even while these situations inspire (or compel) you to dredge your very own depths to find the elements with which to meet and deal with the situation, is clearly a two-way process, self and city becoming mutually constitutive. Taking restrictions and difficulties imposed by the city as challenges to be met is an adventure and women who come from outside soon become aware that all the drawbacks of living independently yet constrained by their social roles as women requires mainly, as the student from Asansol puts it, courage in more than normal doses and the ability to remain calm in situations that seem out of the ordinary but can be dealt with. As this same respondent says, 'Unless something serious occurs, there is no need to suffer from a sense of helplessness'. Wirth (1938: 100) cites Weber's classic study of 'die stadt' and explains this feeling as peculiar to city living: 'The individual gains ... a certain degree of emancipation or freedom from personal and emotional controls of intimate groups, he loses ... spontaneous self-expression the morale and the sense of participation that comes from living in an integrated social whole.' Wirth goes on to connect this with Durkheim's idea of anomie (1951) or the social void, but women who have been through the process have recorded that this experience has actually called up the reserves of strength that an individual can possess, by putting her into situations where this strength is her only support. And that may well be because the inevitable anomie due to loss of community and participation that Durkheim and Wirth seem to associate with the city does not take into account the fact that new networks of friendships, new orders of relationships, indeed new communities and new forms of participation are made available by the city. It is not as if the city offers them to the woman from outside on a platter since she is the one who actively seeks them out and nurtures them, these relationships too become part of the process that the city provides the context for. Kolkata is going through a gradually quickening process of change: its growing capital intensive service industries offer women more scope than before. Besides, the changes from a family-based society are more recent compared to other Indian cities. In the narratives offered here, from women who came to the city forty years ago and are now retired but continue to live here, to those who have come more recently and are willing to move in search of better jobs, we may read a history of women's engagement with the urban, inflected by interactions between local patriarchies on the one hand, and the gradually burgeoning capitalist consumerist global patriarchy on the other.

Generally, the situations described by women in the narratives recorded here are those that different forms of patriarchy attempted to 'safeguard' women against, keeping them unaware of their own strength and thereby preventing them from utilizing it. It is not as if this vast wastage of human resources was not remarked upon earlier; it is just that this project has forced us to take cognizance of the changing nature of control as individual and collective capabilities and aspirations are being harnessed to the service of globalization, without deep-rooted emancipatory transformation. The process of empowerment that feminist practices aspire to cannot be complete without our attempting to bring this wastage onto the agenda. Empowerment for women, it need hardly be said, is not merely the empowerment of women themselves; there is social good that results from it, of which this study has just touched the surface. Women who responded to the question 'What is the most difficult thing about city life and how can that problem be solved?' in terms that evoked the psycho-social dimensions of their experience, indicated that their realization of their own strengths and the joy of using these strengths to establish themselves as individuals as well as forge relationships based upon these very strengths, give them a sense of achievement generally ascribed to the city's role in their lives. The city provides a context, in which those inner resources that patriarchy has concealed from women themselves by professing to 'protect' them, are forced upon the surface, and come into play. It is not as if the city gives it to them as a focus for their thoughts and activities; it acts as a catalyst that makes possible the reaction which will lead to this realization. Their joy in being able to deal with their lives on their own, gives them a confidence that is reflected in their appearance, as the media professional from north Bengal claimed, 'I like the fact that I am a city woman. I know for a fact that I look younger and much more attractive than my counterparts in my home town.'

In consequence, however, sometimes, women who have lived thus for awhile begin to realize that they have outgrown certain places (as the 29-year-old advertising professional felt about her hometown, Jamshedpur) as well as the institutionalized forms of some relationships as they have been structured by patriarchy. For some women this is a fact that must be underlined. As the 27-year-old designer from Siliguri reprimanded us:

> You haven't asked if relations with parents have changed after living alone. I think it has for me. I am taking all decisions myself so I am more independent than my mom/sis, I also know some things better than my father (more tech person than him, have learnt more about investing in mutual funds), I am more confident now than my family members so that's a change. I am given more respect at home and guide my parents also.

This reminds one of the computer professional from Malda, who knows that she can get a salary better than her boss's in Hyderabad but cannot go because her parents only allowed her to come to Calcutta as it was near home, and had a Bengali ambience. She has told us she accepted this restriction to 'maintain family peace'. The change in relationships with parents, structured forever on dependency, is not automatic and inevitable. However, sometimes the 'guidance' or help offered by the daughter staying away from home in a large city is refused. In such circumstances, though she is not open to any compromises as alternative to her attempt to do what she thinks is right for her parents, or for those who were once in a position of responsibility and authority towards her, the woman concerned feels a sense of satisfaction at having been able to offer help or support or a solution; an ability that has been acquired through her struggle in the city as an outsider, as a single woman, A teacher in an English-medium school who is from Chandannagar has been living in Kolkata for 25 years and now has a house of her own, wanted to bring her father here with her, but 'he does not want to come to Calcutta because he cannot adjust at this age. I understand that. I also cannot adjust to my hometown after staying here for 25 years. My family members did not understand or appreciate my opinion because I am an unmarried lady. But what everyone sees now is what I am actually doing for my father, which no one else is doing. So this is my victory.'

These victories actually constitute the experience of Kolkata for a woman who has lived alone in the city. Lefebvre (2003a) and his colleagues have studied the inhabitants of the *pavillon*, a particular kind of dwelling constructed in Paris to house those who are rising up to the lower rungs of the middle class (see Chapter 1). Their project tries to discern how different groups of inhabitants, of different ages and genders manage this for themselves, so that they take part in what Lefebvre calls appropriation, an activity that socializes individual space and individualizes social space. In this study, we have located this process in a specific Indian city and tried to understand how appropriation works in this 'situational space', far removed from where it originated as a theoretical concept. Our subjects have been different from Lefebvre's idealized feminine too; we have considered different groups of women across various strata of the middle class, coming from different areas, with different goals and compulsions, from different age-sets.

It is time, finally, to return to the question that we had raised in Chapter 1 about whether the women who come to the city from outside, chasing a dream into an utopian space, retain the feeling of city-as-dream when that city becomes an inhabited space. Let us recall that Lefebvre tells us that the people expect 'nothing less than happiness' from the pavillon (ibid.: 132). When the woman who has come from outside and made Kolkata her home is asked, 'What has Kolkata given you that you couldn't have got anywhere else?', her answers range from 'a sense of practical realities' and 'self-reliance' to 'Kolkata has given me the ability to recognize the real face of people behind their masks and lots and lots and lots of ... confidence (22-year-old-student from Balurghat, West Dinajpur). 'People who are such good souls, great friends, exposure to a life very different from Durgapur, quality education at an affordable price, a sense of style', in the opinion of the trainee ad professional, from Durgapur. The 29-year-old advertising professional from Jamshedpur says, 'Very special people. People of my wavelength. Jadavpur University pavement booksellers selling *The Color Purple*. Book Fair. Junk Food. Cheap living and transport. A sweet tooth! The ability to breakfast at the Taj Hotel and at a *dadur dokan*[1] with equal ease. Intellectual snobbery.' While this does look like a recipe for happiness that is suitably diverse and almost inexplicable in the affective value of its symbols, one wonders whether this is the kind of utopian happiness that Lefebvre sees the people in the pavillon as expecting from their homes. For example, many women have shared with us the initial stages of their acclimatization to what the university teacher calls the 'city-bred temperament'. As the computer executive from Dhanbad remembers, 'There were a hundred most difficult things every day everything was a problem.' From such a situation, one reaches a stage when, as the media professional from north Bengal says, 'I am now in a better position to articulate my terms and live according to them than before. So I do not need much help. I have developed contacts in different fields through my job.'

This does not fit with Lefebvre's analysis of the bourgeois families who inhabit the pavillon. The pavillon is, ultimately, an abstract location in an abstract theory, a symbol made of many symbols, each of which has to be interpreted according to location of the interpreter, that is, the person who 'inhabits' the city. In fact, this interpretation and its role in fixing goals and aspirations is the process of 'selfing' that we are trying to understand. Women who come to the city either know this, or they learn to appreciate this as they engage with the many facets of city life from finding a job, a place to stay, a system of support for health and emotional needs. They may come from outside to chase a dream but few mistake the city as its fulfilment. Psychic patterns overdetermined by patriarchy may look to home as a feminine space where the man will find both solace and the power of control. The function of the woman in this situation is seen as 'natural' by patriarchy. Though women who come to the city and are forced to set up homes in alien spaces may be acting outside the norms of patriarchy, they are still governed by these norms; they cannot aspire to the unity given by the dream to the dispersed fragments of ego that Lefebvre (2003a) speaks of, assuming his subject (naturally) to be male. Rather, from the discussions of the process of adjustment in the previous chapters, we may agree with Butler's observation (1990: 93) that femaleness is not outside the norms by which it is repressed. The symbolic order within which masculinity and femininity are constructed as binary opposites underlies our own self-perceptions causing the female subject, who breaks the norms deemed proper for her, to describe herself sometimes appreciatively and sometimes deprecatingly, as 'masculine'.

We may remember the doctor from Bardhaman who, after having acquired a car, a house and enviable social standing, says, 'This is just like being a man.' We have tried to unpack these feelings and the social context in which they arise, through the experiences of the women who have spoken about their lives as outsiders in the city. Increasingly, it seems that women come here expecting certain tangible things which they may or may not acquire, but there are many intangible things that they find themselves in possession of, things that they had not apprehended as desires or desirable. We have argued that these are feelings, strengths and attributes that women have been shielded from. They have always possessed these, perhaps, from time immemorial, but not been allowed to exercise or discover these feelings/strengths/attributes within themselves as patriarchy has not provided opportunities or contexts for their realization. Thus the arrival and residence of the woman in the city, even if it is in pursuit of a dream, can never culminate in utopia. She may fulfil her dream, but it is coming to fruition within a patriarchal milieu. In such a milieu, each of her attempts may be bitterly contested and often repudiated as unfeminine, irresponsible, hedonistic or plain selfish, but the utopia imagined by Lefebvre for the bourgeois male pavillon dweller and the female members of his family who have ostensibly been tamed into bourgeois patriarchy, may not be attainable or even conceivable for the woman who lives alone in a city to which she has come from outside.

For one, she does not have a 'home' here unless it is of her own making, a reality that both colonial and local patriarchies would wish to obliterate, because a householder must necessarily be male. Gendering within the home space has been studied by Alam (2011) in this context, but the homes made in the city by women who participated in this study do not fall into that category. A woman coming to the city from the outside must make her own home amongst the many in the city made by men, and in that capacity, she is sometimes construed as a threat to city men (Chapter 9). Her path to this achievement is studded with obstacles that patriarchal social organization has placed there, realities that can hardly be forgotten in the journey to self-fulfilment. The 29-year-old advertising professional remembers these as marking out the difference between Kolkata women/men and outside women, 'In college since I was in charge of my finances, it was assumed by friends who stayed at home that I would pay for things like rolls or bus-fares simply because their families were strict about money.' These are trivial experiences, but they cannot be forgotten because they open the way to a struggle, a journey that cannot be idealized because it has to be lived in the real world. The abstract seamless nature of utopia as a concept, and the women's sense of achievement that is calibrated with reality and dream are therefore at odds with each other, prompting one to ask whether there is another definition of utopia, which is certainly no man's land. Quite literally, it is a land of the real, perfectly possible, that women have been able to craft for and by themselves through negotiations with the limits of patriarchal gender ideology.

And how is it possible to get there? Through a road that is often taken by women who come from outside, littered with realization, adjustments, victories and warnings, which ultimately leads to a perhaps premeditated, perhaps totally unexpected destination. It is impossible to stitch together fragments of splintered Ego on this journey, because the very discovery of the Ego as a possible append-age for a woman is often one of its characteristics; it is impossible to substitute the functional with the symbolic because the functional has to be struggled for at every step, such that it may become a symbol of one's achievement, but then these are only stages of the journey and not the final destination. The process is one which we have striven to understand, because it is still unknown to us, as we were unknown to ourselves until the city 'catalysed' our self-revelation.

Lefebvre analyses the process by which the pavillon habitat is crafted. He designates a 'mythic' level in the thought of the inhab-itants of these houses. We may understand what he means if we remind ourselves of the way in which a certain class is being invited to 'produce' or 'craft' the environment, so that a person may balance work, leisure, wealth and display. This aesthetic pursuit is helped along by the thousands of columns on lifestyle and relationships in every popular medium. After having reached this point in the study, one hopes that the reader will appreciate that one of our aims was to problematize the construction of the 'natural' in the situation of globalized capitalist patriarchy, the situation in which women have taken up roles made 'acceptable' to society by the struggles of feminist movements. There is however partial differentiation in the 'natural-ization' of these struggles and the socialization of these roles. This differentiation is based upon the degree to which the gender roles allocated to women in the previous social formations regulated by patriarchy conflict with those designated in the current time. These roles also differ geographically, culturally and on the basis of class. Thus the 'happiness' that the male pavillon owner finds in his objects of possession, symbolizes his utopia. It is the object that contains his happiness, its possession prompts the owner to experience this happiness. In Lefebvre's view (2003b) the suspension of material labour and productive creativity, or an abstraction of these activities, creates the urban male pavillon owner's experience of happiness signified as a possessed object. As we have discussed in detail with respect to the idea of gendering the concept of utopia, this is different from the pleasure in productive work and creativity recounted in this study by the women who have come into the city to work or wish to stay on in pursuit of success. This success cannot but include the material: in practical terms, the 'achievement' of a convenient place to stay is perhaps the first among many 'material' things that have to be acquired. But this acquisition too entails the initial acceptance of immense hardship, both mentally and physically. The issues of adjustment, the problems quotidian and deep-rooted, indicate that the achievement of 'pleasure' in material possessions, whether rented house, car or credit card, is predicated upon emphasizing rather than eliding the labour involved in achieving them. This also indicates that the right to participate in the workforce on equal terms is an important right on the agenda of feminist struggle, for which women are willing to bear burdens. The joy here is in the intangible satisfaction of being able to achieve material things through one's unaided effort rather than of reducing material to sign.

The naturalization of the human being, though it pretends to be neutral, is gendered. Braidotti's (1994: 187) description of womanhood as the ontological precondition for an individual woman's 'existential becoming a subject' explains this process neatly. What is utopian or mythical for women in the realm of patriarchy? Subservience, being adored as goddesses or home-making? Any of these can be utopian for individual women depending upon the symbolic value a culture has placed upon these roles, and consequently, the opportunities that that culture has given women to exercise their choice to be any one or all of these. Within the scope of this culturally circumscribed choice, it is but natural that the possibilities which have been excluded will eventually not figure in the domain of possibilities at all. What is left over will be the range within which choices can be exercised, and women will have to choose their utopias from among these. The arrival of women from outside into the city to live on their own serves to extend the range of choices even while questioning the limitation of existing choices by patriarchal gender roles. These women question the limitations placed upon the very conception of gender roles and the selective socialization of the gains of feminist struggles with their very presence in the city as 'single' individuals. The utopias that male pavillon owners inhabit are qualitatively different from the pleasures of activity and achievement of single women from outside living alone, whether in Paris or Kolkata. These two categories of women are different through location and through the construction of womanhood or femininity peculiar to their societies, but they also differ, as a group, from men. Lefebvre finds that pavillon owners have lost the effect of pleasure perhaps because they are at the end of a long chain of similar achievement, where the feeling itself is substituted by an object or even, finally, a sign that indicates it. As he says when an aspect of reality is consumed, it becomes a 'value' (ibid.: 76). On the contrary, for women living in an Indian city, if not for their Parisian counterparts, the reality of work and independent existence is still some distance from becoming naturalized or mythified; it still remains an experience not reducible to signs or objects, a continuous process, conscious activity. As the journalist from Bally says, 'It is actually the mindset that needs to be changed. If I live at Kolkata, things are easier, if I live outside, things are difficult; not that one cannot overcome it. If someone wants to groom herself independently, there are ample opportunities in the city of Kolkata. All you have to do is find your way out.'

The idea of a helpline arises from this imperative that the woman has to find her way out since those who can and will help her are so few and it is totally dependent on chance whether she will meet the right people when she needs them. Could it be a solution to have some sort of organization or group that will perform this function even if it is only a place where one can air one's difficulties and feelings to sympathetic listeners? Women often perform this task for other women like themselves who have come from outside. As we have seen, many of those who responded to the survey felt that friendships were made more easily with women like themselves. On being asked to give instances of helping women such as themselves, the respondents pointed out a variety of instances: 'We all used to cut PG ads from *Telegraph* and share them with each other. Even now I mail them and check out how everything is going' (MNC executive, Dhanbad).

> Recently my roommate had to go for a thyroid test, so I spoke to my colleague whose mother is a doctor and she helped out with everything. I always help my roommates and they also help me. We even wear each other's clothes and shoes (marketing executive from Patna).

> I know my 4 roommates. Most of their problems are boyfriend-related. Since they are students they don't manage their money well, so they borrow from me. I have helped my roommates with money and advice as I am their senior. Sometimes I also get help from them like they keep my phone messages, give my clothes to the laundry if I don't have time, etc. (content writer from Jamshedpur).

> We are a network, we pool all information, job-wise or acco-wise. It's a great way to find out stuff, when everyone's working hard you have to give and take to make life easy I think (MNC sales executive, Dhanbad).

> My friends stay in my flat whenever they want. Since I hold a steady job I can also lend them money. We are very close even the married ones (software professional, Bhubaneswar).

> When a woman lands here mostly for a job the main problem is finding a place to stay I and my friend have always been sympathetic towards them and have accommodated them in our flat during the initial days until she has settled down in her job or got used to the city ... we have got help from colleagues who have been staying here for many years (journalist from Bhubaneswar).

> I have had girls from my hometown stay with me until such time as they made their arrangements. Also when it comes to job seeking, I've passed on information and recommended them to people (artist from Agartala).

> Accommodation is a problem if one doesn't have relatives. Learning the ways of Kolkata is a big issue. We are more trusting than Kolkatans so more prone to getting duped. I and the other two

girls [from outside] always tell one another everything. We consult each other before any decision making. We also share tiffin, clothes, accessories (nurse from Contai).

I know a lot of them, Shyamali, Anindita, Dipta, all of them come from outside. Dipta did not get a job for a long time after she had finished her studies; the main problem then became economic. We all used to help her. Then Dipta got a job in a large reputed computer based firm. Even now, all of us take free printouts from her office.

I have been ill a number of times and my friends have looked after me with great care. If I am unable to understand anyone's motives or actions, my friends have helped me to make a rational assessment, quite a few times. In a word, I can say that they fill up the gap left by the absence of family. I too have tried to help them in their times of need—whether I have been able to do this, only they will be able to tell (23-year-old student from Malda).

The idea of formalizing such relational networks that are contingent upon women's location as outsiders in the city, elicited mixed responses; many people who preferred to say that they depended on themselves alone in times of need felt that such a community would be 'artificial', and thought that it would be an imposition to bring people together when they did not naturally veer towards one another. Others felt that they would have very little time for such activities. But a large number also felt that they would welcome such an opportunity because it would allow them to meet more people, and also get some help when they needed it. Mumford (1937) comments on signs, symbols and specialized organs which in the city supplement direct intercourse, and adds many facets to the personality of the citizen. This form of virtual contact has its dangers. We can cite Mumford, though he speaks about a different city in a different time: 'the personality no longer presents a more or less unbroken traditional face-to-face reality as a whole. Here lies the possibility of personal disintegration'. But this is also the site for forging a new kind of sociability: 'and here lies the need for reintegration through wider participation in a concrete, visible collective whole' (ibid.). Respondents have suggested various forms of this new collectivity:

Networking: it should be good for those who are from Bengali medium backgrounds or suburbs. I feel lonely at times so it would be good to connect with others from a similar background and maybe different professions, this community is helpful.... But I am not sure that it is realistic. If there is a full time professional team to coordinate this aspect. Otherwise all efforts will fall flat because we don't have time to organize any kind of community (relationship manager, Chandannagar).

If there is an organization that that is ready to help women who come from outside, it would be good. All the problems could be discussed there, and perhaps ways of solving them can be found. I am ready to help to the best of my ability (21-year-old student, Jalpaiguri).

Organize meetings in regular ways to build up bonds and resist sexual harassment—the most felt pain to any woman. Whether urban or coming to the city for some reason. But mere discussion will not provide a way to promote the living condition of single women. If a cell is created somewhere, we can go and speak properly, seek help, give help in times of need—one of the primary goals of this organization could be to regulate the PGs, the charges there and see that nothing unjust is done by those who take in PGs (23-year-old student, Ranaghat).

I think a network would definitely help, especially in terms of finding affordable and congenial accommodation, solving health problems and also and also fighting other problems like loneliness and insecurities (anonymous survey respondent).

Many women reined in the ambitious plans that some of their compatriots had for an organization/network that was still in its formative stages. They pointed out obstacles which were addressed in an attempt to overcome them by other women who felt that such an organization/network could be the most useful thing that arose out of this study.

Why, really? I don't think anyone would bother if they were not getting extraordinary facilities like housing or job. Because no one has the time. Nowadays people can hardly take out 5-10 minutes from their schedule. First find out if people have any time for network. I work 10 hours a day and I also have to commute twice daily. So I hardly get 2 waking hours to myself, so when is the time for any network, what can it give me (technical writer, Siliguri).

Such a community would help in finding reliable accommodation, and can contain various useful directories … list of doctors, websites of univs/colleges, career counselling, computer centres with course details and price lists, special interest classes—music, languages, fashion designing, interior designing, etc. It could benefit the entire community of single women in Calcutta. Women would know that there is a reliable plus secure virtual space or them in Cal which they can take forward if they want a real space—a club or something. More women from different class and age groups would be e-empowered. They can also find solace and solution from each other without time constraints and the embarrassment of meeting strangers. Minority women, people who are non-Hindus, non-Bengalis or non-heterosexuals can find a voice. Nowadays pink slips have become very common so women who are jobless can post their CV and find a suitable opening through this framework (29-year-old advertising professional, Jamshedpur).

It's a good idea as far as ideas go, but is it feasible? A website might work as one can access it even from office (24-year-old technical writer).

A primarily e-community with added land infrastructure and research for those who need it would be ideal. Nowadays the internet is the easiest and the cheapest and fastest way to communicate with each other. Girls who come to Calcutta from a rural background would initially find the helpline useful, and when they learn to surf, they can also visit the website. Girls who come from towns are e-savvy already and for working girls the Internet is a life-saver. The best part is that it is anonymous. It gives space to build up comfort levels virtually and then it depends on the individual to take it forward (advertising professional from Jamshedpur).

Network of choice: loose informal group not meet face to face, email phone available to others in group. But I would like to choose the

profile of which women I am giving my email id to because I would
not like to mix with people I am not comfortable with over mail
(relationship manager from Chandannagar).

Does that mean that the experiences of women in the city, their
attempts to form a community, whether natural or artificially driven,
have not had any impact at all upon the succeeding generations of
women like them who come from outside the city in order to stay
and work/study there? This was one of the prime concerns that led
to the survey in the first place: that such women needed some kind
of connection to others who were or had been in situations similar
to them, when they were alone in the city and living away from their
families. Despite the fact that the trickle of women from outside
has grown in the last couple of decades to a steady stream, these
connections do not seem to have been forged with any degree of
continuity. Except the 33-year-old executive from Jamshedpur who
said she recalls her own past experiences when young girls come to
her for advice and that she guides numerous younger women, most
women in the 35–55 age group who have responded to the survey
have stated that they either know few women like themselves who
are outsiders, or have not had occasion to help any. How does one
explain this?

On the one hand, they have risen to a certain level in their professions, and they are perhaps too busy to network like the younger
women who party and work with equal zeal, and so make friends in
larger numbers. Secondly, the lifestyle of the forty plus single 'outsider' woman is hemmed in by certain limitations placed upon her
by herself. Either this is the desire to be left alone by nosey neighbours and matchmaking relatives, or it is the careful construction
of a shield around herself for security's sake. Surely, these women
have not been unaware of the struggles faced by younger colleagues
and acquaintances who have come, like them, from outside? Surely,
they have extended help? On the other hand, older women have
imbibed different values and put different defence and maintenance
mechanisms into operation in keeping with the demands of the time
when they first came to the city. As we have seen throughout this
survey, the generation gap in terms of attitudes, coping with daily

difficulties and lifestyles has been quite pronounced. Is this the reason why older women are indirectly often judgmental of the younger women, and prefer to construct a distance between themselves and the younger women?

One of the primary triggers of this survey is the possibility of forging what de Certeau a calls 'generations of subjectivity' (Conley 2000: 57), which we have referred to earlier in the discussion of 'inhabiting' (see Chapter 2). He has not explicitly defined this as male, but given the circumstances, where a certain range of experiences have been historically available only to men in patriarchy, this experience of living alone in the city and fending for oneself has, thus far, been male by default. This is a question I am particularly exercised by because this is where I must locate myself. The question came alive to me when reading the responses I almost dismissed the forty-plus group as 'older women', objectively slotting them as more conservative, and therefore not in tune with the problems the younger women faced. Then, I realized that they were as old as I am and some were actually younger. In fact, there were hardly half a dozen women older than me who responded to the survey, and of these three were my direct contacts. How could they not respond to distress calls, heart-to-hearts, threats and triumphs of students, younger friends and colleagues? Or is it the younger women's attitudes that distance the older women? 'I cannot force myself into someone's life unasked, but I will give vibes that I am there for someone if she needs my guidance. But I have noticed that a working woman in her twenties is too sure of herself and too self-possessed to ask for help. She will make her own choices, especially those who come from outside' (33-year-old hospitality manager). A media executive from Malda says, 'I am very active in informal counselling to younger girls who have come to Calcutta to make a life for themselves. But I would love to do things on a larger scale'.

The doctor from Silchar seems to have thought of this problem deeply, and has weighed the pros and cons of the situation in her answer: 'I think every young girl or boy comes to Calcutta for education and that it is very difficult at first.... They are tender minds who have to adjust.... I will say that girls are not desperate like boys, but I feel sad when I see them getting corrupt by their influences.

Counselling in colleges is very important today. Many unmarried girls want protection or abortion. Earlier young girls were not so knowledgeable. I am not criticizing knowledge but only stressing on the right knowledge.' The effects of this 'knowledge' are also diverse, and being a gynaecologist, she is professionally aware of its consequences: 'Nowadays many women are not getting married at the right age. But as they are more free than women of my age, society has become very westernized. This has some good influences as today this woman cannot be told to obey anyone without her will. So injustice on those women is reducing.' There is also a further consequence, which is not related completely to single women living alone in the city; but it is women like these who seem to be at maximum risk. 'Many working women are having relations with married men by choice. They openly say they know the man is married but no problem as they also don't want to marry. So because of this selfishness many married women and their children are suffering. This is also injustice. I am also blaming the man. But I want to say to the young working girl that if she is earning money she cannot do anything she wants, she also has responsibility of actions.'

Feminist standpoint theorists have argued that the distinct experience of women in a gender-stratified society provide an important resource that enables 'feminism to produce empirically more accurate descriptions and theoretically richer explanations than does conventional research' (Harding 1991: 119). However, this was only the first stage in the journey towards feminist research methodology, as the various dimensions of the relation between experience and gender were elucidated by feminist phenomenology and theories of corporeality. Judith Butler (1990: 144–45), for example, takes issue with an uncomplicated notion of gender, thus: 'Gender ought not to be conceived merely as the cultural inscription of meaning on a pre-given sex…. Even becoming sexed must be conceived in another way.' Feminist phenomenology conceives of maleness and femaleness as styles of being whose attributes cannot be fixed in unchanging forms. Code's critique (1991) of a model of propositional knowledge that assumes a male 'knower' led to her proposal to replace the paradigmatic propositional models of knowledge with a model of testimonial knowledge identified with female knowers. While this essentializing of binary opposites characterizing male and female ways of knowing has not been followed here, we have tried to understand the dialectic between personal/testimonial/experiential knowledge and propositional knowledge with the assumption that this can help unveil the myths surrounding gender ideology and the social performance of gender roles. As Heinemaa (1997: 289–305) has argued, gendered identity is not a collection of actions, but a way of acting, a style of being. There is no core, no specific invariant that will identify an action as male and another as female independent of a context. This last qualifier, the inscription of gender in a context which is both temporal and spatial, encompassing all aspects of being, is the seed from which this study has germinated. I attempted to place these theoretical inputs into the area of practice. This area is also dynamic. Besides, the changes inscribed in the styles of being of women are influenced by gender hierarchies and semiotic systems working within other social forces that are enumerated by Code (1991). The feminist struggle to open up the category of gender, in theory and practice, which is at the centre.

The first generation of women who struggled for emancipation had specific goals ahead of them, defined at that juncture through the inadequacy of: women who were prevented from aspiring for those goals through the process of social gendering. Gradually, their rejection of the goals that society deemed adequate for them led to the extension of scope and opportunity, until the present historical conjuncture when merely the goals themselves are no longer indicative of emancipation, but the means and methods that are used to achieve them are taken into account. This opens up the space for social ethics underwritten by feminist concerns. The consequences of the process of achieving those goals as well as the goals themselves form the social fabric shared by the actors and achievers.

The question that must now be foregrounded is whether those goals were actually brought onto our agenda mainly because we recognized them as thresholds of experience for ourselves, or whether we, as human beings, felt that they were worthwhile markers of our own achievements. It seems, in hindsight, that we did not really discern this subtle difference in goal determination, which might have led us to structure our demands and goals somewhat differently. In fact, the setting of a feminist agenda must encompass the process of change as well as the end-results. The simple reason for this is that a changed goal does not always mean that the process of achieving it reflects the change, and we are still under the impression that there are certain fixed methods that must be adopted for the achievement of certain results. What may be required is revisioning (Cornell 1993), that is, a challenge to the terms and relations on which difference is currently constituted. This occurs with the extension of the area and opportunity available for women's employment. It entails a reorganization of hegemonic gender ideology, and the operation and conception of social roles that go with this reorganization. Achievements that are no longer seen as achievements for women but are now taken for granted, have resulted in some uneven social restructuring that we had not taken into account when feminist agendas were set. Thus the task of feminist theory and of feminist social ethics currently is to address this lacuna. There is no time like the present because now we are in the process of discovering the consequences of emancipation, its effects upon the social fabric, and its resultant effects on women's roles and functions as social beings. Simultaneously, the impact upon the affective economy of the realities of class and caste which inflect gender may well be drawn onto the agenda.

The women in this study have alerted us to the process and its various nuances. As we shall discover in Chapter 9, the attempt to understand their experiences and make their generosity in sharing them with us meaningful to society at large would entail our taking cognizance of the changed circumstances that they have felt and negotiated in their daily lives. These circumstances are results of feminist choices and goals made in the past. This study has been undertaken out of the conviction that these circumstances can be profitably used to underpin practices of social equality, thereby engineering a radical shift in social relationships in the future, if we are able to understand them, discern their importance and prove willing to take them on board.

NOTE

¹ Neighbourhood grocery store run by an old man addressed by the local people as 'grandfather'.

WORKS CITED

Alam, M.S. 2011. 'Unequal They Stand: Decision Making and Gendered Spaces Within the Family', in S. Raju and K. Lahiri-Dutt, eds, *Doing Gender Doing Geography: Emerging Research in India*, New Delhi: Routledge: 231–49.

Butler, J. 1990. *Gender Trouble: Feminism and the Subversion of Identity*, New York: Routledge.

Braidotti, Rosi. 1994. *Nomadic Subjects: Embodiment and Sexual Difference in Contemporary Feminist Theory*, New York: Columbia University Press.

Code, L. 1991. *What Can She Know? Feminist Constructions of Knowledge*, Ithaca: Cornell University Press.

Cornell, D. 1993. *Transformation: Recollective Imagination and Sexual Difference*, London: Routledge.

Conley, Tom. 2000. 'Introduction. Other Cities: Cultural Politics', Part 2, in Graham Ward, ed., *The Certeau Reader*, Malden, Ma: Wiley-Blackwell: 55–59.

Durkheim, E. [1897] 1951. *Suicide: A Study in Sociology*, in George Sampson, ed., trans. J.A. Spaulding and G. Sampson, New York: The Free Press.

England, Paula. 2000. 'Conceptualising Women's Empowerment in Countries of the North', in G. Sen and P. Presser, eds, *Women's Empowerment and Demographic Processes: Moving Beyond Cairo*, New Delhi: Oxford University Press.

Harding, Sandra. 1991. *Whose Science? Whose Knowledge?* New York: Cornell University Press.

Heinämaa, Sara. 1997. 'Woman–Nature, Product, Style? Rethinking the Foundation of Feminist Philosophy of Science', in Lynn Hankinson Nelson and Jack Nelson, eds, *Feminism, Science and the Philosophy of Science*, Dordrecht: Kluwer: 289–308.

Lefebvre, Henri. [1933] 2003b. 'Mystification: Notes for a Critique of Everyday Life', in S. Elden, E. Lebas and E. Kofman, eds, *Key Writings*, Athlone Contemporary European Thinkers Series, London: Continuum: 71–83.

————. [1966] 2003a. Preface. *L'habitat pavillonaire*, in S. Elden, E. Lebas and E. Kofman, eds, *Key Writings*, Athlone Contemporary European Thinkers Series, London: Continuum: 121–35.

Mumford, Lewis. [1937] 2000. 'What Is a City?' in R.T. LeGates and F. Stout, eds, *The City Reader*, New York: Routledge: 92–96.

Shanthi, K. 2006. 'Female Labour Migration in India: Insights from NSSO Data', Working Paper 4, Madras School of Economics www/mse.ac.in/pub/santhi-wp.pdf.

Wirth, L. 1938. 'Urbanism as a Way of Life', *American Journal of Sociology* 44: 1–24.

NINE

The Outsider and Equitable Social Space

It feels good when I find a survey being done on us. It feels that we are important and different. It makes our success more wonderful (27-year-old senior executive Aajtak channel, Shillong).

Angela McRobbie (1982) posits an ontological entity designated as woman, shaped by the lived experiences of women. But she does not conceptualize the 'self' that embodies this entity as produced through the dialectic between individual and world. Later theorists have also begun with accepting the importance of experience and gone on to relate it to ontology. Bodily experience, they have argued, is crucial to the construction of experience itself. We have noted the response to this insight (see Chapter 8) with theorists like Braidotti (1994) Butler (1990) and Heinemaa (1997). Thus how the female being is defined, and inhabits her self is structured by the hegemonic codes of femininity in that particular society. In this study we have tried to discern the overt and intangible changes in women's self-perception related to a number of changes in the social organization of gender. Women have tried to understand and explain the impact these changed perceptions have had upon their lives in social and intimate spheres. This has caused us to reflect upon the extent to which these spheres have been reshaped due to the changes in women's own perceptions of themselves. In the set of narratives we have considered, this is more pronounced because these women come to the city from outside. They have had to find a place and construct a sense of place that could be called a dwelling. Have they then succeeded in finding a dwelling for their spirit within the city that they have adopted as their home?

To engage with this, let us consider the responses to the question: 'Are you still an outsider?'

> I don't think of myself as an outsider anymore; there is something in the people here, or maybe in the very atmosphere itself, that does not allow a person to remain an outsider for too long, provided that the person is not completely artificial (24-year-old student and media freelancer Asansol).

> No I don't feel like an outsider. Kolkata takes into its folds people like us. Initially I did feel I didn't belong to the place but now I feel a part of the crowd, of the crowd which surges out of the buses, trams, metro trains. The feeling is not important but it helps you forget home as one feels part of the city (journalist, Bhubaneswar).

Do you feel like an outsider or a Kolkata person? Or do you think that this feeling is not important?

> This is so difficult. When I go to Jamshedpur, I feel like a Calcuttan, and vice-versa. This feeling is very ambivalent and disturbing and I wish it were not important. Like I am still extremely affected by JMM and BJP in Jamshedpur, yet I am only amused by CPM and Trinamul here. But this is where I have been living for the past 9 years! (advertising professional, Jamshedpur).

I have attempted to understand how the corporeal self forms through the activities that may collectively be called dwelling. Dwelling refers here also to a situational space, which is represented in this study by the multi-layered sign, the city of Kolkata. It is because of this dual approach that the study ultimately foregrounds two sets of related questions. Firstly, given the experiences elucidated by the women who were subjects of the study, what will be the strategies that the women themselves can take in order to negotiate the gap between role and performance expectations, opportunities and choices provided by the urban milieu? This may well be seen as a general question relating to all women in urban space. I want to emphasize strongly its importance for women who come from outside, because for them the finding of a place in the city and making it habitable, both literally and metaphorically, through outer or inner 'adjustments' and negotiations is crucial. The activity and the place are linked together through the narratives, which provide a way of knowing that is different from the kind of propositional knowledge that social 'science' treatises demand. This study has from the outset pointed to the impossibility of quantifying the affective dimension of the processes here studied. Hence the attempt has been to understand them rather than produce conclusions and tabulated findings.

Methods of negotiating the contradictions between gender roles and performances have a separate space within the repertoire of strategies that women use to socialize the gains of feminism and the women's movement. The incessant critique that an abyss between theory and activism characterizes the Indian women's movement and, more specifically, feminist engagement with the lives of Indian women, can be addressed if the experiences and negotiations of women who inhabit these changing realities are brought to light and understood. The experiences foreground certain imperatives and negotiations peculiar to women living alone in an Indian city. The narratives of the women who are the subjects of this study provide a range of practical possibilities and obstructions that arise in the negotiation of a changing urban space. The stories of these negotiations offer us glimpses into a dynamic process of self-construction by the narrators themselves. From the very beginning of this study, the effort has been limited to linking the understanding of geographical 'place' with affective spatialization by asking what space patriarchal urban society offers the woman who enters it from elsewhere. Is there a fundamental lack of fit between the 'natural habitat' of the embodied female self and the somewhat ambiguous dwelling place of the feminine spirit in patriarchal social organization? For everywhere it appears that woman's corporeal body dictates the social implications of dwelling; her being often seems to strain at the margins of the only acceptable 'safe' spaces she is 'naturally' able to inhabit. Modernity claims to 'allow' her the freedom to independently produce for herself a dwelling of both physical and emotional well-being. But like all human beings, she is herself constrained by time and place. Her dreams and desires may be pruned to fit into the space produced for her by capitalist patriarchy. Our attempt has to been to locate this conflict in a modern Indian city: the city which creates opportunities for her as well as puts obstacles in her path when she attempts to take these opportunities. Our respondents relate the process of discovery, production and creation of space in an urban milieu. These intertwined processes constitute 'dwelling' in the city, by fashioning a physical and psychic dwelling for the female self. Each story, like each woman is different: this study has been an effort to make the voices audible to each other and to us all, so that change—directed change—may become possible.

We have assumed throughout this study that the gendering of what appears value-neutral is a process peculiar to patriarchy. In a sense, the stories related by the women who participated in the survey can be contexted in Bat-Ami Bar On's (2008) critique of autonomy as a concept:

> Feminists have attempted to expose received conceptions of autonomy as resting on a gendered male experience and to rework conceptions for male autonomy in such a way so that it refers to women's experience. This reworking construes women's experience positively, but sometimes neglects a critical engagement with the lack of certain experiences that is a function of gender exclusion (208).

Gender exclusion keeps certain areas of experience strictly separate, leading to at least two apparently opposite consequences. One appears to be the fact, as we have seen at the end of Chapter 8, ideas of emancipation are gendered because they are seen as opposed to values that are construed as 'traditionally' feminine, in other words, as constraints. With respect to risk taking, for example, as Featherstone (1995) points out, the 'heroic' life that is wrested, literally, from the jaws of uncertainty and risk, is seen as male, while the avoidance of situations in which risk may be a possibility are construed as the marker of domestic life, befitting for the female. The idea of the home as a dwelling for the spirit, where one is safe, and the family as a place where one 'expect(s) to be left alone or deal with others as (one) choose(s)' (Newman and Grauerholz 2002: 41) is opposed to the scenes of risk, competition and success in the 'public' world. Capitalist patriarchy is predicated upon allocating different spheres to each gender, essentializing the difference based upon biology, and then hierarchizing this difference, placing the 'male' sphere in a position superior to the 'female' in terms of material and affective valuation of labour. This ascription of greater value to the labour of the male is socially concretised through the hierarchization of gender that characterises capitalist relations of production. Though women have come a long way from the traditional role of domesticity, the socialization of these changes has been ambiguous and uneven. Either the double burden of work has become more pronounced, the 'new' public role of wage-earner being added to the modern middle-class woman's self-definition, fuelling a host of consumer goods required to fulfil the needs of the superwoman who manages the public and the private sphere with equal ease. Or, an army of women from lower classes and castes have been recruited to balance the demands of the new middle-class urban woman's role itself, leading to migration of labour from villages to cities (Raju and Banerjee 2009, Banerjee 2011).

The narratives of the women collected here are somewhat differently situated; having to earn their living in the city, they cannot afford to employ other women to manage their daily affairs. Nor do they have family support in the city, since they are here alone, having taken advantage of the education, freedom of movement, equality of opportunity, and so on, that are seen as synonymous with women's march towards equality. One might like to imagine that they face the world as individuals—and the individual is gendered. Such women are among those who have not merely stepped out of their homes to come to another place, they have also stepped out of the confines of the existing gender norm. All the respondents at the time of the survey were single women in a city not their home, without the support of families. Their experiences interrogate the gender roles and the gender ideology that organize sociability in contemporary urban Indian, where this kind of person is not a rarity but still not the norm.

Even while women push at the boundaries of public and private spheres constructed by patriarchy, class mobility plays an aspirational role. A few of the women here are those who have come to Kolkata to ease the double burden of more affluent upper-class women, entering the city to work in the 'private' sphere so that more affluent women can inhabit the 'public' sphere with greater ease. Some of the women outsiders themselves employ lower-class women to ease their own paths. The symbiotic relationship between class and gender practices is merely hinted at in these narratives inflected by the specific characteristics of the location in question. The focus has been on women from different strata of the middle class, but simultaneously a few women from the lower class, who responded, have come to the city as domestic help in affluent households and described their decision to do so as a strategy for upward mobility.

Let us imagine that there is really no gendered division of labour on which the public and the private spheres are grounded. Women are 'allowed' to enter the public sphere with as much ease as men are. Indeed, if such ease of entry was 'expected' by and for them, then the problems ranging from the mundane to the spiritual that follow their entry and continued access, would not have arisen except as individual cases of maladjustment to a 'normal' condition. But that as we have seen is not the case at all. Rather, women's venturing into what we have delineated as the public sphere has caused fissures in the social fabric as well as physical and/or psychic upheavals in the lives of the women themselves. This is a consequence of uncovering the gendered nature of what seems gender-neutral. And to understand that is neither totally exhilarating nor merely depressing, a condition that we shall encounter in the final stages of this chapter.

One of the last questions in the survey was:

What has Kolkata given you that you could not have got any-where else?

Tagore, Biharis, beggars, Kolkata's a melting pot, all thrown in, a novel brew (18-year-old student from Bhopal).

When I was single, I lived in 2 hostels and one PG (Prince Anwar Shah Rd) and in all three there was a lot of interesting happenings which made up for the lack of creature comforts. I was quite happy in all three places. But I was happiest at JU Hostel. Probably because I was taking full advantage of my freedom and enjoying life to the fullest (41-year-old, from Guwahati, currently married and living in Kolkata).

I know many girls/women who are here as singletons and they are pretty happy with their life. There's no mad manhunt on the scene (sales executive in an MNC, from Dhanbad).

Showing us a world ravaged by technology, Heidegger (1971) warns us that a lodging built on the dictates of economy or technology is far removed from a dwelling, as machines are far removed from poetry. But it is as difficult to see the poetry of the contemporary completely excluding machines, real and virtual, as it is to imagine a world without cities, industrial and impersonal. Suffice it to say that Heidegger's dream of transcending technology can be reframed as a negotiation with technology that is adequate to inhabiting the modern world. Can machines and poetry approach each other? As Lefebvre comments (2003a: 212), every mode of reproduction recreates or reproduces space according to its own ideology. The city in the globalized developing world, characterized by the social relations of 'tradition' and 'modernity' in conflict and negotiation, provides our context. But a more troubling, and apparently a more important question remains; how are we to articulate this change that we are witnessing and attempting to understand, which must encompass the very organization of social relations itself? Within this context, we invited women who responded to our questions to demarcate the drawbacks of the city that they have experienced as outsiders, and to suggest what needs to be done in order to make it more amenable to habitation by women like them who come from outside and live here alone. In keeping with our assumption that the affective and the material are mutually constitutive in experience, the drawbacks that our respondents suggested ranged from the practical to the intangible, discernible only to the outsider, obvious only to the woman, or apparent only to the woman outsider:

Traffic and pollution. Salt Lake is a very unsafe part of the city. Roads are miserable in some places (journalist, Aajtak, Shillong).

Eighty per cent satisfied, 20 per cent not really because I feel like a misfit sometimes culturally ... people's attitude is the basic problem. Cruelty and rudeness go together.... A medical student, a girl ... had told me that caste and religion are very important in Kolkata. She left Kolkata after some painful experience. People are difficult even when they look modern (MNC executive from Ranchi).

Cal is facing a brain drain coz Cal lags behind other metros economically. All the best people go abroad/to other cities. Money is better there, job satisfaction and growth are better there. So the govt. must encourage more investment so that more people stay here (ad professional, Durgapur).

The city must shed some prejudices towards women like me. Professionally its esteem has eroded in the last two decades, but I see an upsurge now. It all depends on how much the government is able to bring in foreign investment. Satellite townships like Noida or Navi Mumbai must be thought of seriously because the population explosion will be really harmful in the long run (media professional, north Bengal).

Lefebvre posits a cluster of dwellings, whether we call it city or by any other name, as a system of signification. Whether this system consists of objects or of words, each element, he says, refers to all the others, citing purpose on the one hand and subject on the other which interact to produce totality and meaning (2003a: 132). The dialectical relation between the subject and the meaning lead us into the realm of change. Not surprisingly, this change is practical but not limited to practicalities alone; other suggestions are; 'Keep more policemen in every area' (student from Manipur); 'Number of flyovers and public transport should be increased to prevent traffic jams' (26-year-old MNC executive from Patna[1]); 'More and more flyovers are needed to curb the traffic snarl and Euro III's to curb pollution, also decrease the rush during office hours'. Various other details offered are:

> There should be more Govt-recognized working girls' hostels in Calcutta, it is a need of the hour, or the Govt. can give special Home Loans to working girls, who can think of buying a 1BHK flat to stay, and as an investment also, when they get married (technical writer from Siliguri).

I want women in private and public companies to be given housing allowance and 2–3 metro compartments should be kept for women only, like it is in local trains (29-year-old systems administration executive from Bokaro).

Safety and more safety for women in stations like Sealdah or Howrah in the night, also many landlords and house owners turn hostile when providing accommodation for single working women.... I think Calcutta is still lagging behind in being more open to women (31-year-old artist from Agartala).

Hostels which are safe and inexpensive. Many of my friends live in messes far away from college and undergo a great deal of trouble. In such hostels women from many different backgrounds will live together and remain in touch with one another. A better solution cannot be found (student from Jalpaiguri).

First when a girl lands in Cal alone, it's for studies or a job. Her first thought is safety then health. Then travelling from her place to college/office. In all things she faces problems. I think the first step is good safe acco. It's not easy. The govt. should set up more girls' hostels for students or working girls. All PGs have to be legalized with a contract, as a PG is a good source of income more people can keep PGs but with proper paperwork (trainee ad professional, Durgapur).

There is a dearth of women's hostels of all categories, be it for college-goers or working women. The PG option is not widely available. I think real estate agencies or any agency that can provide information on lodging (depending on budget, area, and nature of lodging) should be made available in the city so that women could at least tackle the initial problem of relocation (31-year-old artist from Agartala).

These are common problems, but the subject and the purpose are related in complex ways, which might be evident from the experience of women in particular kinds of situations. For one thing, the woman who comes from outside is perceived differently when she is young and has just entered the city, and this perception changes as she goes through life, perhaps getting a job and moving up the social scale through better professional positioning, or through a better-paying job. But the circumstances of her employment may not be the only reason why attitudes towards her change. It is possible that she moves to a more upscale and progressive locality because she has a better paying job and now can afford it. Thus she gains what may be called more autonomy, more power than she was used to having when she first arrived. Age, as we have seen, is a crucial factor in people's responses towards the women who come from outside and live alone; profession and age combine, in certain cases to make things easier, and in certain cases with just the opposite effect. The relationships she forms and their outcomes will also affect the change in attitude of people towards her. As the media person from north Bengal says, 'I had more help in my student days than in my subsequent marriage and post-divorced state. Here a student is idealized which is good. But once you are divorced, life becomes extremely tough. I had to undergo any amount of humiliation to find an accommodation after my divorce. People flatly refused.' The entire gamut of this experience seems to be summed up by this comment from the MNC sales executive from Dhanbad, who says, 'What I want changed are some attitudes at work, some men are chauvinists they operate differently when you are a woman, so that should change. City women should look at outsiders with less suspicion, acco ads for women should be totally transparent.' The university teacher from Giridih points to another functional problem that directly relates to women staying alone: 'Institutions in the city are all tailor made for 'families', sometimes even joint families, the gas delivery man, for instance, can never come before 10–30 so what is one to do? Attitudes have to change and make life easier for both single men and women, or in general people who wish to lead a 'modern' city life.'

At bottom, however, the fact that the woman is single and an outsider has a bearing on the changes in attitude that occur as well as their effects upon the women themselves. Women are aware of the stigma attached to the 'single' status and its social implications for women's functioning in the city. But women who come from outside face a particular form of the single-woman-as-predator syndrome because it has an impact upon their basic survival in the city:

One thing I would like to change is the way people think about single women living in the city. Most people are apprehensive (they fear these women would get involved in sexual relationships which would affect them) and avoid letting out houses to single. People in the city should be sensitized towards being more open towards women who come from outside and want to reside in Kolkata. Very few single women even if they have a job, unless married or if they don't have parents moving over to Kolkata can set up home in Kolkata on their own. This is because of the sceptical attitude people have towards singe women which can create tremendous pressure on them mentally (programme coordinator, Ranchi).

Existing laws have to change and maybe even attitudes among women; one has to be prepared to be available to the other (university teacher, Giridih).

As Lefebvre (2003b: 140) comments, the urban space allows confrontation between different strategies of inhabiting, between the global city-life and local practices that may be quite different from the ways in which the global urban is negotiated. This seems especially true of cities in the third world, like Calcutta, which is in the process of physically upscaling an ancient architecture and civic amenities, even while migrants of all classes and a floating population of commuters shape and negotiate this urbanization in their own way. Indeed, these strategies that were suggested by our respondents have directly addressed the patriarchal urban space; even when the underpinnings of patriarchy are not overtly visible the process of inhabiting that the women undertake in the city seems to reveal its subterranean existence. These strategies, or rather tools and means of action as Lefebvre rightly names them, are responses to the workings of patriarchy at minute levels, in the almost invisible daily activities of living. It is not surprising that these are not brought onto the agenda for change, because they are so minute and specific. At the same time, again, it is surprising that they do not occur on the agenda of change because the slightest acknowledgement of their existence would reveal the roots of patriarchy that spread throughout our thoughts and actions. A number of such oversights, some deliberate, some truly unapprehended, also characterized our project. Respondents have alerted us to our lapses:

> You have missed an important facet. Since single women subsist on jobs, a job is very important in her life. You could have devoted a section to jobs—whether it was easy to get and keep, get promoted, whether any sexual harassment/discrimination occurred there. There is a glass ceiling in Calcutta. Some statistics on sexual harassment could also have emerged (media professional, north Bengal).

> I am surprised that there is no separate section on jobs, whether a woman is employed or self-employed, how did she get her job (newspaper ad, website, referrals), whether her co-workers recognize her problems of living alone, whether there is any sexual harassment (36-year-old hospitality manager).

> It is a nice questionnaire but I would have liked a practical edge to it. Questions could have been on these two topics: *(i)* Survival Skills; How have girls like me improved their skills for survival? It can be karate, sweet womanly manipulation, and additional qualifications becoming Net savvy, building contacts, money management, savings schemes and assets. *(ii)* Collation of basic information: Does anyone know a really good gynae/general physician/tailor/beautician/driving instructor/broker for rented houses/diagnostic centre/assembled computer maker/car rental/PG landlady/fast food takeaway/career counsellor/spoken English instructor/feng shui instructor/weight loss clinic/counsellor for depression/blood bank/affordable boutique Living on our own we all build up a bank of information that can be invaluable and if its shared it thus keeps on growing (advertising professional, Jamshedpur).

> When introducing the questionnaire, it is important to mention that this is to build a network/helpline programme for those who migrate to Calcutta. That would have made girls feel obligated to fill up the questionnaire (programme coordinator, Ranchi).

We have recorded here what our respondents perceived as lapses on our part because these serve as indications that these are issues that are important to understand the process that we have tried to study here. Even if we have not collected narratives regarding these issues, the fact that they have occurred to individual women indicate that they have been deemed important on the specific as well as the general level by women who have had first-hand experience of the working of these issues in their daily activities. As far as our own comments on our oversights go, one of our respondents actually summed up our own feeling about the exercise: 'This survey was fun, but it's difficult for us to pen up perhaps because it asked a lot of searching questions. It was too intimate to be strictly academic. This is fine, especially the introduction. I think these findings would help a lot of women, and men too, to understand today's Indian women who are working and urban and walk their talk' (trainee advertising professional, Dhanbad).

One would like to end on a note of reflection: how to articulate these changes? It is time now to specify the question: Is it empower-ment that we desire? A classical definition of power is by Max Weber (1968): 'Power is the probability that one actor within a social rela-tion will be in a position to carry out his own will, despite resistance, regardless of the basis on which that probability rests.' Is the notion of 'power' in empowerment to be differently understood from this notion of power that we already have experienced in patriarchal social structures? It seems to be time to raise this question even while acknowledging the apparent historical absence of this sense of power in the lives of women. Feminism and the women's movements worldwide have attempted to address this lack and, simultaneously, to engage with this definition in order to rearticulate the notion of empowerment which has been conceived of as 'the process by which the powerless gain greater control over their lives: control related to both resources and ideology. The power relations that have to be transformed enmesh women's lives at multiple interlinked levels: the household, the family, the community, the market, the state' (Presser and Sen 2000: 18). England (2000) further emphasizes the relation between the two levels at which empowerment is possible by saying that 'power ... has two interacting components: objective power (economic resources, laws, institutional rules and norms held by others) and subjective power (self-efficacy and entitlement)'. She also raises another crucial question; that of the degree to which self-interest and altruism inflect empowerment. She notes that acting in one's own self-interest is enhanced by the use of power. Clarifying that 'almost all arenas of social life feature a combination of self-interest and altruism with the mixture of the two constructed in part by social factors', she claims that 'the extent to which women have an objective and subjective basis for acting to serve themselves relative to the extent to which men do' will determine the relative level of empowerment of each. But what, if anything, have we as women learnt of the acting of power upon our own lives and selves, fuelled by masculine self-interest and legitimated by patriarchal gender ideology? The degree of self-interest that marks the exercise of power as we have encountered it may very well lead us to ruminate more deeply on the nature of the empowerment that we desire.

And while we think about our desired form of empowerment, we may also note, as Sayer (2000: 185) reminds us, that because we cannot at once address the entire range across which difference operates, equality too becomes a situated concept rather than an abstract one. Classifying difference as 'biological, geographical, imposed, inherited and chosen' he implies that when we aspire for equality as a goal, we must simultaneously identify the level of equality that is desired and with respect to what. How far in practice do we wish for equality, and on whose terms?

In order to begin to engage with such questions, let me recall one of the women who responded to our survey. A 21-year-old student from Kalyani, when asked about any thoughts or feelings she had that we had not addressed in the questionnaire: 'Kolkata has given me the experience how to work or meet or behave with different kinds of people with different mentalities. I have to achieve my goal first at any cost—this is the rule of this city. But I think our result or goal is not our whole life. We have to live in this society with our feelings, values and of course our own life style.' Apparently our questions helped put her experience in the city in a particular perspective. All the elements of social life that have emerged in this study as crucial to the experience of a single woman from outside living alone in the city are contained in her words. The exposure to different people and the growing of a sense of differentiation in interacting with each, the prioritizing of goals and the hard work to achieve them while balancing other trivialities that do not exercise city people because they can be taken for granted, all of these are evident from her comments. Her realization is that these diverse experiences of the city have taught her that it is the woman's sense of her self that matters.

In her view of empowerment, Batlivala (1994) emphasizes the 'growing intrinsic capability, greater self-confidence and inner transformation of one's own consciousness that enables one to overcome external barriers to accessing resources or changing traditional ideology'. The city may be a place of opportunity, dreams, adjustments, aspirations; all these intersect to give affective and material dimensions to the experience of the city. Like all selves, the self of the woman in the city is also intersubjectively formed and dynamic. This same respondent had marked out adjustment as the most difficult thing for an outsider in the city: 'If you have an 'adjustable' mentality, you adjust anywhere, you've no problems then.' But she is also aware that 'it's our responsibility how to treat ourselves'. It is ultimately the self that emerges as concretized through this process. Whether or not it is an aspect or a consequence of empowerment, whether it is unrelated to this or implicated within it, the network of our relations with the world forms the core of our conscious existence, and is subject to change, resistance, triumph, and failure.

Turning to the more tangible outcomes to which this study alerts us, generally women take the attitude, echoed by a 21-year-old student from Durgapur, that 'the single woman from outside will have to change her nature and character spontaneous to herself and adjust with the people of the city'. She will have to identify the difference between the lived and the imagined self. We may read in this statement the adjustments underwritten by patriarchal norms governing the role of woman despite the real change in her circumstances and abilities. There are many possible ways in which this can occur. A woman may come to the city with this insight or perhaps it is the city that teaches the single woman from outside to negotiate relations with a wide variety of Others and choose which networks and communities she can be part of and how she will sustain these 'belongings'. However this occurs, the central concern of this study has been to understand the process by which the woman engages with the institution known as the city, the process which leads her to demand, or request or wish or dream that it inflect itself to her needs. Her arrival as a person, outside the home, upon the streets and in the built-up spaces of the city is an event that is made possible in a particular historical conjuncture as the result of a particular form of struggle. Has the struggle been appropriated by hegemonic social forces and has the woman fallen victim to her own emancipation? Does the endless necessity for compromise and adjustment follow as an inevitable price to be paid for the right to work away from home? Does the woman who finds a job suitable to her skills and temperament away from her hometown have to reconcile herself to insecurity, loneliness, discomfort? Are these supposed to be endured as the price of emancipation?

Our respondents have identified this apparent contradiction in their puzzlement at attitudes towards, and lack of facilities for women like themselves, in their negotiation of social pressures from various quarters. We have only tried to weave some of their narratives into a texture through these contradictions, between what women are naturally 'allowed' to do by patriarchy on the one hand and the conditions and consequences of their actions on the other are articulated and contextualized. Perhaps such articulation of first-hand experiences will begin a process of identifying areas of concern. Addressing these concerns and doing so effectively may contribute towards indicating certain directions of future change and action. Since these changes have been initiated by feminist struggle, it seems natural to think that these may find a place on feminist agendas.

The women's movement has demanded precisely the acceptance, respect and public affirmation that Parekh (2006: 1–2) identifies as the politics of recognition. The demand for recognition goes far beyond the demand for mere tolerance: it is a demand for 'acceptance, respect and even public affirmation of their differences; (some) want wider society to treat them equally with the rest; (some) go further and demand that it should also respect their differences; that is, view them as equally valid and worthy ways of organizing the relevant areas of life or leading individual or collective lives. While acceptance of dif-ferences calls for changes in the legal arrangements of society, respect for them requires changes in attitude and ways of thought'. Within that context, this study has attempted to indicate certain changes in attitude and ways of thought that are necessary if the middle-class working woman is to work and live in a globalizing urban milieu with what she would view as dignity, satisfaction and happiness. This context is shaped by feminist struggles as much as by the changing face of capital and the globalization of the economy. The interaction of various forces fashion this context and consequently the ideas and practices of gender within it. Parekh points out that though some advocates of the politics of recognition limit themselves to the issues of identity and difference, there is no doubt in the minds of others that this cannot be dissociated from wider economic and political structures. The changes in the economic structure and the gains of the movement for women's equality and emancipation have prob-lematized the ideas of gender identity and difference, and some of the issues that have arisen have been testified to by respondents in this study. As Parekh points out, this is not possible 'without the neces-sary freedom of self-determination, a climate conducive to diversity, material resources and opportunities, suitable legal arrangements ... and all these call for a profound changes in all areas of life' (ibid.: 2). These demands and wishes also find an echo in the voices of the women we have heard in this survey. Their voices have indicated to us the need for as well as the scope and nature of, such changes as Parekh calls 'profound'.

Our study has been squarely located in a city in the developing world, and is hence marked by the history of the transformation of capital from colonial to an apparent 'national' and then as appendage to a global variety. We have considered patriarchal gender relations within this changing context. There is a sense of the loss of tradi-tion and the proliferation of the risks of modernity that accompany thinking about and representation of such change. And there is also the dynamic space of the city, moving from the seed of colony to an outpost of empire to the symbol of nationalist resurgence until the present conjuncture in which it is becoming a nodal point for trans-national global capital. Placed at the centre of capitalist expansion in the West, Lefebvre (2003c) hoped for the possibility of a relationship between the fragmented space (in the present, where homogeneity no longer reigns) and the multiple networks that are activated against fragmentation and re-establish, if not a rational unity, at least a (lost?) homogeneity. But desiring homogeneity after we have indicated and established difference is a contradiction in terms.

This leads us to ask whether the city has not changed at all as a result of the presence, needs and contributions of the women who have come here from the outside. Have the contradictions that Lefebvre indicates, the differences that undercut homogeneity, even as a desire, shown themselves in the contours of the city and its relation to the women from outside who now inhabit it? The hospitality manager who lives in the rented flat in Garia[2] senses a change in her locality; after having shown all her identification papers to her landlord when she first came to stay as a single woman, she now feels, 'Nowadays things are pretty much fine because the profile of the neighbourhood has changed, and young families hardly bother about single women living alone, especially if the wives are also working.' The advertising professional from Jamshedpur, who has now moved out of the Bagha Jatin PG[3] and lives in a rented flat with another friend in a different locality, also has noticed the change in her old PG locality:

> Now even Bagha Jatin has an Ekta Heights and a Citi Financials and resident teenage girls whose moms never stepped out of their *chapaa* (printed) saris and *bori khopas* (hair tied back into buns) are dressed in hot pink westerns with cell phones and go for dates at Dakshinapan and beyond.

This means that more and more factories in this once industrial suburb are shutting down finally, and the land on which they were built being handed over to promoters who are building expensive luxury apartments on them. We have earlier (see Chapter 3) considered this process in detail. Read in conjunction with the information provided in Appendices 1 and 2, we will recognize in this comment the aftermath of the death of the small scale industries in the area south of Jadavpur, the reclamation of the land on which these industries, now closed, were housed as spaces for high-cost state of-the-art housing, creating even more pressure on the already fragile and unplanned infrastructure of these areas once known as 'colonies' (see Chapter 4): the example of Ekta Heights that our respondent gave. For her, this change means a change in the neighbourhood, translating into perhaps a change in the attitude that will welcome women from outside who come to live there. There is no avoiding the fact that such a change will not be beneficial to all women or even to all persons, men or women, especially if they are outsiders seeking a place to stay. As this study drew to a close, a friend, who had recently acquired a rented flat in Bijoygarh[4] off Jadavpur, had this experience to narrate about her finding a house. She lives in north Calcutta, but the school where she works is in the south. She is not exactly an outsider to the city, but her flatmate is. Contrary to what we had been told by the programme coordinator from Ranchi, it was not difficult for these two women to find a place to rent. And why is this? There are, according to my friend two reasons: One, of course, is the fact that this locality has for a long time housed many women who are here to study or work: their distinctive lifestyles have made some impact upon the environment of the lower middle-class and middle-class locality that Bijoygarh is. Besides, the building of new apartment complexes have also contributed to a change in the nature of the locality, in a manner similar to the change wrought by Ekta Heights, which our respondent noted.

The other part of the story is sobering: a number of landlords were eager to rent out their places to two single young Bengali girls (without, let us note, the attendant fear of lesbianism) because they did not want to rent to 'Chowmeins': men and women from the Northeast. The irony is that this being a relatively cheap area to live in, with easy access to the Metro and to 8B bus stand (see Figure A2.1) as well as close to Jadavpur University, it has been home to a number of Northeastern students and young people who have recently begun to work in the city. Not all landlords are willing to rent out to Northeastern men and women: we have, in the course of this survey, seen what happens when these men and women are forced to live in a hostile neighbourhood. In the circumstances, Bijoygarh used to be a safe place, with relatively few complications for these men and women from the Northeastern states. But the experience of the two single women seeking a rented place indicates that landlords in the area are now less suspicious of women staying alone. This is, however, accompanied by a narrowing of attitudes to ethnicity: even while conditions seem to have changed, becoming favourable to Bengali women looking for a place to stay, it has simultaneously become worse for men and women from another part of India.

Here we may indicate a major lacuna in our survey: not one of the women who revealed her name (this was optional) as she filled in the questionnaire could be identified as belonging to minority religious communities. Those who participated in the discussions at the various hostels, messes and PG facilities were not required to record their names on tape. Not one of them referred to their religion, either. A question about religion was not a part of the survey question-naire. By this omission, we may have erred on the side of political correctness; we may have spoken to and recorded the responses of many more women from different religious communities without knowing it. But this absence must be recorded such that this fact is taken cognizance of if any description or insight yielded by this study is used in future projects. There may be arguments in support of this outcome; but when ethnicity, religion and caste can clearly be seen as inflecting gender as an analytical category, such an omission must be criticized. So we can only gesture in the final stage of this project, to difference and its consequences in daily living practices in perceptions of self. This story of the general attitude of exclusion towards the Northeastern men and women, coming as it does when the project is being wound up, seems to be another faltering step towards understanding one's own changing habitation of self in a plural society as much as it purports to understand other women's habitation of self and city.

The Telegraph, Saturday, October 28, 2007, carried a report stating that once working women, who had given their household duties priority over their careers because they felt that they would not be able to manage homes as well as the demands of working outside, are now being sought after by certain industries like retail or informa-tion technology. These industries want them to work from home. There is no reason why manufacturing units in the small scale sector which populated the suburbs beyond Jadavpur will restart operations. This is matched by the growth of the technopoles along the Eastern

Metropolitan Bypass, where 'new' information and electronics-based industries are gathering strength. The workforce that feeds these industries now seeks and finds housing in the areas where earlier a different kind of industry flourished: the area south of Jadavpur. An increasing number of the local residents who have been living here for a long time have delinked their daily living from these now closed factories and found other means of income. Perhaps this is good news for women coming from outside the city and looking for cheap PGs in the area, or maybe now the demand for PGs will exceed the supply and the cost of accommodation for these women will also go up. These are major changes which had begun ten years ago, but are now becoming visible in the form of widening gulfs between those who live in Ekta Heights and those who live around its compound walls.

There is no reason to suppose that jobs for women skilled in certain areas will shrink. We can say at once that these are not isolated facts that may be seen as 'good' or 'bad' in themselves. One order of production and its organization of social space is now emerging from another. The chilling fact is that this kind of 'progress' implies a changing neighbourhood through the construction of highrises and young working couples buying high-cost flats on the closest fringes of the city. The kind of development that has facilitated the flourishing of women's accommodation in these areas is related indirectly to the kinds of industries that have created a need for women's skills. These taken together have caused a transformation of urban space and means of production. Lefebvre (2003c: 211), points out that the mode of production organizes society and social space inhabited by the occupants of the city. The third world city seems to be organized by more than just the means of production: time and space are fought over, and occupation, literally and figuratively, is a continuous issue fuelled by population pressure and lack of amenities. This is the 'scape' of a city that is growing by its own logic, where governments have not completely succeeded even when they have intervened to clear the roads of hawkers or food-stalls, move squatters from beside railway lines. Each class has its own Paris, according to Lefebvre, and they are not spatially but symbolically demarcated; they exist in layers, one within, upon, between the other. And a similar thing happens in any city, the city of the pavement dweller is different from the city of the upper-class householder, with all the layers of class difference and area-wise religious or other community concentrations in between. Hence it is not a single city that we inhabit at any given time, but one which is multilayered. The relative alignments of these layers must certainly be different in a first world city like Paris, where Lefebvre's theory is located, and in a third world city like Kolkata where we have found his concepts, naturally, in need of amendment. The layers of the city both as symbol and as material space are deeply implicated within one another rather than being neatly arranged in concentric circles. But the corresponding fact is that the multi-layered nature of the city is a visible reality and passing between these layers is as simple as walking to the bus stop. It sounds contradictory to say that the layers are not physically but materially separate. We have discussed in Chapters 4, 5 and 7 the means and procedures of access to these different layers of social space, dependent on the same factor as anywhere else: affordability. We have tried to show their special implications for women who have to traverse and live within them, as they provide a mix of 'safety' and 'threat' for the 'outsider'.

The binaries of centrality and marginality do not serve to explain these spatial distinctions, and as the women who came from upper middle-class homes into lower middle-class PG areas have related, class itself is relative and fractured in the city. The class of the woman from outside is no longer determined by the class of the family she has left behind. Rather, inasmuch as she has proved herself capable, whether it is academically or through some acquired skill or through natural efficiency or some other quality or resource that is useful to the burgeoning of a particular kind of capital, the woman can apparently construct her own class position. It may articulate itself symbolically in the nature of her employment and the area where she can afford to live. The city provides enough anonymity for the achievement of this task. That is not to say that it will unfailingly treat the woman with sympathy when like her unconventional sexual preference, her lower-class background is revealed, simply because cities are assumed to be sophisticated and progressive.

The changing relations of production in the southern part of Kolkata, which also happens to be very popular for providing cheap accommodation for women from outside, is undergoing a movement beyond a particular class. This is not in any way related to the inhabitants of these areas but to 'outsiders' to the neighbourhood; the area is being built up in order to accommodate those who will raise its tone, its standard of living; and thereby, its perception in the class-divided cityscape. In other words, through the indirect agencies of the very women who found space to stay here cheaply, of the industries that provided them with jobs that led them to migrate to the city, the industries that were locked out and so forced the sale of factory land for highrises, and simultaneously increased the number of homes that were forced to take in boarders to supplement vanished income, the city which contains these diverse set of people is changing. The process outlined here connects the people through the city: their locations, professions and perceptions of self are also changing.

And so, as the story of the landlords' preference for (even?) female Bengali tenants over Northeastern ones of either sex shows, enhanced facilities for one set of participants in this change does not necessarily connote either general well-being or depression across the range of people and processes that are consequent upon it or affected by it. For example, a more accommodating attitude towards single women living alone in the city will not necessarily result in increased facility for visibly marginal groups in general. This leads one to conclude that the fulfilment on the functional and attitudinal level of the demands made by women as a homogeneous group upon both state and society, does not necessarily ensure increased tolerance for cohabitation, let alone acceptance, respect and public affirmation of lives and lifestyles practiced by all people who are identifiably different, within the hegemonic socio-economic structure. Women, as we have seen, may have recorded some hard-won gains: but have these been at the cost of others who are markedly different, in terms of class and ethnicity? Should women then cease to increase the scope of their actions such that what England (2000) would call their self-interest will be furthered? Or should they consider the degree to which they will accept that feminist demands are humanist only in the narrow sense that women are also part of the human race? Perhaps we can say that the acknowledgement of the humanity of women was a first and crucial step towards a larger goal: a step that still has not been fully taken. Even so, the consequences of this fledgling step are becoming evident. So our responsibility is to think about the preparations we must take to continue in the direction of the humane. Can woman as category remain the sole focus of our thought, action and commitment? How shall we envisage the future?

We cannot deny that foundations for process of women's 'selfing the city' had been laid with the oldest respondents who came thirty years ago, and has proceeded apace even while this book was in the throes of production. It may not be the 'older' women who have begun to take the initiative to form networks and communities, but the 'younger' women who, though young in years, are now older than their age in terms of experience. Can we argue that this too is a gift of the city? Let us take the case of the content writer from Durgapur, 23 years old, who wishes to install her 'mom in place of her khadoos landlady'. She and her roommates seem young enough to take this as a game. When asked how she has helped any woman like her from outside the city, with city living, she replies, 'I help my roomies all the time to make life hell for khadoos landlady and they return the favour.' But though she had been in Kolkata less than 365 days when she answered the questionnaire, by her own admission, city life had already taught her a few hard lessons. Away from home, she has realized that now she lacks 'enough money to spend on the happening places in the city, giving treats and so on. So much money goes to the PG landlady. And my salary isn't enough to maintain the kind of life style I had at home.'

This is just an obvious example of 'growing up' as an independent city woman. If we want an example that appears more serious, then we may remember that in the current sample, as we have seen in Chapters 5 and 6, a number of women have clearly indicated their desire to take on the responsibility of getting other younger female relatives over, to go through the same experience that they themselves have gone through, only this time round, they are there to provide the security of accommodation, counselling and the support system that they had themselves lacked. But the experiences and the insights that they have earned are yet to be made available to others like them immediately outside their close circle. Social realities seem responsible for this; emancipatory movements have enabled women to work, instilled in them the desire to move out of known and familiar locations to do so, appointed them on jobs that have irregular hours: all steps in the direction charted out by the ideology of the women's movement; but here, as in most other spheres, women walk this path negotiating conflicts in their lives and their choices. Thus, after making the most difficult adjustments and negotiations, women look upon their feats in silent and personal satisfaction—not a meagre return by any means—but they are still reluctant to make this unique experience a part of the general process of social change by highlighting their struggles and triumphs, making it part of social knowledge by sharing them out over a wider circle, and part of 'normal' sociability wherein the dilemma not complaining about her son's unwelcome advances to the landlady in order to keep a suitable PG accommodation, need not arise.

These questions have arisen in conjunction with the changing contours of urban space. We have argued above that this is fuelled by the changing patterns of production, which include the changes in the gender composition of the workforce. In relation to productive work is fashioned our consciousness of the personal and our ideas of inner life and self. This survey is a set of questions to be written up; it has also been, as some of the resource persons, all outsiders to the city themselves, put it, an adventure, a process of making friends, and an attempt to bring the unrecorded (female) heroics of 'selfing' the city to common notice. Patriarchy had denied/shielded women from work and its effects, good and ill, until the pressure of capital brought women into the sphere of paid work beyond the domestic even while the women's movement demanded the rights that women as workers ought to enjoy, whether at home or in the workplace or in the larger public or more intimate private sphere. However, the various impacts of this process are now visible in the knots and rents in the social fabric that have resulted from the contradictions between women's right to work and society's providing them with conditions wherein these rights could have some effect including the economic upon their lives.

We shall not pause to explore the nature of paid work which can bring more than an economic wage in the form of intangible confidence, self-sufficiency, independence. We shall not ask how domestic work, even waged, does not seem to provide the same comforts even if it can provide economic independence. We shall not even ask the basic question about the difference between 'work' and domestic work. We shall only note that the primary difficulty is represented by sweeping these contradictions under the carpet of normalcy. This difficulty is constructed by the refusal of a patriarchal gender organization to acknowledge the changed conditions under which women live, and the conflicts that arise between their changed self-definition and the gender roles that they are expected to live by. The reason why Lefebvre, as a thinker, has been so crucial to our project is because his work attempts to provide the conscious and unconscious crafted as a result of these changed and changing relations with, literally, a habitation.

It is true that understanding the world, as Marx put it so pithily, may remain just that: an understanding that is not used to make change. Though we cannot claim any great breadth of philosophical conception as Lefebvre describes it, we have attempted to apply the method he has outlined to articulate his conceptual frame to the realities of our location, in order to explore this question: for how long can society's demand for submissive, feminine 'stay at home' women be forced upon those who have actively done just the opposite? Women working outside the home may be the cause of middle-class upward mobility and status as modern and emancipated, but the women we have here considered come from smaller towns and cities, suburbs and villages, where their venturing into the city is still looked upon as a step forward, which they often have to fight to justify. After having won that battle, begins the one that we have attempted to share with them here: the battle to become a part of the city, building a life from scratch without conventional support bases or networks, and perceived as outsiders. We have studied this experience and the consequences it must have on social norms. The women who have shared their experiences with us have themselves tried to suggest ways of socializing those consequences such that we can strive towards a more just and equitable social space.

This might be an appropriate note on which to end this chapter, except that there is still another variety of experience that we have encountered in the course of the survey that might make us pause to think in a different way. It arises out of a condition that has been thus far associated with men, and quite admiringly: all the romantic heroes of fiction are such individuals, part of whose charm lies in the fact that they cannot remain housebound, they cannot settle and be constrained by domesticity. Does this remain as romantic and as acceptable when the same condition is feminized?

My mother had a transferable job: she used to stay in Bolpur first, when I was young, then she got transferred to Bardhaman. Now there are three rooms in this house; parents have one, my brother and his wife have the other and there is another small one, which they are saying is the study. So where is my room? They are pressurizing me to get married; my parents don't want this, they think I should finish my studies and earn. The people in small towns are different, they will interfere, but in Kolkata your area of operation may be small, but still you can mingle with the crowd; now I feel rootless, I don't feel at home, not here not in Shantiniketan.

Cannot think of any place as home—when I am able to have a house of my own, from the money I have earned myself, then that will be my home (25-year-old student).

Does this feeling encapsulate the basic homelessness of the Indian woman? Is she still taught that her home is not her own, it either belongs to her parents or to her husband, and her role in both is to be subservient to the will of others, mainly men? Does the male sibling always have the greater right in the natal home? Is the feeling of belonging not a state of mind? One of our respondents defined home as 'a place where I can sleep in peace'. Another defined it as 'a place where my mother is'. The responses to the question 'Which place do you call "home" and why?' were varied:

With most women like us, we have homes in plural. My room in my parents' flat, my first childhood home, and this rented place. The 1st, because it is ready and waiting for me, 2nd, because I dream of it still though we left it when I was 11, and 3rd, because I live my own way here (advertising professional from Jamshedpur).

My home is the home of my friend Manorama. They had the tendency to make me one of the family right from the start, but then there is a coriander leaf savoury that is made in their house which is exactly like the same savoury made in our house in Asansol (student and media freelancer, Asansol).

Neither of these definitions is limited to the purely geographical; and this leads us to wonder whether the opening of the doors to the inner house, evocatively constructed on celluloid by Satyajit Ray's *Gharey Bairey*, that was mentioned earlier, has indeed led women into the outer world and exposed them to all the vagaries of patriarchy including the ennui and angst of the public space that were till recently strictly male preserves. Or are we reading the situation from behind gendered lenses: ennui was a human rather than a male condition, and we did not associate it with women earlier because women had not the experience of expressing their ennui, taking it as natural to their lot to be sequestered and hence bored?

The city has given us many things that we as women who have come to it from the outside and succeeded in staying on have revelled in, but perhaps what we are finally left with is this sense of homelessness even as we are conscious of our achievements, knowing that we have achieved these heights within a form of psycho-social organization that has used both men and women, hierarchizing them and splitting them from being complete human beings into becoming gender roles, fixed or mobile. As the student from Bolpur says, 'I do not think of myself as completely secure anywhere, let alone Kolkata. For complete security we will have to empower ourselves.' From many aspects of this survey, arises this sense of unbelonging, even in the very depths of satisfaction, joy and fulfilment: for maybe the woman has acquired the ability to draw in her reserves of courage and remain calm in the face of all odds, but cannot forget that she is a woman in a patriarchal space which can articulate itself to her being only through her own struggle to change it.

Life has its own peculiar demands. The word 'relationship' expresses a lot of what it entails, though not all of it. I have left much of these relationships back in my hometown, I think—this vacuum, this loneliness cannot be easily overlooked. In the midst of all the progress and success, or in the midst of all the pressures of daily living, this loneliness cannot be wiped out from your mind. Many people know things, understand me, try to convey many things to me, but no one can share this space of loneliness because perhaps it is almost impossible to do so.

Walking alone in the crowded streets of the city,

I saw a splintered labyrinth [it was London]; I saw, close up, unending eyes watching themselves in me as in a mirror; I saw all the mirrors on the earth and none of them reflected me; I saw in a backyard of Soler Street the same tiles that thirty years before I had seen in the entrance of a house in Fray Bentos (Borges, 1973).

London, the first city of the industrialized capitalist world; the urban space in which for thirty-odd years, trapped in a strange bourgeois labyrinth, in wretched poverty, lived the man who diagnosed, even then, the cityscape of the future, where 'man is at last compelled to face with sober sense, his real conditions of life, and his relations with his kind' (ibid.). But who is this man on whom sober sense has now dawned, the I who walks the streets of this city? For us, women who come to the city from outside, we recognize another I; she is the woman who arrives, much after the supposed dawning of man's sober sense, when the city itself dominates all. And she too faces the real conditions of her life, and her relations with her kind.

Like many of us before her, she too comes to that splintered labyrinth that is the city and its endless, multiple reflections of our selves that we have discovered in its back alleys and cemeteries, its vegetable markets and tramlines, in the eyes of everyone we meet. They stare at us for are we, women, supposed to walk here alone? Is this our city?

It consists of spaces that we have appropriated and engaged with, the spaces of our poiesis, the spaces of our selves among all that we cherish the most. In every mirror that the city holds up, we see our faces: but 'none of them reflected me', because we have forever changed, life in the city has forever changed us, and perhaps will continue to do so. As we walk in the city, we walk towards a future through the years.

Into another city. A changed city. Changed, if we have the resources and the will to change it.

NOTES

[1]   We might note that this is an obvious solution, absent earlier, which is now being done.

[2]   See Figures A2.2 and A2.8.

[3]   See Figure A2.8.

[4]   See Figures A2.3 and A2.4.

WORKS CITED

Bat-Ami, Bar On. 2008. 'From Hegelian Terror to Everyday Courage', in P. DesAustels and R. Wishnant, eds, *Global Feminist Ethics*, London: Rowman and Littlefield.

Banerjee, Arpita. 2011. 'Mobilities and Spaces: Gendered Dimensions of Migration in Urban India', in S. Raju and K. Lahiri-Dutt, eds, *Doing Gender Doing Geography: Emerging Research in India*, New Delhi: Routledge: 89–109.

Batlivala, S. 1994. 'The Meaning of Women's Empowerment: New Concepts from Action', in G. Sen, A. German, and C. Lincoln, eds, *Health, Empowerment and Rights: Population Policy Reconsidered*, Cambridge: Harvard University Press.

Borges, J.G. 1973. *The Aleph and Other Stories (1933–1939)*, trans. J.L. Borges, Adolfo Bioy Casares and Norman Thomas de Giovanni, London: Picador: 11–30.

Butler, J. 1990. *Gender Trouble: Feminism and the Subversion of Identity*, New York: Routledge.

Braidotti, Rosi. 1994. *Nomadic Subjects: Embodiment and Sexual Difference in Contemporary Feminist Theory*, New York: Columbia University Press.

England, Paula. 2000. 'Conceptualising Women's Empowerment in Countries of the North', in P. Presser and G. Sen eds, *Women's Empowerment and Demographic Processes: Moving Beyond Cairo*, New Delhi: Oxford University Press.

Featherstone, M. 1995. *Undoing Culture: Globalisation, Postmodernism and Identity*, London: SAGE Publications.

Heidegger, Martin. 1971. 'Poetically Man Dwells', in *Poetry, Language, Thought*, trans. Albert Hofstader, New York: Harper and Row: 213–29.

Heinämaa, Sara. 1997. 'Woman–Nature, Product, Style? Rethinking the Foundation of Feminist Philosophy of Science', in Lynn Hankinson Nelson and Jack Nelson, eds, *Feminism, Science and the Philosophy of Science*, Dordrecht: Kluwer: 289–308.

Lefebvre, Henri. [1966] 2003a. 'Preface'. *L'habitat pavillonaire*', in S. Elden, E. Lebas and E. Kofman, eds, *Key Writings*, Athlone Contemporary European Thinkers Series, London: Continuum: 121–35.

———. [1970] 2003b. 'Levels and Dimensions', in S. Elden, E. Lebas and E. Kofman, eds, *Key Writings*, Athlone Contemporary European Thinkers Series, London: Continuum: 136–50.

———. [1986] 2003c. 'Preface to the New Edition, *The Production of Space*', in S. Elden, E. Lebas and E. Kofman, eds, *Key Writings*, Athlone Contemporary European Thinkers Series, London: Continuum Elden: 206–13.

McRobbie, A. 1982. 'The Politics of Feminist Research: Between Talk, Text and Action', *Feminist Review* 12: 46–57.

Newman, D.M., and Grauerholz, E. 2002. *Sociology of Families*, Newbury Park, Ca: Pine Forge Press.

Parekh, B. [2000] 2006. *Rethinking Multiculturalism Cultural Diversity and Political Theory*, London: Palgrave-Macmillan.

Presser, P., and G. Sen, eds. 2000. 'Women's Empowerment and Demographic Processes: Laying the Groundwork', in *Women's Empowerment and Demographic Processes: Moving Beyond Cairo*, New Delhi: Oxford University Press.

Raju, S., and A. Banerjee. 2009. 'Gendered Mobility: Women Migrants and Work in Urban India', *Economic and Political Weekly* 44, 8 (July 11): 115–23.

Sayer, Andrew. 2000. *Realism and Social Science*, London: SAGE Publications.

Weber, M. [1922] 1968. *Economy and Society: An Outline of Interpretive Sociology*, trans. E. Shils and M. Rheinstein, New York: Simon & Schuster.

The Survey

SELFING THE CITY: GENDER AND URBAN SPACE (2004–07)

Profile of respondents

I. Language of response: English
   a. General occupation: Working

Age range	No. of respondents
Up to 19	1
20–29	44
30–39	17
40–49	5
50–59	3
60 plus	4
Total	74

   b. General occupation: Student

Age range	No. of respondents
Up to 19	12
19–29	18
Total	30

II. Language of response: Bangla and Hindi
   a. General occupation: Working

Age range	No. of respondents
Up to 19	
20–29	13
30–39	
40–49	2
50–59	
60 plus	1
Total	16

b. General occupation: Student

Age range	No. of respondents
Up to 19	2
20–29	14
Total	16

History of the City

- Established in the late seventeenth century by Job Charnock, an agent of the East India Company, amalgamating three villages, Gobindopur, Sutanuti and Kalikata after the East India Company's factory at Hooghly was destroyed. The British leased the land from the Sabarna Raichaudhuris at Rs. 1,300 annually, and built Fort William.
- At the end of the fifteenth century, a reference to Kolkata was found in the narrative *Manasa Mangal* written by Bipradas. The character of *Chand Saudagar* in the narrative paid a visit to Kalighat to offer puja to the Goddess Kali on the way to Saptagram.
- When the Portugese first began to frequent Bengal about the year 1530, the two great centres of trade were Chittagong and Saptagram.
- In *Ain-i-Akbari*, a work written in 1596 by Abul Fazal in the court of Emperor Akbar, a reference to Calcutta is noticed under the Government of Satgaon (Saptagram).
- **1690:** August, Job Charnock, an agent of East India Company (established 1600) settles in the village of Sutanutee.
- **1693:** Charnock died.
- **1696:** Fort at Calcutta Factory commenced.
- **1698:** East India Co. bought three villages (Sutanuti, Kolkata, Gobindapur) from local landlord Sabarna Chowdhury.
- **1699:** East India Company started developing Calcutta as a Presidency city.
- **1715:** British people completed building the Old Fort.

- **1717:** The Mughal emperor Farrukh-Siyar granted the East India Company trading privileges in return for a yearly payment of 3,000 rupees.
- **1726:** A royal charter established the Mayor's Court with judicial functions.
- **August 12, 1726:** The East India Company was granted the *diwani* of Bengal, which gave them the right to collect taxes and imposed a moral obligation to provide civic services.
- **1727:** Following the orders of King George I, a civil court was set up. The city corporation was established and Hallwell became the first mayor of the city.
- **1756:** Alivardi Khan died and Siraj-ud-Dawlla (Mirza Muhammad) became the Nawab of Bengal. Siraj-ud-Dawlla attacked and captured Calcutta. He changed the name of the city to Alinagar.
- **1765:** Clive took Bengal, Bihar and Orissa from Badsha Alam II (Delhi) with an agreement of paying excises.
- **1772:** Calcutta became the capital of British India when the first Governor General, Warren Hastings, transferred all important offices to the city from Murshidabad.
- **1773:** A conservancy system and police force were set up, governed by the Collector (British administrative official who 'collected' revenue).
- **1775:** Nandakumar, a local landlord was hung in a false allegation when he accused Warren Hastings of corruption.
- **1794:** Justices of the Peace were appointed.
- **1773–1800:** Old Fort shifted to present site of Fort William. The city grew from north to south, including the salt water areas in the east and stretching up to the Sunderbans. The Chitpore Road connected the north to the south and formed a spine for the city. The area around the Kalighat temple was settled.
- **1800:** The city's population was 600,000.
- **1803:** Transformed from a mercantile complex into a colonial city, with 33 bathing ghats constructed along the Ganges.

- **1814:** A lottery commission set up, which funded the building of north-south arterial roads, tanks and squares.
- **1850:** Kolkata only river port in India.
- **1854:** Setting up of the Howrah rail terminus and development of jute and iron works in the Howrah area.
- **1890:** Increase of industries outside Kolkata, setting up of the Kidderpore docks.
- **1911:** Setting up of the Calcutta Improvement Trust.
- **1921:** King Edward VIII inaugurated the Victoria Memorial building.
- **1870–1921:** Setting up of the General Post Office, development of the Chowringhee-Dalhousie area where the offices are located, renovation of Writers' Buildings from which the bureaucracy functioned, establishing of Victoria Memorial, New Market and the Indian Museum. Growth areas in this period: Tollygunge, Maniktala, Kankurgachi, Phoolbagan, Ultadanga, Entally, Paddapukur, Baghbajaar.
- **1850–1930:** Setting up of a pontoon bridge across the Hooghly, heavy engineering industry began in tandem with the development of the railways at Howrah.
- **1941:** Construction of the Howrah Bridge; census gave the population as 21,08,891.
- **1966:** Basic Development Plan for the city.
- **1979:** Calcutta Metropolitan Development Authority designated as the statutory Planning and Development Authority for the Calcutta Metropolitan Area under the Town and Country (Planning and Development) Act of 1979. Development of East Calcutta (647 acres) and Baishnabghata south of Jadavpur (297 acres).
- **1982:** Eastern Metropolitan bypass became operational.
- **1984:** Metro, the first underground railway in India, started from Tollygunge to Esplanade 36 km of tracks of the circular railway became operational.
- **1990 onwards:** The satellite township Rajarhat (3,075 ha) was planned for a population of 7.5 lakhs; 100 ha of land at Sector V at Salt Lake was earmarked for industrial use.

> • **2001:** Calcutta was officially renamed 'Kolkata' from 1st of
> January.
>
> *Sources:* 1. Official website of the Kolkata Corporation.
> 2. Kolkata Metropolitan Development Authority
>   Presentation, 2004, "Chronology of Planning and
>   Devlopment Activities in Kolkata".
> 3. http://www.calcuttaweb.com/history.shtml
> Prepared by Angana Mookerjee, Research Fellow, University with
> Potential for Excellence Programme (Phase II), Jadavpur University.

Figure A2.1 Calcutta: A condensed civic history

BASIC STATISTICS

Location: longitude: 88° 30'E latitude: 22° 33' N.

Altitude: 9 mt (30 feet) [from the mean sea level]

Climate: Maximum temperature rises during the summer months
of May–June up to 24–42°C and the minimum temperature falls
during winter months of December–January up to 8–26°C on an
average. Climate is humid varying from 85–65 during the summer
and exceeding by pleasant in winter. From June to September average rainfall in Kolkata is 158 cm.

Area:

Old Kolkata Boundaries:

Sutanuti—Chitpur, Baghbazar, Sobhabazar and Hatkhola.
Kolikata—Dharmatala, Bowbazar, Simla, Janbazar.
Gobindapur—Hastings, Maidan and Bhowanipur

New Kolkata Boundaries:

North—Sinthi, Cossipore and Gughudanga
South—Tollygunge, Khidderpore and Behala
East—Salt Lake, Beliaghata and Topsia
West—Hooghly River

Greater Kolkata: Baruipur to Bansberia and Kalyani to Budge Budge.
Area in kilometers: 1,480 sq. km. (London 1,580 sq. km.) 185 sq. km. is within Corporation Area.
Population (2011 census): 4,486,679 (Mumbai: 12,478,447).
Density of Population: 24,000/ sq. km. (Mumbai 20,694/ sq. km).
Ratio of Population: Male: 1,000; Female: 956.
Literacy Rate: 81.31%.
Mother Tongues: Bengali 55%, Hindi 20%, English 10%, Others 15%.
Position: 7th largest city of India in area and population.

Prepared by Angana Mookerjee from Official website of the Kolkata Corporation (https://www.kmcgov.in/KMCPortal/jsp/ KMCAboutKolkataHome.jsp)

Figure A2.2 Kolkata city and suburbs

Source: Maps of India. ©2014 www.mapsofindia.com. Reproduced by permission from mapsofindia, Compare Infobase, New Delhi.

This figure is not to scale. It does not represent any authentic national or international boundaries and is used for illustrative purposes only.

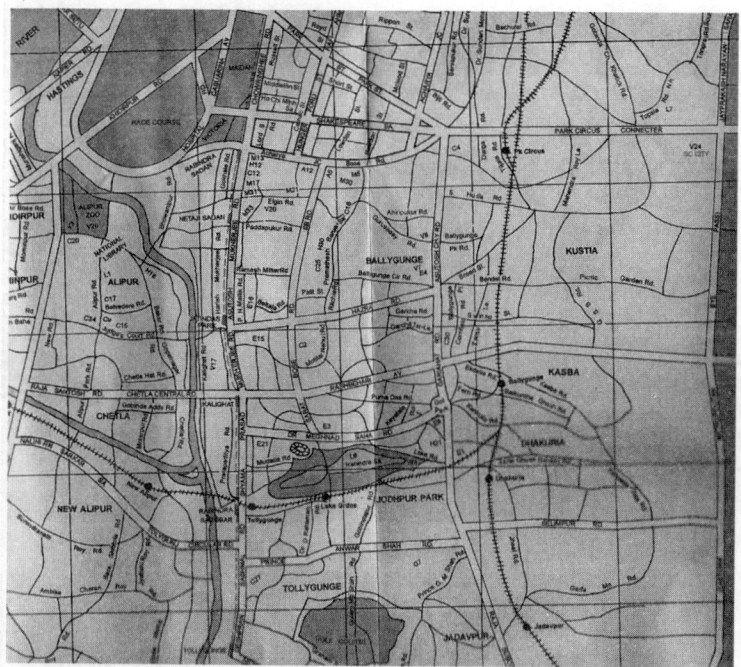

Figure A2.3 Calcutta South, Park Street to Tollygunge

Source: Calcuttaweb, maps of Kolkata/Calcutta. ©2001 Calcuttaweb.com. Reproduced by permission from mapsofindia, Compare Infobase, New Delhi.

This figure is not to scale. It does not represent any authentic national or international boundaries and is used for illustrative purposes only.

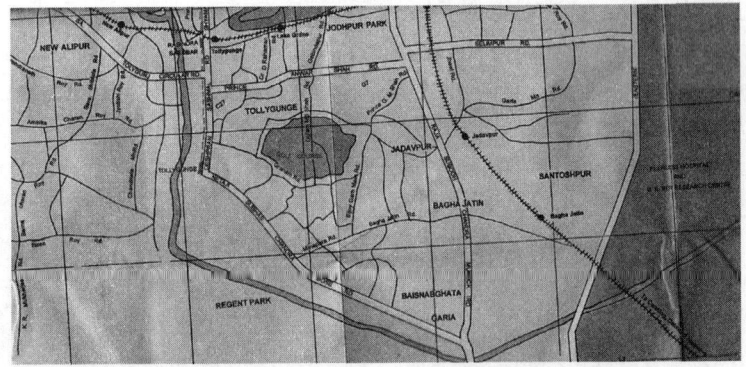

Figure A2.4 Kolkata south of Jodhpur Park

Source: Calcuttaweb, maps of Kolkata/Calcutta. ©2001 Calcuttaweb. com. Reproduced by permission from mapsofindia, Compare Infobase, New Delhi.

This figure is not to scale. It does not represent any authentic national or international boundaries and is used for illustrative purposes only.

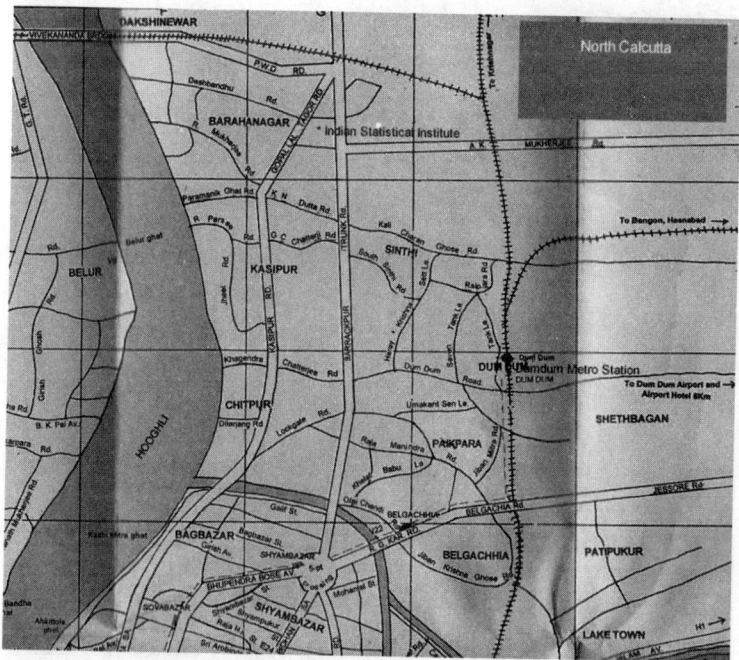

Figure A2.5 Kolkata—North (Shyambazar to Dakshineswar)

Source: Calcuttaweb, maps of Calcutta/Kolkata. ©2001 Calcuttaweb. com. Reproduced by permission from mapsofindia, Compare Infobase, New Delhi.

This figure is not to scale. It does not represent any authentic national or international boundaries and is used for illustrative purposes only.

Figure A2.6 Kolkata—North Central (Entally to Bagbazar)

Source: Calcuttaweb maps of Calcutta/Kolkata. ©2001 Calcuttaweb.com.
Reproduced by permission from mapsofindia, Compare Infobase, New Delhi.

Notes:

V22	Pareshnath Jain Temple	E11	Circarina Theatre
E24	Radha Cinema Hall	E12	Kashi Viswanath Mancha (Theatre)
E14	Star Theatre	L3	Bidhan Sishu Udyan (Childrens Park)
E13	Rang Mahal Theatre	L5	Central Park(Salt Lake)
E10	Biswarupa Theatre	L6	Mahajati Sadan

This figure is not to scale. It does not represent any authentic national or
international boundaries and is used for illustrative purposes only.

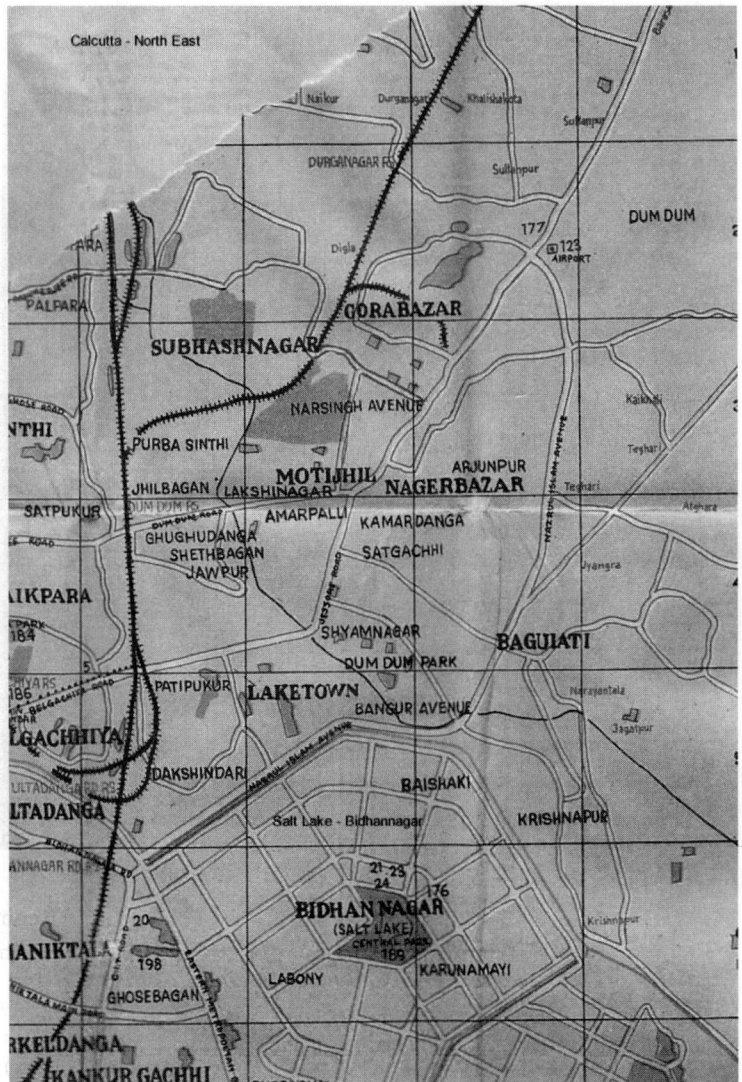

Figure A2.7 Calcutta North-East

Source: Calcuttaweb maps of Kolkata/Calcutta. ©2001 Calcuttaweb.com.
Reproduced by permission from mapsofindia, Compare Infobase, New Delhi.

This figure is not to scale. It does not represent any authentic national or
international boundaries and is used for illustrative purposes only.

Figure A2.8 Salt Lake City guide map

Source: Calcuttaweb maps of Calcutta/Kolkata. ©2001 Calcuttaweb. com. Reproduced by permission from mapsofindia, Compare Infobase, New Delhi.

This figure is not to scale. It does not represent any authentic national or international boundaries and is used for illustrative purposes only.

Post-Partition Refugee Settlement in South Calcutta

BRIEF FACT SHEET AND BIBLIOGRAPHY

- 'More than 3 million Hindus may have migrated from East Pakistan following the Partition of British India in 1947' (Heitzman and Warden 1989).
- Colonies were set up within the area under the jurisdiction of the Calcutta Corporation in the southeast part of Calcutta.
- Areas comprising the southeast under the Calcutta Metropolitan Development Authority: Jadavpur, Tollygunge, Kasba, Santoshpur.
- Basic Development Plan for the city, 1966: 'city in crisis'. Externally imposed urbanization by colonizers, delinked from rural areas. The city stretched in the 1940s. The famine of 1943 and ensuing illness led to migration to the city. The estimate of the loss of lives due to famine and related causes varies between 1.5 and 4 million (Dyson and Maharatna 1991).
- The second large refugee movement into the city followed Partition: 25 percent of the population of the urban agglomeration named Calcutta were 'refugees' and between 1941 and 1951, the population went up by 20 percent in the areas with refugee presence. The population in Tollygunge area rose by 41 percent. One of the reasons was education: in undivided Bengal, students came to study in Kolkata and the phenomenon of the 'mess' was born.
- The Policy towards refugees in independent India was to disperse them outside Bengal. But there was resistance to this move among the middle class, who took over the marshy lands and set up squatter colonies, which were by 1955, known as *jabardakhal*' land, or land seized through force. By the West

Bengal legislature's Act XV of 1951, squatters were protected from eviction.
- Between 1947 and 1971, the eastern low lying areas of Tangra, Topsia, Tiljala and Kasba were settled by refugees.
- The Suburban areas consisted of Garden Reach in the south, north and south Dumdum, Baranagar, Kamarhati and Panihati in the north. The number of colonies was 350, and the population, 5,50,000
- Calcutta metropolitan district.

Works Cited

Chatterji, Joya. 2007. *The Spoils of Partition: Bengal and India 1947–1967*, Cambridge: Cambridge University Press.

Chatterji, Monidip. 1975. 'A Broad Outline of Action Programme for the Development of Refugee Colonies in CMDA Area', CMDA Publication (August): 20.

Dasgupta, Biplab. 1987. 'Urbanisation and Rural Change in West Bengal', *Economic and Political Weekly* (February 14) 278–79.

Dyson, T., and A. Maharatna. 1991. 'Excess Mortality during the Great Bengal Famine: A Re-evaluation', *The Indian Economic and Social History Review* 28, 3.

Ghosh, Benoy. 1973. *Metropolitan Mon: Metropolitan Mon o Moddhobitto Bidroho*, Kolkata: Orient Longman.

Goswami, Omkar. 1990. 'Calcutta's Economy: 1910–1970: The Fall From Grace', in Sukanta Chaudhuri, ed., *Calcutta The Living City*, vol. 2, New Delhi: Oxford University Press: 88–96.

Heitzman, James, and Robert Worden, eds. 1989. *Bangladesh: A Country Study,* Washington: GPO for the Library of Congress.

http://countrystudies.us/bangladesh/27.htm. The accounts of closure of industries located in southern Calcutta and in the other suburban areas between the 1980s and 1990s are based upon the documentation of Nagarik Mancha entitled *Locked Out Factories, Plight of Workers and Urban Space* available at *http://www.nagarikmancha.org/images/1211-Reports-%20LOCKED-OUT%20FACTORIES,%20PLIGHT%20OF%20WORKERS%20AND%20URBAN%20SPACE.pdf*

Index

About the Author

Ipshita Chanda is Professor at the Department of Comparative Literature, English and Foreign Languages University, Hyderabad. She has been ICCR Visiting Professor of Indian Culture, Georgetown University (2013–14). A member of the Faculty Team in the International Faculty Exchange Programme of the Virginia Council for International Education and the Virginia Community College System, 2008–09, she has written extensively in books/journals including the edited volume *Shaping the Discourse: Women's Writings in Bengali Periodicals: 1865–1947* (Stree, 2014); *Packaging Freedom: Feminism and Popular Culture* (Stree, 2003). She is also a SAGE author.